T0361348

77 Pillars of Quality and the Pursuit of Excellence

This book offers a basic and practical guide for any manager, quality practitioner, or anyone interested in learning and understanding the fundamental principles, concepts, tools, and techniques of quality management and process improvement. This book enables managers to have a strong foundation for effective management and improvement of operations. It strengthens quality practitioners' approach to people, products, or services and process improvement, to influence without authority. It provides practitioners with a comprehensive understanding of the contemporary concepts of quality, guiding principles, and quality tools and techniques and on successfully implementing them. It helps enhance how practitioners perform their work and inspires them to strive for excellence.

The book begins with an introduction and an overview of quality, followed by listing and explaining the selected 77 pillars (basic principles, concepts, and tools) of quality, grouped under the themes of quality, Six Sigma, and Lean Management. It examines the logical understanding of these pillars and how to implement them, providing practical examples and beneficial real case studies. The stories are based on the learning and practical experience of the author—a certified Lean Six Sigma Master Black Belt, a quality manager, and a university lecturer.

This book benefits employees, partners, and customers of any organization, offering a great reference for practitioners and academics alike. It serves as a call to reflect on basic quality pillars first, before embarking on a quality improvement journey. It provides a solid foundation for managers and practitioners to exceed their customers' expectations and excel in managing their business operations.

77 Pillars of Quality and the Pursuit of Excellence

A Guide to Basic Concepts and Lean Six Sigma Tools for Practitioners, Managers, and Entrepreneurs

Souraj Salah

Routledge
Taylor & Francis Group

A PRODUCTIVITY PRESS BOOK

First published 2024
by Routledge
605 Third Avenue, New York, NY 10158

and by Routledge
4 Park Square, Milton Park, Abingdon, Oxon, OX14 4RN

Routledge is an imprint of the Taylor & Francis Group, an informa business

ISBN: 978-1-032-68836-7 (hbk)
ISBN: 978-1-032-68835-0 (pbk)
ISBN: 978-1-032-68837-4 (ebk)

DOI: 10.4324/9781032688374

Typeset in ITC Garamond Std
by Apex CoVantage, LLC

To my beloved parents, Qasem Salah
and Mariam Ali; my darling wife, Majd
Abdallah; my wonderful sons, Albara and
Bahauddin; my wonderful daughter, Sura;
and my dearest brothers, Danial, Muhammad,
Anas, Yazeed, Suhaib, and Mosab.

To my respected teachers and mentors,
especially Dr. Abdur Rahim and Dr. Juan
Carretero. To my friends and extended
family everywhere, in Canada, the USA,
the UAE, Jordan, and Palestine.

To all of those learners and practitioners who
challenge the status quo, carry goodness in
their hearts, are passionate about quality,
inspire everyone else through their positive
attitude, and are proud of their efforts to make
people's lives easier and more prosperous.

Souraj Salah

Contents

PART V CURRENT AND FUTURE QUALITY IMPROVEMENT TRENDS, RECOMMENDATIONS, AND CONCLUSIONS

APPENDICES

Foreword

Over the past 50 years, quality management has been the focus of many researchers and practitioners. However, some organizations adopt a chosen improvement methodology without necessarily reflecting on whether the preliminary foundation is in place. In the fast-paced world of today, it is essential to get the basics right and not overlook the potential impact of what the basic principles and tools can bring. This book is a good referential source for various tools and techniques, such as quality management, Six Sigma methodology, and Lean or Japanese quality improvement.

I am delighted to introduce this comprehensive book on quality, which offers a practical guide for any learner or reader interested in understanding the fundamental concepts of quality management. It is an invaluable resource for quality practitioners aiming for business excellence through the application of Lean Six Sigma tools and quality principles. It assists academicians in offering courses on quality tools and techniques, Lean Six Sigma, and quality management.

The author carefully selected 77 pillars of quality and discussed practical examples based on his learning and practical experience. With a wealth of knowledge and experience in the field of quality management, the author provided insights into the fundamental principles that underpin the pursuit of business excellence and the successful implementation of process improvement tools and techniques.

The book is structured in a way that makes it easy for readers to navigate and find the information they need, whether they are new to quality management or experienced practitioners. It emphasizes the importance of reflecting on the basic quality principles before starting a quality improvement journey. It also reflects on Quality 4.0 advanced technology tools and the future of quality improvement.

I am proud to have supervised the author during his PhD studies, and I highly recommend this book, as it will bring more inspiration and knowledge to help achieve higher levels of business excellence.

Abdur Rahim
Professor of Quantitative Methods
Faculty of Business Administration
University of New Brunswick
Fredericton, New Brunswick
Canada

Preface

This book begins with an introduction and overview of quality followed by various chapters covering relevant topics on quality. These sections are based on a careful selection of basic quality pillars, which are in turn based on quality principles and concepts. These pillars are examined for logical understanding and supported with a discussion of how they can be implemented through various practical and real case studies, examples, and stories. The book covers a wide variety of quality tools and techniques such as Lean and Six Sigma tools, which are used for quality and process improvement.

Part I of this book consists of Chapters 1–2, which cover the introduction and literature review. The main contribution of this book includes the introduction and discussion of the 77 pillars of quality, which are illustrated in Parts II, III, IV, and V. These parts cover Chapters 3–12.

Part II covers Chapters 3–5 and discusses the pillars related to quality, in general; change management; and strategic quality management.

Part III covers Chapters 6–8 and examines the pillars related to Six Sigma, its structured approach, basic tools, relevant techniques, and other tools.

Part IV covers Chapters 9–11 and examines pillars related to Lean Management, its tools, Value Stream Mapping (VSM), and some additional tools.

Part V covers Chapter 12, which examines the pillars related to current and future trends of quality, including integrated management system (IMS), advanced technologies of Industry 4.0, contemporary issues related to quality, and an overall conclusion and recommendation.

Appendices A and B provide two actual case studies of practical value related to the various pillars explained earlier.

Preface

Acknowledgments

All thanks are due to God who bestowed upon me His great blessings and generosity to be able to complete this book, which I hope will be valuable for practitioners and academics alike or for any reader who is interested in learning about quality and its potential to change the way we think, communicate, and operate.

I would like to thank my parents, my wife, my sons, my daughter, my brothers, and my family for their endless encouragement, support, patience, and faith in me.

I would like to thank Dr. Abdur Rahim for his great mentorship and Dr. Juan Carretero for inspiring me.

I would like to thank all my teachers and mentors who contributed to my development over the years.

I am grateful to Dr. Abdur Rahim for writing the foreword for this book.

I am indebted to all my colleagues and friends who supported my efforts in different aspects to accomplish this book.

I am indebted to all who supported me in publishing the book.

I present this work seeking Allah's acceptance and reward for conveying my humble knowledge in the hope that it will be of benefit to all humanity.

Souraj Salah
Associate Faculty, Business and Quality Management
Hamdan Bin Muhammad Smart University
Dubai, United Arab Emirates

About the Author

 **Dr. Souraj Salah** received his BSc in mechanical engineering, specializing in industrial production engineering from Jordan University of Science and Technology; a master's degree of engineering in mechanical engineering, specializing in industrial engineering from Concordia University, Montreal (with great distinction); and a PhD in mechanical engineering, specializing in industrial engineering management from the University of New Brunswick, where he won the Graduate Student Merit Award twice. He is currently a part-time adjunct professor at Hamdan Bin Mohammed Smart University and also at Abu Dhabi School of Management (teaching courses like Japanese quality, quality tools and techniques, TQM fundamentals, and operations management). He also serves as a member of the Industrial Engineering Advisory Committee at the American University of Sharjah, United Arab Emirates. He also serves as a member of the advisory board for the Faculty of Engineering at the University of Sharjah. He is a business process improvement manager working in the logistics, contracting, services, and manufacturing sectors internationally. He worked for various local, multinational, and Fortune 500 companies across North America and the Middle East. His main research interests are quality control, Lean, Six Sigma, TQM, quality culture, operational excellence, and management systems. He has coauthored a book, published by Springer, titled *Integrated Company-Wide Management Systems Combining Lean Six Sigma with Process Improvement*. He has also authored and coauthored more than 30 papers that have been published in various international journals (the best of which has been cited over 470 times) and has over 23 years of industrial engineering experience. He is also certified as a Six Sigma Master Black Belt and Lean Leader, trained by the Juran Institute, Lead Advisors, Alignment Strategies in Canada, and Johnson Controls

International in the United States, and as a Quality, Health, Safety, and Environment Management Systems' (ISO 9001, ISO 14001, ISO 45001) Lead Auditor by Bureau Veritas. He has led and coached several Green Belt and Black Belt practitioners in executing numerous Lean Six Sigma Projects, delivering millions of dollars in savings from the cost of poor quality. In 2015, he won the United Arab Emirates Quality Professional Award by the American Society for Quality (ASQ).

Abbreviations

3D	Three-Dimensional
8D	Eight Disciplines
4Vs	Volume, Variety, Velocity, and Veracity
5Ms	Manpower, Measurement, Machine, Method, and Material
6Ms	Manpower, Measurement, Machine, Method, Material, and Mother Nature
5S	Sort, Set in Order, Shine, Standardize, and Sustain
5S+1	Sort, Set in Order, Shine, Standardize, and Sustain plus Safety
A	Availability
ADAEP	Abu Dhabi Awards for Excellence in Government Performance
AHP	Analytical Hierarchy Process
AI	Artificial Intelligence
AND	Activity Network Diagram
ANOVA	Analysis of Variance
API	Application Programming Interface
AR	Augmented Reality
ASQ	American Society for Quality
BB	Black Belt
BE	Business Excellence
BEM	Business Excellence Model
BIA	Building Industry Association
BoE	Bill of Entry
BoL	Bill of Lading
BPR	Business Process Reengineering
BSC	Balanced Score Card
CA	Clearing Agent

CEO	Chief Executive Officer
CI	Continuous Improvement
CMM	Computerized Maintenance Management
COBOT	Collaborative Robot
COPQ	Cost of Poor Quality
COQ	Cost of Quality
COVID-19	Coronavirus Disease of 2019
CPM	Critical Path Method
CPS	Cyber-Physical System
CQI	Continuous Quality Improvement
CRM	Customer Relationship Management
CSF	Critical Success factor
CT	Cycle Time
CTC	Critical to Cost
CTD	Critical to Delivery
CTQ	Critical to Quality
CWQC	Company-Wide Quality Control
DCP	Dynamic Control Plan
DDW	Drill Deep and Wide
DFSS	Design for Six Sigma
DGEP	Dubai Government Excellence Program
DLT	Distributed Ledger Technology
DMADV	Define, Measure, Analyze, Design, and Verify
DMAIC	Define, Measure, Analyze, Improve, and Control
DO	Delivery Order
DOE	Design of Experiments
DPMO	Defects per Million Opportunities
DPU	Defect per Unit
DQA	Dubai Quality Award
EDI	Electronic Data Interchange
EFQM	European Foundation for Quality Management
EOQ	Economic Order Quantity
ERP	Enterprise Resource Planning
EVOP	Evolutionary Optimization
FF	Freight Forwarder
FFF	Fuse Filament Fabrication
FIFO	First-in-First-Out
FMEA	Failure Mode and Effect Analysis
GB	Green Belt

GE	General Electric
GES	Government Excellence System
GPS	Global Positioning System
GUI	Graphic User Interface
HCI	Human-Computer Interface
HHT	Handheld Tablet
HOQ	House of Quality
HR	Human Resources
HSSER	Health Safety Security Environment Risk
I4.0	Industry 4.0 (Fourth industrial revolution)
ICT	Information and Communication Technology
ICWMS	Integrated Company-Wide Management System
IDOV	Identify, Design, Optimize, and Verify
IIoT	Industrial Internet of Things
IMR	Individual Moving Range
IMS	Integrated Management System
IMVP	International Motor Vehicle Program
IoT	Internet of Things
ISO	International Organization for Standardization
IT	Information Technology
JIT	Just-in-Time
JUSE	Japanese Union of Scientists and Engineers
KPI	Key Performance Indicator
KPIV	Key Process Input Variables
KPOV	Key Process Output Variables
KT	Kepner-Tregoe
LAN	Local Area Network
LPWAN	Low Power Wide Area Network
LSL	Lower Specification Limit
LSS	Lean Six Sigma
MBB	Master Black Belt
MBNQA	Malcolm Baldrige National Quality Award
MES	Manufacturing Execution System
MIT	Massachusetts Institute of Technology
MS	Management System
MSA	Measurement System Analysis
NA	Not Applicable
NGT	Nominal Group Technique
NIST	National Institute of Standards and Technology

NPS	Net Promoter Score
NVA	Non-value-Adding
OC	Operational Characteristic
OEE	Overall Equipment Effectiveness
OT	Operational Technology
P	Performance
PCF	Process Classification Framework
PDCA	Plan-Do-Check-Act
PDPC	Process Design Program Chart
PERT	Program Evaluation Review Technique
PEST	Political Economic Social Technological
PLM	Product Life Management
PO	Purchase Order
PT	Process Time
Q	Quality
Q4.0	Quality 4.0 (Fourth quality revolution)
QA	Quality Assurance
QC	Quality Control
QCD	Quality Cost Delivery
QE	Quality Engineering
QFD	Quality Function Deployment
QI	Quality Improvement
QLF	Quality Loss Function
QM	Quality Management
QMS	Quality Management System
QPS	Quality Planning Sheet
QR	Quick Response
QS	Quality System
R and R	Repeatability and Reproducibility
RFID	Radio Frequency Identification
ROI	Return on Investment
RPA	Robotic Process Automation
RPN	Risk Priority Number
RTY	Rolled Throughput Yield
SC	Supply Chain
SCM	Supply Chain Management
SDCA	Standardize-Do-Check-Act
SHI	Smart Human Interface
SIPOC	Supplier-Input-Process-Output-Customer

SKGEP	Sheikh Khalifa Government Excellence Program
SLA	Service Level Agreement
SLRA	Simple Linear Regression Analysis
SLT	Stereo-Lithography
SMART	Specific Measurable Achievable Realistic or Relevant Time Bound
SMED	Single-Minute Exchange of Dies
SOP	Standard Operating Procedure
SPC	Statistical Process Control
SQC	Statistical Quality Control
SWOT	Strengths-Weaknesses-Opportunities-Threats
TIPS or TRIZ	Theory of Inventive Problem Solving
TOS	Terminal Operating System
TPM	Total Productive Maintenance
TPS	Toyota Production System
TQC	Total Quality Control
TQM	Total Quality Management
UAV	Unmanned Aerial Vehicle
USL	Upper Specification Limit
UT	Uptime
VA	Value-Adding
VOC	Voice of the Customer
VR	Virtual Reality
VSM	Value Stream Map
WBS	Work Breakdown Structure
WEF	World Economic Forum
WIP	Work-in-Process
WMS	Warehouse Management System
X-bar and R	Average and Range
YB	Yellow Belt

Figures

Tables

Abstract

Today's world is becoming increasingly interconnected, to the point it is often described as a small village. Customers can access the global marketplace and order products or services with the simple click of a button. This has formed a new reality, which is creating fierce competition among organizations for not only meeting the market demand but also improving customer experience and innovating ahead of others to ensure the sustainability of their businesses. An essential way to ensure that is by setting up a solid foundation for an understanding of what quality pillars are about. Without these basics, many organizations would lose much potential for achieving higher rates of improvement and levels of success.

Total quality management (TQM) has been a fundamental management concept for continuous improvement (CI), utilizing Deming's basic approach of plan-do-check-act (PDCA). The measurement of efficiency and effectiveness, cost of quality, loss to society, quality assurance (QA), innovation, change management, effective communication, and quality culture are all critical aspects of quality management (QM). Six Sigma is a well-disciplined and structured methodology used to improve process quality and performance. It is based on the deployment of an effective program using various graphical and statistical analysis tools to achieve process stability and capability. TQM and Six Sigma share similar goals of pursuing customer satisfaction and business profit. Another state-of-the-art process improvement methodology is Lean, which is proven to help organizations achieve timely delivery while reducing the various types of waste. It focuses on streamlining processes using value stream mapping and various other tools such as Kaizen and visual management. Lean and Six Sigma can be integrated and thought of as toolboxes filled with various tools that can be selected depending on the nature of the challenges faced. Management systems (MSs) are ways to run a business that are developed to meet the requirements of quality management, health, safety, environmental management, *etc*. Recently, different MSs have gained more attention, as they form a critical infrastructure for improving and controlling the different operation systems of an organization. Numerous studies pointed out that most of the implementation efforts of CI methodologies had failed. One important foundation for an effective CI implementation lies in the setup of an integrated company-wide management system (ICWMS), which is based on a framework for formulating and modeling an integrated approach for all management systems in any organization. This includes strategic quality management, management commitment, and the adoption of self-assessment quality models.

There is a genuine need to return to the basics of quality so that improvement efforts for processes, products, and people's lives can be further enhanced. The lack of understanding of such basic tools and pillars will lead to limited improvement, which will not be optimal or effective, as much of waste and redundancy will still exist. The pillars covered in this book consist of various interconnected ideas of financial significance and real business value. The aforementioned topics are easy to understand and implement and, thus, worth considering and evaluating. Moreover, focusing on quality basics paves the way for another important phase explored at the end of this work, which is related to future quality trends, including advanced technologies of Industry 4.0 and Quality 4.0, such as Big Data, blockchain, robotic process automation (RPA), artificial intelligence (AI), and virtual reality (VR). All these topics cover various pillars and tools, which are introduced, explained, and illustrated using real cases and stories based on the author's literature review and own experience.

INTRODUCTION AND LITERATURE REVIEW

1 INTRODUCTION AND LITERATURE REVIEW

Chapter 1

Introduction and Overview

1.1 Introduction and Motivation

It is widely accepted among quality practitioners and process improvement managers that it is essential to implement quality tools and techniques for organizations to continuously improve and be successful. These tools and techniques are commonly used by organizations working in various domains, such as manufacturing, retail, contracting, service, and logistics. The implementation of continuous improvement (CI) approaches is necessary to the success of several stakeholders, including business owners, managers, quality practitioners, employees, customers, and society, in general.

Many organizations today are not realizing their full potential in terms of improvement and profitability. There are several reported cases of limited success or even failure in the implementation of improvement initiatives. This leads to losses in effort, time, and resources, which not only negatively impact the profitability of an organization but also its own employees' morale as well as the whole society.

The reason for that lies in the lack of understanding (by many managers, practitioners, or employees) of some of the basic pillars of quality, which, if implemented properly, can help transform organizations into healthier and sustainable businesses that effectively align all employees and engage them. This will naturally help drive the right decisions and the desired employee behaviors. It will also help enhance communication among teams to ensure their alignment toward a united vision.

In order to achieve this desired transformation, it is important to focus on understanding the basics of quality improvement so that managers from

DOI: 10.4324/9781032688374-2

different backgrounds, as well as quality practitioners, can speak the same language of quality and then properly utilize the understanding of the basic quality pillars to achieve higher levels of performance excellence.

1.2 Objectives and Contribution

The objectives of this book can be summarized into the following:

- To clarify the various basic pillars related to quality, in general; change management; strategic quality management; Six Sigma; basic quality tools; additional Six Sigma–related tools; Lean tools like value stream mapping (VSM); visual management tools; and additional related Lean tools.
- To provide a solid foundation for learners and entrepreneurs to understand the basics of quality and its tools and techniques.
- To enable managers, quality practitioners, and employees, in general, to better understand the basic pillars of quality and how they can be implemented in practical life.
- To propose ways to managers and quality practitioners on how to embark on a journey for continuous improvement (CI) and achieve high levels of business excellence.
- To rationalize that quality pillars are simple to understand, not difficult to implement, match with common sense, and promote a logical approach to CI.
- To demonstrate how managers and quality practitioners can excel in achieving high levels of excellence, using real cases, stories, and examples.
- To introduce some emerging technologies and future trends related to Quality 4.0 and provide some insights and examples on how they can be utilized to enhance operations.

1.3 Book Organization

This book is organized as follows:

Part I includes Chapters 1–2. Chapter 1 covers an introduction to the book. In the second chapter, a literature review is conducted, including various topics such as quality management (QM), Six Sigma and Lean management.

Part II covers Chapters 3–5. Chapter 3 discusses several pillars related to quality, in general, such as the pillars related to the topics of measurement of efficiency and effectiveness, cost of quality, quality loss to society, quality assurance, and innovation management. Chapter 4 introduces the pillars related to change management such as the topics of culture change, effective communication, employee engagement, and quality culture. Chapter 5 covers the pillars related to strategic quality management, an integrated company-wide management system (ICWMS), and the sustainability of quality.

Part III covers Chapters 6–8. Chapter 6 examines the pillars related to Six Sigma in general, including its structured define-measure-analyze-improve-control (DMAIC) approach and deployment program. Chapter 7 discusses basic quality tools and techniques, as well as basic management tools. It also provides a discussion of process stability and capability Chapter 8 covers additional tools that are also used within the DMAIC framework of Six Sigma. This includes statistical and graphical analysis tools, such as concentration diagrams, box plots, multi-vari charts, and main effects plots).

Part IV covers Chapters 9–11. Chapter 9 examines the pillars related to Lean management, in general, and its principles and tools, including line balancing and value stream mapping (VSM), which can be considered as a framework for CI. Chapter 10 examines visual management and other related Lean tools such as 5S (sort, set in order, shine, standardize, and sustain), supermarket, and Heijunka. Chapter 11 discusses additional tools form the Lean management tool kit, including standardization, Kaizen, Poka-Yoke, Jidoka, total productive maintenance, quick changeover, cell layout, quality function deployment (QFD), and the Kano model.

Part V contains the last chapter (Chapter 12), which examines the pillars related to the current and future trends of quality, including integrated management system (IMS) and advanced technologies of Industry 4.0 (such as Big Data, blockchain, robotic process automation, virtual reality, and artificial intelligence), as well as contemporary issues related to quality, an overall conclusion, and recommendation.

Appendices A and B provide actual case studies of practical value, which are related to the various pillars explained in this book.

Chapter 2

Literature Review

2.1 A Brief History of Quality Control (QC) and Quality Improvement (QI)

Quality has always been an integral part of all products and services. Over many years, the awareness of quality and the introduction of formal methods for continuous improvement (CI) and quality control (QC) have gone through an evolution. Here are some milestones related to the history of quality methods (Montgomery, 2001):

- Before the 20th century, quality was largely dependent on the individual craftsmen' efforts.
- In 1875, Frederick Taylor introduced scientific management principles to divide complex processes into smaller components, which are easier to accomplish through standardization, leading to increased productivity.
- In 1924, Walter Shewhart used statistical process control (SPC) to monitor the behavior of processes with the aim to stabilize them.
- Genichi Taguchi started his studies and approach to experimental design in 1948. However, his work appeared in the United States for the first time in the 1980s.
- In 1951, Armand Feigenbaum introduced total quality control (TQC).
- In 1960, the concept of zero defects was introduced in some industries in the United States.
- Between 1975 and 1978, total quality management (TQM) evolved in North America.
- In 1988, the Malcolm Baldrige National Quality Award (MBNQA) was established by the US Congress.

 DOI: 10.4324/9781032688374-3

- In 1989, Six Sigma methodology implementation for process improvement (PI) began at Motorola.
- In the 1990s, the International Standards Organization (ISO) evolved.
- In the 2000s, the Lean Six Sigma (LSS) methodology evolved.

Quality evolved in the following phases: operator quality control (QC), or custom-craft quality practiced before the industrial revolution, foreman QC, inspector QC, statistical quality control (SQC), TQC and TQM (Feigenbaum, 1991), and techno-craft quality (Kolarik, 1995). In the 21st century, technology is becoming more prevalent as part of the emerging knowledge age and digital economy. Customers are exposed to more information and are becoming more demanding. Thus, companies need to be more innovative, anticipate future desires, be more flexible, and ensure the designing and building of quality products and services (Hassan *et al.*, 2000).

Nowadays, new technologies of Industry 4.0 as well as Quality 4.0 are increasingly becoming popular in helping resolve different quality problems (see Chapter 12).

2.2 The Leading Contributors to Quality

Several people have contributed to the development of TQM, SQC, and CI practices. Here is a brief background and summarized philosophy of selected gurus, who are considered to be among the main leaders and contributors to the field of quality (Montgomery, 2001; Oakland, 2003; Dahlgaard *et al.*, 2007; Foster, 2007; Goetsch and Davis, 2013; Evans and Lindsay, 2020):

- Edwards Deming: After World War II, Dr. Deming became a consultant for various Japanese companies, where he managed to convince managers of the importance of statistical tools and quality in overcoming competition. He believed that the responsibility for quality resides with managers, as their action is required for quality to improve. He introduced a chain reaction focused on quality improvement (QI) as a way for businesses to succeed. He also introduced a system of profound knowledge. His philosophy for quality and productivity improvement is summarized in his famous 14 points of management, which include mission clarity; learning the modern philosophy of quality; understanding the purpose of inspection; focusing on quality, not price alone; CI;

training; leadership; driving out fear; teamwork; eliminating slogans and quotas; instilling pride; self-improvement; and executing transformation. It focused on reducing uncertainty and variability. He was also famous for his plan-do-check-act (PDCA) cycle of QI.

■ Joseph Juran: Dr. Juran is one of the founders of the field of statistical quality control (SQC). He worked for Dr. Walter Shewhart at the American Telephone and Telegraph Company (AT&T). Dr. Shewhart is famous for his plan-do-study-act (PDSA) cycle and for being the father of SQC charts, which were implemented industrially in the 1930s (Ishikawa, 1985). Dr. Juran's philosophy is based on the implementation of change or improvement through managerial breakthrough or problem-solving process. He also believed that management could address most of the opportunities for QI. He introduced a QC handbook and defined quality as the fitness for use and freedom from deficiencies. He addressed variation types and sources. Also, he emphasized the importance of trust, pride, and motivation. He introduced Juran's quality trilogy, which consisted of quality planning focused on products, customers, and processes; QC focused on conformance to specifications; and QI focused on developing an infrastructure of teams and tools to successfully execute projects.

■ Armand Feigenbaum: Dr. Feigenbaum introduced the concept of company-wide quality control (CWQC) in his book titled *Total Quality Control*, which was first published in 1951. His book influenced the Japanese TQC philosophy. His focus was on organization structure more than statistical methods. He introduced three steps to quality: quality leadership focusing on planning, modern quality technology across the entire workforce, and organizational commitment supported by training and motivation.

■ Kaoru Ishikawa: Dr. Ishikawa is the foremost leader in Japanese QI. He provided various tools such as the famous fish-bone diagram for root cause analysis and worked within the Deming and Juran frameworks. Through his leadership of the Japanese Union of Scientists and Engineers (JUSE), he focused on training and the involvement of all employees in improving quality through the understanding of statistical analysis and data interpretation. He is credited for coining CWQC. Dr. Ishikawa emphasized the importance of taking care of the internal customers within any company, as well as the external customers, through his axiom: "The next process is the customer" (Berling, 2001).

■ Philip Crosby: Crosby has been the most successful in marketing his expertise in quality. In 1979, he founded one of the world's largest and most successful consulting companies in quality, named "Crosby and Associates", and managed to capture the attention of many top company leaders by measuring the cost of quality (COQ) in dollars. He is famous for his book titled *Quality Is Free*, in which he explains that managing quality can be a source of profit for an organization. He is also well known for his 14 steps to QI, which underline his zero-defect approach. His absolutes of quality management included the following: conformance to clear requirements, proper problem definition by individuals who cause them, doing the job right the first time is always cheaper, and companies typically spend 15%–20% of their sales dollars on quality cost. His QI approach emphasized behavioral aspects more than statistical aspects. However, he did not promote the same type of strategic planning approach proposed by Deming and Juran.

■ Genichi Taguchi: Dr. Taguchi proposed a QI method, which is a continuation of the works of Shewhart and Deming, and is comparable to the works of Ishikawa. Among the unique aspects of his methods are Taguchi's definition of quality, quality loss function (QLF), and robust engineering design. Taguchi stressed that a loss in quality is a loss to the whole society. Taguchi defines ideal quality for a product or service as a reference point or target value for determining the achieved quality level. Ideal quality is delivered if the product or service performs up to its intended purpose without loss to society. Taguchi is famous for proactively disagreeing with the notion of allowable variation or the traditional view of quality as conformance to specifications. His concept of robust design proactively states that products and services should be designed so that they are defect-free.

More on the differences between gurus is provided by Martinez-Lorente *et al.* (1998). Juran, Deming, Crosby, and others have developed different QI approaches, which share the philosophy of quality and focus on customer satisfaction (Ekings, 1988). There are differences and similarities between Deming, Juran, and Feigenbaum. However, they all stressed the importance of quality, customer satisfaction, statistical methods, and the role of management (Montgomery, 2001).

2.3 Quality Dimensions and Perspectives

The quality of a product is an important factor for customers to consider when choosing a supplier. QI efforts can be applied to any area of a company for any type of process, whether providing a product or service. Quality engineering (QE) is concerned with the activities done to ensure the product of a process is meeting specifications. QI and QE efforts could be based on TQM, Six Sigma, Lean, *etc.* (Montgomery, 2001).

Traditionally, quality efforts had the problem of being too internally oriented when considering the supply chain (SC) where value flows. Across the SC, there are several dimensions and definitions for quality depending on where the stakeholders are located within that SC. Even within the same firm, employees from different functions often view quality differently, and managers need to recognize that fact to be able to improve communication. David Garvin found that most definitions of quality were either transcendent, product based, user based, manufacturing based, or value based. Using these five classes of the definitions of quality, Garvin developed the following list of eight quality dimensions (Garvin, 1988; Foster, 2007):

- Performance: refers to the efficiency at which a product achieves its intended purpose.
- Features: attributes of a product that supplement its basic performance.
- Reliability: the tendency for a product to perform consistently over its useful design-life.
- Conformance: the numerical dimensions for product performance, such as capacity, speed, size, durability, and color.
- Durability: the degree to which a product tolerates stress without failing.
- Serviceability: the ease of repair.
- Aesthetics: the subjective sensory characteristics, such as taste, feel, sound, look, and smell.
- Perceived quality: customers instill products and services with their opinion or understanding of their goodness.

On the other hand, here are the service quality dimensions (Foster, 2007):

- Tangibles: include the physical appearance of the service facility, equipment, personnel, and communication material.
- Service reliability: differs from product reliability in that it relates to the ability of the service provider to perform the promised service dependably and accurately.
- Responsiveness: the willingness of the service provider to be helpful and prompt in providing the service.
- Assurance: the knowledge and courtesy of employees and their ability to inspire trust and confidence.

■ Empathy: the individual attention and care paid to customers by the service firm.

Also, Dale *et al.* (2016) listed the following service quality determinants:

■ Tangibles: physical evidence.
■ Reliability: getting it right the first time and honoring promises.
■ Responsiveness: willingness and readiness.
■ Communication: keeping customers informed.
■ Credibility: honesty.
■ Security: physical, financial, and confidential aspects.
■ Competitive: possession of required skills.
■ Courtesy: politeness, respect, and friendliness.
■ Understanding: knowing the customer's requirements.
■ Access: ease of approach and contact.

A summary of the quality as well as service dimensions can be seen in Table 2.1. According to Foster (2007), quality-related activities can be classified into the following:

a. Upstream activities, which include supplier qualification (using grading approaches, such as ISO 9000:2000 and acceptance sampling), supplier

Table 2.1   Product and Service Quality Dimensions

Garvin's product quality dimensions	Service quality dimension
Performance	Tangibles
Features	Empathy
Reliability	Service reliability
Conformance	Assurance
Durability	Responsiveness
Serviceability	Availability
Aesthetics	Professionalism
Perceived quality	Timeliness
	Completeness
	Pleasantness

Source: Adapted from Foster (2007)

development (including the use of electronic data interchange (EDI) to link customer purchasing systems to the supplier enterprise resource planning (ERP) systems).
b. Core process activities, including CI and value stream mapping (VSM) activities.
c. Downstream activities, which include logistics, customer support, and after-sale activities.

Quality is a multifaceted entity. Traditionally, it is the fitness for use from two aspects: quality of design and quality of conformance. The modern definition is that quality is inversely proportional to variability. QI is about the reduction of variability and waste in processes and products. As variation decreases, quality improves, and warranty cost decreases. Also, repair, waste, and rework decrease (Montgomery, 2001).

Additionally, here are some differing functional perspectives on quality (Foster, 2007):

■ Engineering perspective.
■ Operational perspective.
■ Strategic management perspective.
■ Marketing perspective.
■ Financial perspective.
■ Human resources perspective.

2.4 Statistical Methods for Quality Improvement

Statistical methods for QC and QI mainly include three areas: acceptance sampling, SPC, and design of experiments (DOE). A major type of DOE is factorial design, in which all factors' inputs are varied together to test all possible combinations. A designed experiment is a major offline QC tool. Once the dynamic relationship between inputs and outputs is understood, the process can be routinely adjusted through engineering control (also referred to as automatic control or feedback control). Acceptance sampling includes incoming inspection and outgoing inspection (raw and finished products, respectively). Rejects are classified into either scrapped or recycled items, through rectifying inspection. Quality assurance (QA) systems focus more on SPC and DOE than on acceptance sampling. For SQC and statistical quality improvement (SQI) tools to be effective, they need to be part of a quality-driven management system (MS) that directs the improvement philosophy and ensure its application to all aspects of the business. Some managerial frameworks used to achieve this are CWQC, TQM, QA, and Six Sigma (Montgomery, 2001).

However, additional statistical tools are widely used within the define-measure-analyze-improve-control (DMAIC) phases of Six Sigma for QI. For example, whenever an analysis is conducted to test a sample of data against a certain targeted value or against another sample collected after the implementation of improvement actions (or for another supplier or department), a hypothesis test is constructed. Then statistical tests are used along with graphical analysis to find out if there is enough statistical evidence of a significant change or difference in the process. If that is the case, the null hypothesis is usually rejected in favor of the alternative, which is often what the quality practitioner is hoping to confirm. Software applications like Minitab, for example, are widely used to easily perform such tasks.

Often, not enough attention is paid to achieving all dimensions of an optimal process. These dimensions are related to economy, efficiency, productivity, and quality. To increase productivity and reduce cost, QI is essential. The use of statistical quality tools of process control can help reduce variability and defectives, which results in an enhancement in quality and the overall process yield or productivity (Montgomery, 2001).

2.5 Quality Management (QM)

Quality Management (QM) is about process improvement, efficiency, and effectiveness (Nanda, 2005). QM evolved through the stages of inspection, control, assurance, TQM (Mangelsdorf, 1999; Basu, 2004), continuous improvement (CI) (Kaye and Anderson, 1999), Six Sigma, and other forms (Anderson *et al.*, 2006). Basu (2004) viewed the new, evolving CI methodologies as being embedded in holistic programs of operational excellence and QM, which need tools and techniques in order to be realized. Organizational excellence is a result of building quality into people, processes, and products (Dahlgaard and Dahlgaard-Park, 2006). Ultimately, the aim of QM is to set up a management system (MS) and culture that ensure organization-wide quality, CI, leadership, employee fulfillment, customer focus, human focus, management structure, quality tools, supplier support, and teamwork. From a strategic alignment perspective, QM is defined as the integration of all business activities involving all participants through CI (Mellat-Parasat and Digman, 2007).

2.6 Total Quality Management (TQM)

TQM is an organization-wide strategy for managing QI activities, which began in the early 1980s based on Juran and Deming's philosophies (Montgomery, 2001). One of the reasons for the origin of TQM is the replacement of total quality control (TQC) because of the belief that quality has to be managed, not simply controlled (Martinez-Lorente *et al.*, 1998). It has been a dominant management concept for CI, utilizing Deming's basic concepts of PDCA. TQM can be defined as a quality management system (QMS) or corporate culture continuously evolving and consisting of values and tools focusing on customer satisfaction and the use of fewer resources (Anderson *et al.*, 2006). Short and Rahim (1995) viewed TQM as a philosophy used by organizations to drive CI across their business activities.

There are seven quality control (QC) tools and seven management tools frequently mentioned in TQM literature (Arnheiter and Maleyeff, 2005). The seven quality tools are control charts, histograms, check sheets, scatter plots, cause-and-effect diagrams, Pareto charts, and data stratification (which is replaced by process mapping in some references). The seven management tools are affinity diagrams, interrelationship diagraphs, tree diagrams, matrix diagrams, prioritization matrices, process decision program charts, and activity network diagrams (Salah and Rahim, 2019). These tools will be covered later in this book (see Chapter 7, for example).

Furthermore, TQM is considered a management process that applies management principles to improve all processes within an organization (Jitpaiboon and Rao, 2007). TQM became more popular as organizations started to integrate quality into their MSs (Evans and Lindsay, 2002). The holistic approach is a key feature for TQM, which includes strategic, process, and technology management (Castle, 1996).

Some of the reasons why TQM had moderate success are the lack of widespread efforts to use technical tools to reduce variation, lack of management support, lack of specific objectives, lack of focus on specific technical education, and lack of understanding of statistical tools (Montgomery, 2001).

2.7 Quality in the Service Industry

The service sector is a generic term, which includes many industries such as banking, education, insurance, and health care. The QI approach seems to be more relevant to manufacturing processes than service processes, as their performance is typically easier to measure. For example, it is challenging to assess the degree of achievement of goals at an educational organization, such as the provision of education for a community. However, the fact that quality is about organizational culture makes it applicable to both manufacturing and service organizations (Atkinson and Murray, 1988).

The use of the QI approach in service industries has lagged behind its use in manufacturing sectors due to the difficulty in objectively defining the quality of a service or tangibly assessing its output. Service industries have unique features, as work itself is a commodity supplied and consumed at the same place, and at the same time. Also, work is directly assessed by customers, is expected to rise to the occasion, and is employee dependent to a large extent (Kaneko, 1988).

Obstacles facing QM implementation in service industries include resistance to change, lack of quality-related information, and poor communication (Savell and Williams, 1988). Nevertheless, several service organizations succeeded in using TQC techniques (Wyckoff, 1984).

In the example of the hotel business of Takasago-Kanko Co. Ltd. in Japan, given by Kaneko (1988), the services and goods offered are classified into three categories: services for guests, facilities, and food. For measuring the services, the preparatory work for a banquette served in a hotel restaurant is analyzed objectively using industrial engineering approaches. The process was taped, and an analysis was performed on the postures, time, and distance traveled through the process. Tremendous improvements were implemented, and their significance was demonstrated (Kaneko, 1988).

2.8 Quality Engineering (QE)

Quality engineering (QE) is a technique used to improve performance and reduce functional variations caused by three types of noises: namely, outer noise of environment, inner noise of deterioration, and imperfection in manufacturing. It is about the manufacturing of products that are robust to noise factors (Taguchi, 1985). QE is an interdisciplinary science including engineering design, manufacturing operations, and economics. QE sets the focus and direction for further development of products. It refers to the hard technologies, which play a tremendous role in the creation of quality, as opposed to QM, which refers to the soft aspects of quality. Taguchi is among the very few prominent quality gurus who are recognized for their contributions toward the engineering aspects of quality (*i.e.*, QE), unlike QM contributions that many gurus are noted for (Hassan *et al.*, 2000).

Every product has quality characteristics that jointly describe what customers think about in relation to that product. Quality characteristic types are physical, sensory, and time oriented such as reliability and durability. QE is a set of operational, managerial, and engineering activities that a company uses to ensure that the quality characteristics of its products are at the nominal or required levels. These targeted or desired values usually range from an upper specification level (USL) to a lower specification level (LSL) or engineering tolerances. The primary objective of QE is to systematically reduce variability in key product characteristics to improve product performance and enhance competitiveness. Variability sources are materials, machines, methods, and operators. The inherent variability in raw materials should be taken into account for design specifications (Montgomery, 2001).

Taguchi *et al.* (1989) classified QC activities into two types: online QC and offline QC. Offline QC is about identifying customer requirements, product design, and process design (using tools as such as quality function deployment and DOE). Taguchi introduced an approach that has three tiers for product and process design, which include system, parameter, and tolerance designs. Online QC is about process control during production (Taguchi *et al.*, 1989). Figure 2.1 shows these QE components.

Quality control (QC) is the collection of activities to achieve, sustain, and improve the quality of a product or service (Besterfield, 1994). Quality

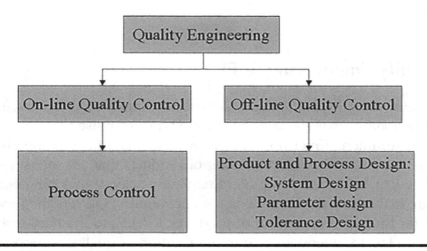

Figure 2.1 QE components as adapted from Hassan *et al.* (2000).

assurance (QA) is concerned with ensuring that quality is what it should be. SQC refers to data collection and analysis within quality control activities (Hassan *et al.*, 2000).

2.9 Six Sigma

More than at any other time in history, companies compete fiercely for market share at the global, not local level. Moreover, modern applications on mobile phones made it easier for customers to shop from different suppliers. Additionally, COVID-19 forced more customers to switch to online shopping for safety and health reasons. Thus, companies must look for ways to improve their processes and cope with modern business changes, so as to gain an advantage over their competitors. Today, there is more focus on reducing defects and exceeding customer expectations due to global competition. This competitive climate, along with the fact that statistical software technology has improved and become more user friendly, is very suitable for process improvement methodologies to spread. One of these great methodologies is Six Sigma.

Empirical-based research indicated that it is more effective to use a structured approach in process improvement (Ried, 2006). Methodologies such as Six Sigma are groups of activities performed in a prescribed way to reach targeted values (Anderson *et al.*, 2006). It is defined as a breakthrough change for increasing the rate of improvement in processes and products (Bellows, 2004). It represents a new wave of the QM evolution (preceded by TQM evolution) toward operational excellence (Basu, 2004). Additionally, it is a collection of process improvement tools used in a series of projects in a systematic way to achieve high levels of stability. It embraces key values such as process focus, customer focus, CI, and the use of facts and data (Tannock *et al.*, 2007).

The term "sigma" is from the Greek letter σ that is usually used to refer to the standard deviation, which is a measure of the variation in a process output around its mean value, μ. Quantitatively, Six Sigma quality means only two defects per billion opportunities fall outside the USL and LSL. This is almost a defect-free level (or a perfect process capability). Table 2.2 shows Six Sigma levels and their corresponding defects per million opportunities (DPMO). The long-term values listed in Table 2.2 correspond to the typical 1.5-σ shift of the process mean to account for process drifting (Breyfogle,

Table 2.2 Six Sigma Levels and Their Corresponding DPMO

Short term		Long term			
σ level	DPMO based on a centered process	Process yield	σ level	DPMO based on worse side	Notes
6.0	0.002	99.99966%	4.5	3.4	A Six Sigma process; the necessity to operate at such a low level of defects may not always be economical.
5.0	0.6	99.97700%	3.5	230	
4.5	6.8	99.86500%	3.0	1,350	
4.0	63.5	99.37900%	2.5	6,210	
3.0	2,700	93.32000%	1.5	66,800	Most companies operate at this level (Kwak and Anbari, 2004).

Source: **Adapted from Sheehy** *et al.* **(2002) and Raisinghani** *et al.* **(2005)**

2003). This process shift, however, is criticized for not being always applicable.

However, at high-yield companies, such as Motorola, producing electronic products consisting of numerous components, each of which has a probability to cause the whole product to fail, achieving an almost defect-free level is very necessary so that the combined probability for failure (based on all these components) stays as low as possible.

In 1987, Motorola's Six Sigma Quality Program was created by William (Bill) Smith (Devane, 2004; Kumar *et al.*, 2008) and Mike Harry (Harry and Schroeder, 2000). Antony (2008) indicated that Six Sigma helped organizations reduce defects rates, decrease cost of operation, and increase value for customers and shareholders. Jack Welch, who was a former CEO of General Electric (GE), claimed savings of hundreds of millions of dollars were achieved as a result of embracing a Six Sigma methodology for process improvement. This reported success helped spread out this methodology (Raisinghani *et al.*, 2005).

2.9.1 Six Sigma Principles

Six Sigma principles include (Friday-Stroud and Sutterfield, 2007) the following:

- Aligning key processes and customer requirements with the strategic goals of the organization.
- Identifying champions for each project, obtaining necessary resources, and securing help to overcome the resistance to change.
- Instituting a standard measurement system and identifying appropriate metrics.
- Training and deploying improvement teams and setting up stretched improvement goals.
- Utilizing a structured methodology based on the five DMAIC phases.

2.9.2 Six Sigma Phases

Motorola created the following steps to achieve Six Sigma (Dahlgaard and Dahlgaard-Park, 2006):

- Identify customer requirements.
- Identify critical product characteristics.
- Determine how they are controlled.
- For each characteristic, determine the maximum range and process variation.
- Redesign material, product, and process if capability is less than a value of 2.

These steps were later replaced by the GE four phases of measure, analyze, improve, and control. After that, the define phase was added before the measure phase to form the well-known DMAIC process: *i.e.*, define, measure, analyze, improve, and control. This may be regarded as a short version of Deming's PDCA cycle—*i.e.*, plan, do, check, and act (Dahlgaard and Dahlgaard-Park, 2006).

In the following sections, the DMAIC phases are explained. Various tools from the Six Sigma tool kit were already known prior to Six Sigma. These tools were smartly arranged to be used in a structured approach following DMAIC. These phases and the tools used within them are generally acknowledged among different organizations, certifying bodies, and consultants who apply Six Sigma. However, there are some differences between them with regards to the tools used in terms of what phases they belong to.

2.9.2.1 Define Phase

The Six Sigma methodology starts with the identification of the need for an improvement project. In the define phase, the problem statement as well as the goal of the project are formulated. Every Six Sigma project has a charter that includes statements describing the specific process under investigation. It typically explains the problem without any indication of its causes, as it is too early at this stage. It also explains the problem without any statement blaming people, as it can lead to early opposition by the team and eventual failure.

A key step in the define phase of Six Sigma is the financial analysis including cost of poor quality, or COPQ. The concept of "quality cost" was developed based on the works by Juran, Feigenbaum, and Freeman, and it was later popularized by Crosby's publication of *Quality Is Free* (Han and Lee, 2002). A financial analysis is performed to quantify the project's expected financial impact. This is typically estimated based on an improvement target for a certain performance measure of the outcome of a process. The financial analysis gets validated by business accountants who are assigned as members of the team. The project charter also includes a project timeline and lists the team members as well as stakeholders.

Moreover, the define phase includes the usage of an important tool called the supplier-input-process-output-customer (SIPOC). This tool is a great tool that helps the team understand the voice of the customer (VOC). It is a high-level process map that typically uses four to seven steps to describe the process under consideration. It leads to the exercise of finding the characteristics at each process step, which are critical to quality (CTQ), critical to delivery (CTD), and critical to cost (CTC). Also, a project management tool or Gantt chart is used to show the different stages of the project as initially planned. It is later updated to show the actual progress compared to the plan.

2.9.2.2 Measure Phase

The first step in this phase is to measure the baseline performance of the process output in terms of its average and standard deviation. The brainstorming is conducted in this phase to identify a list of the potential process inputs. Some of the tools used in this phase (which will be explained later in the book) are statistical process control (SPC) charts, Pareto charts, process capability analysis, histograms, box plots, process flowcharts, cause-and-effect or Ishikawa diagram, failure mode and effect analysis (FMEA), measurement system analysis (MSA), data collection plans, and quality function deployment (QFD) matrix.

The cause-and-effect diagram is famously referred to as the fish-bone or Ishikawa diagram. It is a brainstorming tool often used in the measure phase of Six Sigma to identify the potential causes for a problem. It was invented by Ishikawa to better understand process inputs. The brainstorming process is guided by six areas often referred to as the 6Ms: method, measurement, manpower, machine, material, and mother nature (environment). Cross-functional teams are formed to find the potential factors influencing the process output or the key performance indicator (KPI) under investigation, by using brainstorming and voting techniques. These few potential factors are then taken to the analyze phase in order to be verified using various statistical analysis techniques.

Another tool often used in the measure phase is the Pareto diagram. A Pareto diagram can be used to find the prioritized or the most frequent issue that is worth brainstorming about. This issue can typically be a maintenance or customer complaint issue. Also, a Pareto diagram can be used later in the analyze phase to drill down and test some potential root causes and verify whether they are indeed frequent and critical or not.

Similarly, FMEA is a well-known Six Sigma tool used to identify the potential product or process failure modes, their rate of severity, rate of occurrence, and rate of detection. These rates are multiplied in order to calculate a risk priority number. The prioritized issues are then added to what resulted from other tools like the Ishikawa diagram to be taken to the analyze phase for verification. FMEA was initially used by the US military to evaluate the impact of failures on a mission's success (Su and Chou, 2008). It aims at identifying and prioritizing the potential failures so that they can be eventually eliminated. This leads to the improvement of product quality and reliability.

2.9.2.3 Analyze Phase

One of the main deliverables of the measure phase is the list of the potential process inputs or parameters, which might be affecting the process output.

In the analyze phase, these potential inputs (from x_1 to x_n) are investigated by data analysis, one at a time, to verify which among them are the critical root causes contributing to the examined problem and negatively affecting the process output (Y), as described in Equation 2.1:

$$Y = F\left(x_1, x_2, x_3, \ldots, x_n\right) \qquad (2.1)$$

The main step in this phase is to design a data collection plan that lists all these potential inputs or x's, indicates what data are needed, and what hypotheses are to be tested. An important step in the analysis is to understand the data patterns and distributions, which will lead to the decision of what the next steps could be. Comparisons of proportions, means, and variances are often tested relative to certain targets or to other groups of data. These comparisons are examples of the statistical tools used in this phase. Graphical analysis tools are also used, such as histograms, main effects plots, box plots, multi-vari charts, correlation, regression, interval plots, and analysis of variance (ANOVA).

Table 2.3 shows a list of the basic and common tools used in graphical data analysis. The result of this phase is a list of the few critical x's or inputs that were statistically proven to be significant. In these cases, there is typically enough statistical evidence, at a satisfactory confidence level, to reject the null hypothesis in favor of the alternative. Sometimes when data are not available or easily obtained, the team may decide to proceed based on voting done in the measure phase, as a sufficient verification for a critical input in order to be examined during the next phase of improvement. This is also acceptable when a quick solution is already known and does not cost much time or effort to be implemented.

2.9.2.4 Improve Phase

In this phase, the verified critical inputs are examined to determine the best approach for developing solutions that would counteract the negative effect of these inputs. This may incorporate the usage of additional quality tools, such as statistical methods, evolutionary optimization (EVOP), simulation, pilot testing, regression analysis, and design of experiments (DOE).

Developed in the early 1920s by the British statistician Ronald Fisher, DOE is a powerful technique used to study how several process parameters affect the response or the quality characteristic of a process or product (Rowlands and Antony, 2003). It helps identify the critical factors similar to

Table 2.3   A List of the Basic and Common Tools for Graphical Data Analysis

Tool	What	Why	When
Dot plot	A graph that shows each data value plotted as a dot along a continuous scale of values.	To show how data points are distributed and see the center of tendency as well as the amount of variation.	Variable data
Histogram	A bar graph in which data are grouped into classes. The height of each bar shows how many data values fall in each class.	To show the center of tendency, the amount of variation, and shape of data.	Variable data
Box plot	A rectangular box showing the median and the extent of normality of the data. Unusual or outlying values are typically highlighted.	To show the center of tendency, the amount of variation, shape of data, and any potential outliers.	Variable data
Line graph	A graph showing every data point plotted in a timely order from left to right.	To verify if the process is changing over time.	Variable and sometimes attribute data
Scatter plot	A graph of paired data (x, y).	To see what kind of relationship exists between the two variables (x and y).	Variable data
Pareto chart	A tool to display categorical data in bars that are ordered from the highest count to the lowest. The bar height represents the frequency of the category.	To separate the vital few from the trivial many categories.	Attribute data (categorical)
Pie chart	A tool that is used to display categorical data represented in pie slices. The size of the slice represents the proportion of the corresponding category.	To see the main contributors to the whole.	Attribute data (categorical)
Concen-tration graph	A graphical tool used during data collection to display the location where the defects occur within the parts themselves.	To determine if there is a pattern related to the physical location of defects.	Attribute data

Source: Adapted from Six Sigma Training, personal communication (2008)

what was done in the analyze phase and then the settings for these factors to get the best response from the process. DOE can be used as a control measure for achieving a high level of product design quality. It helps create a robust design that is less sensitive to the inherent noise in input variables. It can also help in the design of tolerances (Breyfogle, 2003). It is often used within the improve phase of Six Sigma to design and optimize a process or product. Additionally, DOE is much superior to the traditional way of experimenting with one parameter at a time, because it considers the parameters' effects as well as their interactions.

According to Dale *et al.* (2016), here are the basic steps in DOE application:

■ Identify the factors selected for evaluation.
■ Define the levels of these factors, which will be used during the experimental runs.
■ Create an array for experimental design..
■ Conduct the experiment.
■ Analyze the results, and conclude the experiment.

Quick hits are usually fixed once identified if they do not require further analysis. Any obvious source of variation could be eliminated directly without delay. For example, this might include the introduction of a new standard operating procedure, employee training, new measurement system, visual monitoring of process performance, and empowerment of employees with proper tools to regulate the process output.

Generally, process inputs tested in this phase might be factors or variables affecting the output. In addition, alternatives are tested, where the process could be examined in different ways. If the inputs (x's) are continuous variables, solutions can be reached by developing and testing a mathematical model. On the other hand, if they are discrete variables, the best combination of factors' settings could be determined using DOE or simulation.

A key deliverable of this phase is the improvement plan, which describes the final list of actions needed to improve the process outcome. It also describes the person responsible for each action and its deadline. Capability and control charts are also used in this phase to show the improvement and achievement of targets, as compared to the baseline performance. In this phase, Antony (2006) recommends to develop potential solutions and evaluate their impact and associated risks. Some solution options could be to optimize the process flow, standardize the process, and develop a practical solution to the problem faced using pilot studies and benchmarked best practices.

2.9.2.5 Control Phase

In this phase, the focus is on ensuring that the inputs and/or outputs of the improved processes are monitored on a day-to-day basis. It is necessary to confirm that the anticipated gains are being held and the achievement is proven by the end of the project, based on the data in hand. By this time, new standards and controls are in place, and the failure mode and effects analysis (FMEA), as well as the measurement system analysis (MSA), is validated.

Capability charts, as well as control charts, are used in the measure phase and later in the improve phase to compare the status of the process before and after the implementation of the improvement actions. These charts are also checked again in the control phase to confirm and validate the sustainability of the improved performance. Before studying the capability of the process to meet its specification limits, it is important to ensure that the process performance is predictable. The process performance cannot be predictable unless its behavior is stable—*i.e.*, the performance average and standard deviation are under statistical control. If the process is not stable, a prediction of the number of defects per million opportunities (DPMO) cannot be correctly determined (Montgomery, 2001).

In addition, a control plan is developed that includes the setup of controls, running controls (specifying when to stop or start), product control, and facilities control (mainly maintenance schedules). After achieving the targets, the control plan is handed over to the process owner who follows it day by day, to ensure it is being implemented.

One of the main barriers in Six Sigma is people's resistance to change. That is why it is important to have the right approach technically and socially. The early involvement of key people is critical to success and to hold the gains after the project is completed.

2.9.3 Design for Six Sigma (DFSS)

Customer requirements do change and vary over time. Therefore, companies need to continuously revise their designs (Ishikawa, 1985). The DMAIC improvement approach taken in a Six Sigma project is typically used when a product or process already exists but is failing to meet some of the customers' requirements (Banuelas and Antony, 2003). On the other hand, if the product or service under consideration is still in the early stages of development, or if major design changes are required to reach higher customer satisfaction, then Design for Six Sigma (DFSS) becomes the used approach. Its five phases are define, measure, analyze, design, and verify (or DMADV). Sometimes these phases are called identify, design, optimize, and verify (IDOV). The goal of DMADV is to achieve a Six Sigma level from the early project stages, and it normally applies the principles of concurrent engineering, where specialized team members from different disciplines work together, concurrently (Montgomery, 2001). According to Harry and Schroeder (2000), organizations that implemented Six Sigma and achieved a five sigma level (*i.e.*, 233 defects per million opportunities) need to implement DFSS to exceed that level. They have also indicated that IDOV helps create stable, reliable, efficient, and satisfying products. Banuelas and Antony (2004) indicated that DMAIC is concerned with continuous improvement (CI), whereas DMADV is concerned with continuous innovation.

Six Sigma stresses the importance of using QFD, cross-functional design, and design for manufacturing (Schroeder *et al.*, 2008). It has a strong emphasis on customer satisfaction through its focus on what is critical to quality (CTQ) from the customer's perspective (Klefsjo *et al.*, 2001; Schroeder *et al.*, 2008).

DFSS is a structured methodology based on the use of analytical tools to predict and prevent defects, starting at the product design stage. It is used to make a new, reliable, and defect-free product and, thus, increase profits. It passes through five phases: define the design problem and customer requirements; measure the CTQ characteristics; analyze the high-level technical requirements of the design in order for them to meet the customers' needs; develop the detailed, optimized design; and finally, verify the design performance and ability to satisfy the customers' specifications. De Feo and Bar-El (2002) have summarized the seven elements of DFSS as follows:

- It drives the customer-oriented design process with Six Sigma capability.
- It predicts design quality at the outset.
- It matches requirements flow down with capability flow up.
- It integrates cross-functional design involvement.
- It drives quality measurement and predictability improvement in the early design phases.
- It uses process capabilities in making final decisions.
- It monitors process variances to verify that customer requirements are met.

Thus, DFSS aims at satisfying the customer's needs and optimizing the process of designing a new product or service. Some of its benefits include decreasing the time to market new products, reducing the costs of new product development, improving the quality and reliability of products, and decreasing warranty costs (Antony, 2002).

2.10 Lean Management

Lean can simply be described as a methodology that focuses on the elimination of waste, variation, and work imbalance. Variation is related to any activity that deviates from the target or standard, causing defects. Lean can also be described as a philosophy and way of thinking aimed at reducing the time from order to delivery, by the elimination of waste in the value stream (Bhasin and Burcher, 2006). Also, the National Institute of Standards and Technology (NIST) defines Lean as a systematic way to eliminate waste by pulling products from the supplier, just in time as required to achieve CI (Anderson *et al.*, 2006).

There are three types of activities in any work environment:

■ Waste: any activity that consumes time or resources while being unnecessary to meet the needs of the customer.
■ Incidental work: any activity that does not add value but is currently necessary due to the limitations of the process or legal requirements.
■ Value-adding work: any activity transforming the part, product, or service, which a customer is willing to pay for, if given the choice.

The Lean solution for the value-adding activity is to streamline it, for the wasteful activity is to eliminate it, and for the incidental wasteful activity is to streamline it in the short term and eliminate it in the long term. Also, Lean is unique in the way it focuses on enabling people to see things from the perspective of the customer, product, or service and the whole value stream.

2.10.1 Where Did Lean Start?

The term "flow" in production was used by Henry Ford in the early 1900s. In the 1940s, the Toyota Production System (TPS) came into existence. It was based on the idea of production material flowing like a water stream.

Anything preventing the material from flowing is a waste that should be removed. The TPS was developed by the Japanese engineer Taiichi Ohno to become the first Lean manufacturing system. He made use of various ideas from the West (Holweg, 2007), including Ford's production techniques, and good expertise of his Japanese mentors. He did much experimentation to come up with TPS, which has been evolving through the years. It became known initially in the West as just-in-time (JIT) (Reichhart and Holweg, 2007). Eventually, in the late 1980s, the generic term "Lean" was introduced and made popular by the International Motor Vehicle Program (IMVP) researchers of the Massachusetts Institute of Technology, or MIT (Devane, 2004).

2.10.2 How Does Lean Work?

Lean is self-funding and is much superior to mass production, since producing more and batching often leads to work imbalance and increased waiting times and prevents products from flowing. These negative aspects of batching work are not acceptable from a Lean perspective. Lean enables employees to rethink the way they do things and engages them in the process improvement approach. It focuses on training employees to be able to see waste and also empowering them to implement changes. Another unique feature of Lean is that it focuses on teamwork and seeing more than only one's task.

2.10.3 Types of Waste

According to (Bhasin and Burcher, 2006), there are seven types of waste:

- Overproduction: Producing faster than the customer demand rate can lead to overproduction. Pushing and batching leads to queues of finished products or intermediate stocks, which are linked to other types of waste such as waiting and inventory. Also, a long changeover time can lead to this type of waste.
- Waiting: Slower response and unavailable resources can lead to employees, machines, and documents waiting for information, approvals, *etc.* This typically occurs between the process steps. An example of it is when employees become idle until information is received.
- Transportation: This is caused by poor layout, distant vehicle travel to locations of material, documents, clients or stakeholders, and multiple handoffs of goods or documents.

■ Inappropriate processing or overprocessing: This type of waste is often caused by bureaucracy, unnecessary details or reports, complex procedures, repeated mistakes, fear of mistakes, unresolved root causes, and lack of trust or empowerment. It leads to other types of waste such as waiting and defects.

■ Inventory or bottlenecks: Inventory ties up cash, consumes space and resources, and may end up obsolete. It is typically caused by economic order quantity (EOC), a long lead time, absent resources, and filing of documents that are in progress.

■ Unnecessary motion: This is caused by poor layout, poor organization, searching for files and tools, lack of visual management, lack of standard procedures, and tools not located at the point of use. This can lead to employee frustration and fatigue.

■ Defects or rework: Defects are caused by variation, complexity, not doing the task right the first time, missing information, wrong information, delayed information, improper information format, miscommunication or mixed messages, management by feeling or hunch, reviews of information, reentering data, repeating the same steps, and discrepancies. They can lead to customer dissatisfaction, employee frustration, and high warranty cost.

In addition, the following types are sometimes added:

■ Reprioritization: This is caused by multitasking and leads to wasting time in shifting back and forth between various tasks. Other types of waste like defects can cause a transaction to be put on hold while starting to process another transaction. Once processing is done, the employee has to switch back to find the previous transaction that was put on hold, get familiarized with where it was left the last time, and then restart the handling process of that transaction.

■ Inferior process: This type of waste is caused by not using standard best practices and the proper tools that are safely designed for the task. It leads to delays, incidents, defects, and employee frustration.

■ Employee's skills or poor employee utilization: This is caused by not trusting in employees' capabilities, not using their potential abilities, not engaging them, not empowering them, reassigning resources before tasks are completed, using hands and ignoring minds, not valuing their ideas, not working as a team, resisting change, and struggling for power or self-protection. It leads to low morale and a slow rate of improvement.

■ Other resources: This type of waste is caused by not using the equipment's ability, not utilizing material, not utilizing energy, overconsumption of energy, not utilizing facilities, failing to properly maintain machines, failing to use resources economically, failing to recycle, leaving machines idle, leaving lights turned on unnecessarily, and lack of a quality culture and sustainability awareness. It can lead to lower return on investment, extra cost, more failures, environmental damage, and more scrapped items.

The challenge is to be able to see waste, ask why it exists, and come up with solutions to eliminate it.

2.10.4 Five Lean Principles

To become Lean is a major transformation in the way any business operates. However, it is simply based on five principles, as identified by Womack and Jones (Hines *et al.*, 2004; Bendell, 2006):

Principle 1: to understand what is of value to the customer.
Principle 2: to map the current value stream of all activities from the initial stage of raw material to the delivery stage.
Principle 3: to make value flow by striving for a continuous and one-piece flow as well as waste elimination.
Principle 4: to pull products from the supplier, just in time for use.
Principle 5: to seek perfection by CI and transform the operation from a current state to a future state.

2.10.5 Value Stream Mapping (VSM)

Value stream mapping (VSM) is recognized as one of the most important tools used in a Lean journey. It can be considered an improvement framework used to transform processes from a current state to a future state. In the mapping exercise, a team goes to the Gemba (*i.e.*, the place where work is performed and value is added) and walks through the production steps. Following the flow of how the process is currently done, the team observes cycle times at each step as well as the staged inventory and waiting times between those steps. Opportunities are identified across the value stream as *Kaizen events* for CI. After that, the team works on enhancing the design of a future-state map where everyone innovates on how the process should look like. Then the team makes an implementation plan, which is used to manage the details of the migration from the current state to the future state. It typically includes detailed information of the improvement actions to be taken, employees assigned to execute those actions, and when they are expected to happen. These actions could be quick-fixes or just-do-it fixes, full projects, two-day improvement events, *etc.* After implementing the future state, the cycle repeats itself to achieve the CI vision.

2.10.6 Kaizen Events

Kaizen events were largely initiated and deployed by the Japanese consultants Shingijutsu and their followers (Hines *et al.*, 2004). *Kaizen events* or blitzes are CI changes that utilize various parts of the Lean tool kit. The word "Kaizen" is taken from two Japanese words: "kai" means change, and "zen" means for the better. A cross-functional team typically gets together for one to five days and starts to brainstorm and identify quick, economic, and effective solutions to a problem. The team is actually empowered to implement most changes even before the event ends, quickly and without bureaucracy.

2.10.7 Lean Tools

Here are some of the common and generally acknowledged Lean tools:

- Value stream mapping (VSM): A map of all the steps in the process from the moment customers make an order to the moment they receive the finished product. It also includes information about communication and time metrics such as lead time, cycle times, and waiting times.
- Mistake-proofing: A method used to prevent specific defects or mistakes from happening.
- Visual workplace: A method for ensuring abnormal conditions in the workplace are visible at a glance. It makes it easier to track work progress against expectation.
- Total productive maintenance (TPM): A method for ensuring all employees in a facility know how to use, maintain, and clean machines in a way to prolong their life span.

- 5S+1 (*i.e.*, sort, set in order, shine, standardize, sustain, and safety): An approach used to organize workplaces, where waste can be easily found and eliminated. It enhances the work environment and cleanliness and heavily depends on employee self-control.
- Standardized work: An approach for ensuring work is properly controlled and follows a standard best practice. It describes the best possible method of work with the least amount of waste and lowest cost. It is usually described by process experts and experienced practitioners.
- Quick changeover or single-minute exchange of dies (SMED): A method to ensure that the changeover time between production tasks or transactions is kept as low as possible. This is usually achieved by listing all the steps of the changeover, eliminating the unnecessary ones, combining what can be combined, switching from doing them in series to parallel, and by externalizing as many of these steps as possible (by staging or doing them prior to the actual changeover).
- Work cell design: Redesigning the production cell and rearranging the location of machines to follow the sequence of the steps in order to minimize waste, especially motion.
- Kanban: A method for controlling the production flow between steps without any schedules. It enables customers to pull products by using cards or physical empty spaces, as an example, to authorize sending work to the next station or replenishing stock.

2.10.8 Lean Measures

Most of the Lean measures are simple and nonfinancial. To quantify the financial savings resulting from Lean initiatives, an additional effort is required. Traditionally in CI, the focus lies on cost control with full utilization of resources (such as labor and machines). The measures are primarily financial and cost oriented, while inventory is considered an asset that helps in dealing with variation in customer demand. However, the objective of Lean is to maximize flow with a pull from the supplier to maximize customer value, resulting in reduced costs. In Lean, inventory is considered as waste that hides many problems within the system. Some of the key Lean measures include the following:

- Lead time, which is the time measured from the moment customers make an order to the moment they receive it.
- Cycle time, which is the time it takes for a certain product to be made at a certain process step as seen by the customer of that step.

- Percentage of customer satisfaction.
- Percentage of on-time delivery as a measure of process effectiveness.
- Inventory turns.
- Takt time, which equals the available time of work divided by the customer-demanded quantities.
- Waiting time between production steps.
- Percentage of employee satisfaction.

Bhasin and Burcher (2006) gathered the following benefits of Lean implementation from different references: 90% reduction in lead time, 90% reduction in inventories, 90% reduction in cost of quality (COQ), 40% reduction in waste, 60% reduction in changeover, and 50% increase in labor.

2.11 Management Systems (MSs)

According to Deming (1993), a system can be defined as a network of interdependent components that function together and should be managed to achieve a unique aim. Moreover, management is the integration of all resources into a total system to achieve an objective (Johnson *et al.*, 1964). The process of management involves planning, coordinating, developing standards, and organizing experiences so that the performance can be improved (Cunningham, 1979). Deming (1993) proposed a management theory called a system of profound knowledge, which consisted of the awareness of all connecting parts of a system and its variations, awareness of the people as they form part of the system, and awareness of the idea that management is about prediction. Management concepts take two recurring approaches (Harnesk and Abrahamsson, 2007):

- rational focusing on work control through surveillance and improvement, and
- social focusing on the quality of the relation between the employees and their manager.

Burns and Stalker (Keller, 1978) claimed that there are two types of management systems (MSs):

- mechanistic, which is highly structured and suitable for a stable business environment; and

- organic, which is less formal, more empowering, and suitable for a dynamic business environment.

As indicated by Spencer (1994), there is a third model called cultural MS, in which leadership shares control, and human development is valued.

An MS is an approach or a plan of running a business that can be considered formal when documented and communicated (Salah and Rahim, 2019). Generally, MSs are developed to fulfill the requirements of various management disciplines, such as quality, health, safety, and environment (Scipiono *et al.*, 2001).

2.12 Quality Management Systems (QMSs)

A QMS like ISO 9001 aims to integrate quality into the practices and procedures of running an operation. These systems are based on the principles of customer focus, leadership, people involvement, process focus (including mapping, documentation, risk management, and performance indicators), a management approach focused on systems of processes, CI, decisions based on facts, and supplier relationship (Pfeifer *et al.*, 2004).

A QMS such as ISO 9001 should not be considered a substitute for a CI methodology and philosophy such as TQM, but they both need to be integrated to improve the business performance (Sun, 2000). A QMS needs to address issues of a technical and nontechnical or behavioral nature, such as leadership styles, conflicts, and change management.

ISO 9001 and other quality standard series had been developed by the International Standards Organization (ISO) with quality systems as their primary focus, including components such as management responsibility for quality, design control, documentation, data control, purchasing management, product identification, inspection, testing, process control, handling of defective items, corrective actions, handling of products, control of quality records, internal audits, training, and statistical methodology. Many organizations today attempt to obtain ISO certification, as it is a requirement for many customers. ISO is criticized for focusing excessively on formal documentation and not enough on variability reduction. Also, many third-party consultants or auditors are not well educated in technical quality tools. The return on investment (ROI) of the billions of dollars spent on ISO certification worldwide is not clear (Montgomery, 2001). However, various organizations managed to quantify tangible savings based on their efforts to review, enhance, and document their processes as part of ISO certification initiatives.

Quality award models, such as the Malcolm Baldrige National Quality Award (MBNQA) and the European Foundation for Quality Management, *i.e.*, EFQM, or BEM (Business Excellence Model), are used by many organizations to conduct self-assessment audits. These models can be considered QMSs (Salah and Rahim, 2019).

MBNQA consists of three basic components: strategy and action plans, system, and information and analysis (Kaye and Anderson, 1999). It includes seven areas of quality measures: leadership, information and analysis, strategic quality planning, human resources (HR) development and management, management of process quality, quality and operational results, and customer focus and satisfaction (Beatty, 2006; Jitpaiboon and Rao, 2007). EFQM is based on the following principles: results focus, customer orientation, leadership, management by facts, people involvement, improvement, and social responsibility (Ricondo and Viles, 2005). The implementation of these quality award models is the second step after adopting QMSs (Mangelsdorf, 1999). TQM is perceived as the umbrella for quality tools or approaches like ISO 9001 and MBNQA (Leonard and McAdam, 2004; Harnesk and Abrahamsson, 2007).

The emergence of these models helped identify areas for improvement and put TQM in a model form (Ricondo and Viles, 2005). They enabled organizations to monitor and improve their TQM efforts (McAdam *et al.*, 2008). Leonard and McAdam (2004) have proposed that TQM interacts with strategy, quality tools, and award models and that TQM is considered a catalyst for the implementation of award models. TQM is more comprehensive than MBNQA (Jitpaiboon and Rao, 2007). The MBNQA and the EFQM holistic models encompass definitions of TQM in a broad sense. Self-assessment against these models can help organizations achieve excellent performance. However, even organizations that use self-assessment auditing against business excellence models, such as MBNQA and EFQM (which have much in common), are failing to sustain improvement, especially between audits (Kaye and Anderson, 1999).

EFQM lacks some key drivers such as clear mission, critical success factors, and specific aims, which are important to focus management commitment and attention in the right direction. The competitive CI model, presented by Dyason and Kaye (1995), had been developed to overcome these weaknesses but still, as suggested by Kaye and Anderson (1999), lacks other key critical success factors. Kaye and Anderson (1999) incorporated those critical factors in a new CI model they developed, which was revised again to stress the management role. They proposed an adjusted model, which they had seen as preparatory and complementary for the more complex models such as MBNQA. These more complex models are useful where an organization already has a base and culture for improvement and wishes to build on them. They suggested that their revised model still needed to be refined and expanded. In addition, Lean Six Sigma (LSS) itself can be thought of as a MS (McAdam and Evans, 2004). It represents a new wave of the QM evolution (Basu, 2004).

2.13 Company-Wide Quality Control (CWQC)

CWQC can be considered a system of means to economically produce goods that satisfy the customer's requirements of quality and value for money, dividing the benefits among consumers, employees, and stockholders while enhancing the quality of people's lives (Ishikawa, 1983). The traditional literature in the United States refers to the cost of quality (COQ) as the cost of quality assurance and management of material defects. In CWQC, quality cost is the cost to society determined by design, manufacturing efficiency, sales, and services (Sullivan, 1988). Figure 2.2 shows the seven stages

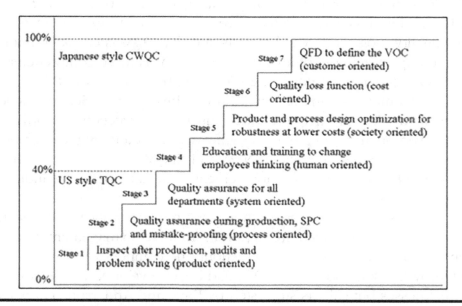

Figure 2.2   The seven stages of quality as adapted from Sullivan (1988).

in CWQC. The US-style total quality control (TQC) only covers the first three stages of CWQC.

2.14 Integrated Company-Wide Management System (ICWMS)

The use of a well-structured system that engages the organization in CI is essential to survive and stay ahead of competition. ICWMS, proposed by Salah and Rahim (2019), can be considered an organization governance system that provides the capability to align the employees and the whole operation in the same strategic direction. This is realized through the integration of different MSs to achieve total control in an "entrepreneurial and ethical way" (Hilb, 2006) in order to fulfill the desired targets. Also, ICWMS promotes the CWQC approach, creates an environment of participative management, and builds a culture of total quality and cooperation. In the literature, different components of management systems can be found under different names. These MS components have not necessarily been used together. ICWMS encompasses various aspects of the management disciplines. It primarily draws on five MSs that are subdisciplines of management. The tools used within these components are generally acknowledged. However, the grouping and connection of these components with each other represents the novelty of ICWMS. These five components are strategic quality management, quality project management, daily (operation) quality management, process management, and quality performance management. A brief description of these components of ICWMS will be highlighted later in this book (see Chapter 5, Section 5.4). However, Salah and Rahim (2019) introduced a detailed and comprehensive review of ICWMS.

2.15 Cost of Quality (COQ)

The knowledge of cost is essential in order to define quality (Ishikawa, 1985). Quality definitions have ranged in scope from narrow definitions such as "meeting engineering specifications on the shop floor" to large society-level definitions (Kolarik, 1995). The definition of quality by the ISO 9000 (1992) standards indicated that it is the totality of features of a product or service that bear on its ability to satisfy the stated or implied needs of customers. Quality practitioners along with financial accountants have to work hand in hand to help estimate, validate, and then report the QI financial savings in an organization. The purpose for quantifying the cost of quality (COQ) includes (Juran and Godfrey, 1999) the following: to present quality projects and programs in a language understood by the top management, to identify and prioritize cost reduction opportunities, to identify product stability threats and customer satisfaction opportunities, to expand budget and cost controls, and to stimulate improvement. According to Dowd (1988), COQ is important because it typically accounts for 10%–25% of sales turnover.

Taguchi defines "value" in terms of the losses imparted by a product to the society from the time of shipping. Some observers believe societal losses should include losses before a product is shipped. Either way, quality must be described from the perspective of the whole system of product manufacturing and use, not local accounting perspectives. This involves costs of rework, scrap, and loss of productivity because of inefficiencies due to variation such as maintenance, downtime, excess inventory, excess processing, and waste of time. The worst costs and the most difficult to evaluate are those incurred by customers because of reliability and durability issues. From the view of his conceptual framework for QI, Taguchi's ideas can be condensed into two concepts: quality losses must be defined as deviation from the target and measured system wide (loss to society), and quality must be designed to ensure that high system-quality levels are achieved economically, by focusing on systems, parameters, and tolerances (Gunter, 1988). Manufacturers are becoming more aware of their products' life cycle costs (involving maintenance, labor, spare parts, and aftermarket failures) and the importance of communicating COQ using the language of management (*i.e.*, money). Quality costs are costs linked to producing, identifying, avoiding, and repairing defective products (Montgomery, 2001) (see Section 3.4 for further discussion related to COQ).

2.16 Quality Loss Function (QLF)

The selection of a QLF is an essential issue in quality engineering to relate the product's key quality characteristics to its quality performance. QLF depends on customer specifications, and it computes the quality loss on an economic scale (Teeravaraprug, 2002). Various QLFs have been discussed in the literature such as DeGroot (1970), Taguchi and Wu (1980), Taguchi (1986), Spring (1993), Drain and Gough (1996), and Li (2003). However, a quadratic QLF may be reasonable in several cases (Taguchi *et al.*, 1989; Teeravaraprug and Cho, 2002).

The traditional step-loss function is the simplest form of QLF. If the product quality characteristic *y* falls within the USL and the LSL, the customer is satisfied. If *y* falls outside these limits, the customer is dissatisfied. This QLF can be described as (Salah and Rahim, 2019):

$$L(y) = 0, \ if \ USL \ <= y <= LSL, \ R \ otherwise, \tag{2.2}$$

where L(*y*) is the quality cost related to the characteristic *y* and R is the cost of rejecting a defect. The step-loss function is shown in Figure 2.3.

Another QLF was introduced by Taguchi in the form of a quadratic relationship, which unites the financial loss with the functional specification. His QLF changed the way people think about quality and funding QIs (Sullivan, 1988). Taguchi's function consists of three models: smaller the better, where zero is considered to be the best target value; larger the better, which considers some larger value as the target; and nominal the best,

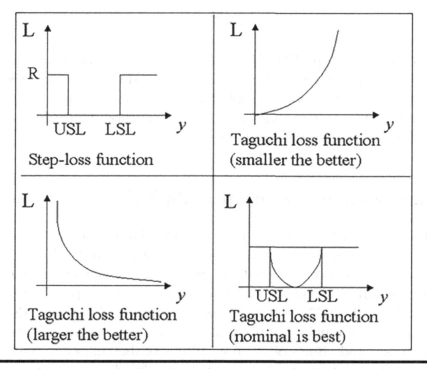

Figure 2.3 Step-loss and Taguchi loss functions as adapted from Teeravaraprug (2002).

where a deviation from the target value in any direction is treated the same. Examples of the smaller-the-better type include deterioration, wear, noise level, and shrinkage. Examples of the larger-the-better type include strength of materials, life of a system, and fuel efficiency (Teeravaraprug, 2004). The loss functions are as follows:

$$L = k \times (y)^2, \text{ if smaller the better} \tag{2.3}$$

$$L = k/(y)^2, \text{ if larger the better} \tag{2.4}$$

$$L = k \times (y - T)^2, \text{ if nominal the best,} \tag{2.5}$$

where L is the loss to society due to the deviation from the nominal target value T, y is a random value that represents the quality characteristic measurement; and k is a company-specific and composite cost constant (loss coefficient) that depends on the internal costs, warranty costs, field costs, the cost to customers, and the cost to society. Taguchi's three models are shown in Figure 2.3. For the smaller-the-better type, as Taguchi classifies static quality characteristics:

$$k = R/(USL)^2 \tag{2.6}$$

R is the quality loss at the USL. However, for service quality (or nonmanufacturing), the requirements differ by customer, and thus, the coefficient k of the QLF is not constant. One example for the smaller-the-better type in the service sector is the waiting time (Li, 2003). See Section 3.6 for further discussion related to quality loss to society.

2.17 Supply Chain Management (SCM)

A SC is the entire network of activities of a firm that connects suppliers, warehouses, factories, stores, and customers. Beside material flow, these activities include services, information, and funds. It is sometimes referred to as the distribution of logistics. The term "SCM" was developed by Procter & Gamble in the early 1980s as they started tracking the flow of goods in their distribution channels (Nahmias, 2009). SCM is about the integration of the processes and efforts of all stakeholders of the chain like buyers and suppliers to improve material flow through the chain; add more value to customers; reduce lead times and materials costs; and improve quality, responsiveness, and pricing (Kannan and Tan, 2005). Besides being fast and cost effective, a superior SC is agile, adaptable, and aligns with all its partners' interests (Lee, 2004).

SCM focuses on the coordination of the manufacturing, logistics, material, distribution, and transportation and on how companies utilize their suppliers' capabilities to enhance their competitive advantage. It helps firms improve product development through utilizing suppliers' capabilities and improve quality, delivery, and waste elimination (Tan *et al.*, 2002). Examples of operational SCM key performance indicators (KPIs) include cycle time, utilization rate, forecasting accuracy, and lead time. Financial KPIs include sales, material, transportation, and inventory (Yang *et al.*, 2007). The objectives of SCM are productivity improvement; inventory reduction and cycle time reduction in the short term; and the improvement of customer satisfaction, profit across the whole SC, and market share in the long term (Tan *et al.*, 1998).

2.18 LSS and SCM

There are various benefits for utilizing and integrating Lean Six Sigma with SCM such as the DMAIC project discipline, sustainability of results, a well-established human resources framework using the LSS belt system, and a quantitative analysis strength (Yang *et al.*, 2007). Within LSS, the Six Sigma tools ensure that products are of high quality resulting from a capable process, and the Lean tools (including VSM) ensure efficient flow through the SC, taking into account inventories, schedules, and demand quantities. LSS tools, in general, target reducing cost, waste, and non-value-added activities and satisfying customers across the SC. Also, LSS encourages good relationships with customers and suppliers, including partnering for problem solving (Salah and Rahim, 2019). One important concept in Lean, which is linked to VSM, is seeing the value stream from the perspective of the whole enterprise SC (Foster, 2007). Just-in-time (JIT) delivery is necessary for the success of JIT production. Products need to be delivered on time, at low cost, with the right quality, and in the right quantity. The Lean approach to SCM can also be described as Lean logistics, aiming at reduction of inventory, waste, and lead time. Parveen and Rao (2009) recommended some considerations for Lean SC, including stakeholders' collaboration, inventory optimization, and continuous improvement. Also, training is an important factor for succeeding in the integration of Six Sigma and SCM, as it helps establish an educated and committed workforce that is willing to change and embrace the quality strategy (Salah and Rahim, 2019).

2.19 Requirements for Successful Continuous Improvement (CI)

At present, there is a crisis in organizational improvement programs, particularly in their execution and sustainability (Devane, 2004). Much has been written about the necessity for QM and CI; however, no one has provided a solid foundation for sustainable success (Johnson, 2004).

Self-assessment auditing against business excellence models, such as the MBNQA and the EFQM, has enabled organizations to monitor and improve their TQM efforts (McAdam *et al.*, 2008). However, organizations that use these audits have failed to sustain improvement, especially between audits (Kaye and Anderson, 1999). MBNQA is useful where an organization already has a base and culture for improvement and wishes to build on that (Kaye and Anderson, 1999).

One enabler and a core component for the success of CI initiatives is an effective approach of culture change management, which is a key part of the well-structured ICWMS. Some great culture-related advantages of integrating CI methodologies with ICWMS are overcoming the resistance to implement change, increasing the speed and commitment to CI, increasing adaptation to external events, increasing motivation, ensuring that proper alignment and timely information exist, transforming the culture of the organization to a culture of cooperation and innovation, and defining everyone's roles and responsibilities.

A QMS includes all the procedures needed to integrate QM practices into an organization, and it supports communication and improvements (Nanda, 2005). It needs to address issues of a technical and nontechnical (behavioral) nature, such as leadership styles, conflicts, and change management. Its success not only depends on the quality system, including the procedures and administration of records, but also on their sensitivity to organizational values, expectations, behaviors, and relationships (Pheng and Alfelor, 2000).

ICWMS is a comprehensive MS that encompasses quality and culture management as part of its various aspects. The culture change management is a primary component that needs to be stressed and considered in order to properly execute initiatives.

Some culture change management–related requirements and foundations needed for the successful deployment of CI, as found in the literature include human integration and employee involvement (Kaye and Anderson, 1999; Hines *et al.*, 2004; Anderson *et al.*, 2006; Antony, 2006); a stable and enabling organizational infrastructure (Chapman and Hyland, 1997; Anderson *et al.*, 2006); a supportive organizational culture of innovation, lesson sharing, and empowerment (Chapman and Hyland, 1997; Kaye and Anderson, 1999; Antony, 2004; Anderson *et al.*, 2006; Antony, 2006; Bhasin and Burcher, 2006; Dahlgaard and Dahlgaard-Park, 2006); training, incentives, and project management approach (McAdam and Evans, 2004; Basu, 2004); trust and cooperative learning (Mellat-Parasat and Digman, 2007); and an initiative management approach linking projects to customers and finical impact for accountability and including proper project selection and prioritization (Antony, 2004, 2006). The alignment of the operations with the business mission, pursuit of CI, removal of barriers between individuals and departments and unity of purpose, development of a culture of flexibility, and training are all keys to achieve productivity improvement and customer satisfaction (Terziovski, 2006). ICWMS strengthens the people and system approach to improvement. It ensures that proper alignment and timely information is in place, facilitates cultural change, optimizes the overall performance of the organization, and enhances the rates of improvement. Various sections of this book will later consider different aspects related to an effective culture change management and the ICWMS culture-related practices.[1]

Finally, CI successful deployment is about the following:

■ Management commitment and allocation of resources.
■ Structured approach.
■ Strong foundation (quality culture).
■ Skilled team to set up and run the program, including planning, training, and progress monitoring.
■ Proper selection of projects and project leaders.

Note

1. Chapter 2 is partially prepared based on my literature review from my thesis titled "Total company-wide management system: A framework for Six Sigma and continuous quality improvement", 2009, available at the library of the University of New Brunswick.

QUALITY
MANAGEMENT

Chapter 3

Fundamental Pillars Related to Quality

3.1 Quality Pillar # 1: If You Cannot Measure, You Cannot Improve. Start Measuring in Order to Manage, Improve, and Control Your Processes

Assuming a scenario where an individual is envisioned to participate in a football game where the score does not attract the attention of any of the players, it is likely that the experience would be perceived as tedious and uneventful. In such a circumstance, the lack of a competitive atmosphere and the absence of a sense of achievement could significantly diminish the enjoyment and motivation of the player. In the event that a team is significantly behind on the score and is no longer invested in keeping track of their progress, players may become disinterested in the game. Conversely, in a highly competitive setting, all individuals involved in the game would remain acutely aware of the score, with the ultimate goal of emerging victorious. This approach is directly applicable to the operations of business teams. Much like the football team, such teams must adopt an active approach to measuring and tracking their performance, creating a dynamic and engaging workplace environment that inspires passion and fosters a commitment to quality and excellence.

Upon the completion of their first Lean Six Sigma (LSS) Green Belt project, junior industrial engineers experience an unforgettable sense of achievement. For the first time, they are able to quantify their contribution to the organization in tangible financial terms, which are successfully validated by

DOI: 10.4324/9781032688374-5

the finance department. This realization highlights the significant impact of Lean Six Sigma methodologies and the diligent efforts of the practitioners in changing the prevailing culture, which can be a formidable challenge. They are heroes who patiently, steadily, and persistently strive to change the status quo and create a better future.

One popular quote states: "[I]f you cannot measure it, you cannot control it". In order to manage, improve, and control a process, it is essential to start measuring it. A measurement system is formed of a person who measures, a measuring instrument, a specimen to be measured, and a method to follow for measurement. For measurements to be precisely close to the true or real values, the variation in the data shall be resulting from the variation among the measured specimens themselves. The variation in the data shall not be due to variation in the measurement method or the people who perform the measurements. In addition, it definitely shall not be resulting from the tools or gauges used in measurement, due to issues related to bias in measurements, nonlinearity over the scale of measurement, inaccuracy in relevance to the true value, precision or consistency, stability over time, or lack of calibration. All these may result in errors. Thus, one of the important initial steps in any improvement project is to ensure that data is authentic, accurate, and reliable. That is why the measure phase in Lean Six Sigma (LSS) methodology emphasizes performing a measurement system analysis (MSA) prior to performing any data analysis. Otherwise, if corrupted data is used as an input, corrupted inferences will result as an output. MSA typically uses a gauge repeatability and reproducibility (R and R) study (Breyfogle, 2003). In such an analysis, the repeatability and reproducibility of measured data are evaluated. Repeatability means that the same result will be obtained if a measurement is repeated by the same examiner using the same measuring instrument and the same specimens (randomized while tracked to minimize potential bias). On the other hand, reproducibility means the same result will be obtained if another examiner measures the same specimen using the same instrument. In addition, stability of the measurement system indicates its consistency over time. Both accuracy and stability can be addressed by calibration. This can also help in comparing various gauges with each other.

In order to conduct a variable gauge repeatability and reproducibility study, around 10 parts that represent the full range of variation are typically selected. The order of runs is randomized to minimize the risk of bias. Also, a minimum of two operators are required to perform the measurement of each part for at least two times (not successively but randomly so that the operator is not aware of or memorizing the previous measurement result).

Using statistical software packages like Minitab, analysis of variance (ANOVA) as well as the X-bar and R charts can provide reliable estimates of the variation of the measurement system. However, the ANOVA method is more accurate, as it considers the interaction between the operator and the part. What a quality practitioner tries to evaluate is the relative portion of the variation due to the gauge repeatability and reproducibility (or Gage R&R), compared to the total variation in the study. As a rule of thumb, if this portion is less than 9%, the measurement system is considered good (Farmer and Duffy, 2017). Also, if it is between 10% and 30%, the system might be acceptable, as a general guideline. If it is above 30%, the system is rejected and requires revision (Six Sigma Training, personal communication, 2008). MSA can be used as a quality tool on its own to improve a process. When comparing different assessors, it can be clear if one of them is harder or softer than the rest based on measuring the same units or similar units from the same batch. This can result in type I or type II errors. In a type I error, the risk is attributed to the producer, where the assessor may be oversensitive and incorrectly reject a good part and end up costing the company a fortune. On the other hand, in a type II error, the risk is endured by customers who may receive a defective unit due to the earlier failure of an assessor to reject it (being too soft in his/her assessment).

It is essential in the measure phase of the LSS methodology to measure the baseline performance of the key performance indicator (KPI) or metric under investigation and then compare it to a best-in-class target or benchmark (Salah *et al.*, 2010). Measuring the process performance after introducing improvement actions is also essential to establish how effective these actions are, as well as to continuously monitor the behavior of the process and act accordingly as per the famous Deming's plan-do-check-act (PDCA) cycle (Juran and Godfrey, 1999). Figure 3.1 shows a depiction of the PDCA cycle adapted to reflect the importance of measurement within the approach of continuous improvement (CI).

Furthermore, it is mainly through the measurement of indicators that an organization can realize its vision and strategic objectives progressively. Performance measurement is a key part of the strategic planning process, which is about understanding where an organization stands and where it is heading. Moreover, Hoshin Kanri, or strategy deployment, is about cascading down the KPI targets to all employees at all levels, in a company-wide approach (Juran and Godfrey, 1999). This is essential in aligning the various teams to the corporate strategy so that all of them work as a united team in one direction.

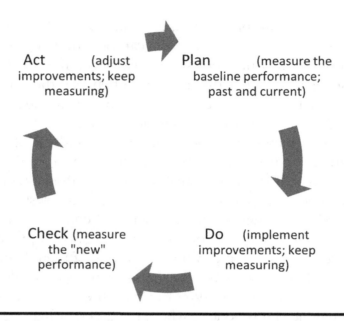

Figure 3.1   Deming's famous PDCA cycle reflecting the importance of measurement in CI.

Continuous monitoring of the behavior of the process over time is a key task that can help anyone working within a process to control and improve that process. Statistical process control (SPC) charts are among the basic quality tools used as a process behavior measurement tool (Montgomery, 2001). Using this tool enables organizations to clearly hear the voice of any of their processes. Through the measurement of variation, one can verify if assignable causes exist or not and then take the necessary steps to bring the process back under control to be only governed by the natural causes of variation, which are inherent in the process. Thus, the process would become stable or under statistical control. This means that its behavior in the future can be predictable. Only then can its behavior be compared to the specification limits dictated by subject matter experts, regulators, customers, or consultants to verify if the process is capable of satisfying these tolerances or not (for more information on SPC charts, see Section 7.5).

Edwards Deming proposed 14 points of management (Montgomery, 2001), which in many ways were ahead of his time in terms of how progressive and futuristic they were. While Deming opposed setting production quotas as per one of his 14 points due to the negative aspects of target setting at that time, it is widely accepted today to use balanced score card (BSC) metrics, as introduced by Norton and Kaplan (Kaplan and Norton,

2006). The use of BSC metrics include setting up KPI targets, which form an essential part of running any business. Deming was indeed ahead of his time. He opposed treating people as machines and forcing them to deliver quantified targets or else face getting fired. This, in his opinion, took out pride in quality, as employees lost the meaning of the value of their work. They fearfully focused on quantity only. Today, quality targets need to be emphasized in a positive approach in order to motivate employees to be proud of delivering the best quality for the products they make or the services they deliver. As per Rouillard (2009), targets need to be specific, measurable, action oriented or achievable, realistic or relevant, and time constrained or time bound (*i.e.*, SMART). If a target is missed, it is treated as an opportunity, not as a problem. The goal is to encourage learning, innovating, and striving for success. Admitting there is an opportunity to improve is the first step in improvement, which is not always easy to establish. Moreover, it is indeed useless to set up targets that are easily achieved and represent no challenge whatsoever.

The lack of performance measurement negatively impacts the team members' productivity and motivation to enhance quality. If the management system (MS) does not quantitatively recognize the performance differences between employees, then it does not matter anymore whether an employee works well or not. Measurements can be used to drive the right behavior by rewarding employees who perform well, intrinsically recognizing them or paying them an incentive. However, team-based targets are better to start with than individual-based targets, depending on the level of maturity in an organization, in terms of its quality culture.

Measuring the voice of the customers is also essential. Using customer satisfaction rate measurement such as the net promoter score (NPS) is a great way to start assessing the voice of customers (Bernstein, 2018). However, a survey may not provide the full picture of what the customer really wants. Thus, it is recommended to couple it with other means of data collection and innovation techniques such as interviews and customer-focused group discussions.

Sometimes, it can be challenging to choose a proper metric for evaluating a product or a process performance. Some managers may present this argument as an excuse for not being able to come up with a proper metric for a certain process. To overcome that, the following example can be considered.

How can pepper spiciness be measured?

Well, Wilbur Scoville was able to answer this question. Dried pepper is dissolved in alcohol and then diluted in sugar water gradually until the burning taste disappears. Scoville units are used based on the quantity of sugar water added (Parthasarathy *et al.*, 2008). Thus, there are always creative ways of measuring even when it seems very challenging. Sometimes the success of an LSS project lies merely on fixing the measurement system itself, which enables the team to realize most of the improvements and the lessons learned from the project right after the measure phase of a Lean Six Sigma (LSS) project.

Finally, it is much better to start measuring performance instead of giving up to complaints about a negative process or making excuses about a process being impossible to measure. Data can help elevate discussions form what may seem like a personal argument into a professional dialogue. In conclusion, here is a famous and anonymous saying: "In God we trust. All others must have data".

3.2 Quality Pillar # 2: Manage Your Operation by Focusing on Its Efficiency and Effectiveness

In his book *Gemba Kaizen*, Masaki Imai explained that "Gemba" means the real place where action or value is created to satisfy customers (Imai, 2012). He introduced three main elements for managing the Gemba, which are essential for measuring any process performance: quality, cost, and delivery (QCD) (see Figure 3.2). First, quality refers to the number of defective items

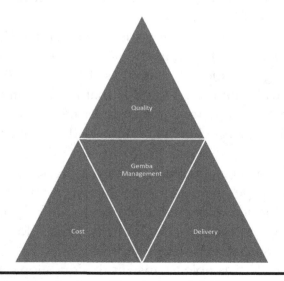

Figure 3.2   Gemba management: quality, cost, and delivery.

or defects per shift or day, percentage of defects, *etc.* Second, cost refers to the cost per unit produced, the number of products made per unit of time, productivity, utilization, *etc.* Third, delivery refers to time or durations such as lead time (total time from receipt of customer order till customer receipt of finished order), cycle time (total time elapsed between two successive products), and processing time (total time elapsed for one operator to finish working on one product). Cycle time and processing time are often used interchangeably, but they differ when more than one operator is performing the same operation to produce more products. Time-related metrics can include the percentage of on-time delivery as an example of the effectiveness of product or service delivery. For example, in a procurement department, the following can be measured:

a. Quality: Number of purchase requisitions returned due to missing or incorrect information, as a measure of defective inputs. Also, the number of issued purchase orders that were later rejected by the requestor, as a measure of a defective process output.
b. Cost: The cost per issued purchase order, or the number of created purchase orders per buyer per day. Obviously, if the count of purchase orders is increased for the same number of buyers, the cost will be less per order. This means better productivity and higher efficiency.
c. Time: Lead time from the moment a purchase requisition is received to the moment the purchase order is sent. Also, the processing time it takes for a buyer, uninterruptedly, to create a purchase order.

Improving the quality of a process typically results in fewer defects, less rework, shorter lead time, and less required resources. Consequently, this results in lowering the total operational cost. The quality of a process is about the way products or services are delivered. It is about managing the resources at the Gemba, including man, machine, material, method, mother nature or environment, and measurement (6Ms). Enhancing quality and minimizing cost are compatible. Actually, quality can be considered the basis for enhanced cost and delivery. The old philosophy indicates that quality does cost more money (expensive machines, testing equipment, and more resources to perform rework and inspections) and leads to higher prices. The new competitive approach indicates that better quality and lower cost are compatible, and the new resulting product can be of equal or higher quality while at a lower price. The priority for managers is to achieve better QCD simultaneously, with a focus on quality first. Managers need to resist the temptation to cut costs at the expense of quality or sacrifice quality for faster delivery. Competitive advantage must not be built on unit cost or price alone, but on a total approach reflecting QCD, as they are closely interrelated (Imai, 2012).

What companies need to focus on is cost management, not cost cutting or cutting corners. Cost cutting includes firing employees, poor restructuring, and beating up suppliers, all of which end up in quality deterioration (Imai, 2012).

Other important measures for any process, which are generally emphasized in various quality award models, are efficiency and effectiveness. Efficiency is about maximizing the output using the same or even less input (see Equation 3.1). It is about the utilization of all resources and exploiting every second to ensure the production of all potential units that are planned for the available production interval. So it is well associated with the enhancement of QCD. Effectiveness, on the other hand, is mainly focusing on comparing the output to the customer requirement in terms of QCD and ensuring they match. Figure 3.3 illustrates the meaning of process efficiency versus effectiveness. Another common term used in manufacturing, which can be applicable to any process, is the overall equipment effectiveness (OEE) (Juran and Godfrey, 1999; Breyfogle, 2003; Pyzdek and Keller, 2019). OEE comprises availability (A) or uptime, Performance (P) or occupancy, and Quality (Q) metrics (see Equation 3.2). Ideally, OEE amounts to a 100% value where there is a defect-free process (such as having invoices or transactions without errors) and a zero cost of poor quality (COPQ) (see Section 3.4 for more details about COPQ). In addition, effectiveness of a process is about its capability to satisfy its customers and thus can be evaluated by measuring the percentage of customer satisfaction, such as meeting

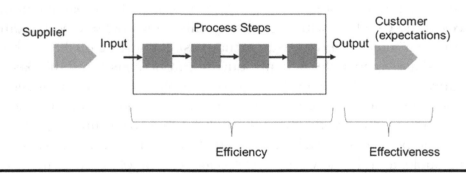

Figure 3.3 Process efficiency versus process effectiveness as adapted from Six Sigma Training, personal communication (2008).

the goals of a service level agreement (SLA), delivering on time as promised, and complying with budgeted cost plans. Other common metrics include productivity and utilization. Productivity improvement is concerned with maximizing the production rate or the number of produced units per day. For example, in a purchasing department, productivity can be measured by tracking the number of purchase orders issued per buyer per day. Utilization is concerned with maximizing the productive hours of adding value, compared to the total hours scheduled. For example, in a facility management company, the technicians' utilization can be evaluated by tracking the number of billed hours, per technician per week, out of a total of 40 hours of scheduled work, per technician per week.

$$\text{Efficiency} = \text{Output} / \text{Input} \tag{3.1}$$

$$\text{Effectiveness} = \text{Overall Equipment Effectiveness} = \text{OEE} = A \times P \times Q \tag{3.2}$$

where:
- A = Actual operating time or uptime (without downtime) / Planned time or total shift time
  = 1 − % downtime
- P = Ideal productive cycle time / Actual cycle time based on available time, including all waste
  = % fill rate
  = % un-idle
- Q = Acceptable output (without defects) / Total output
  = 1 − % defective

3.3 Quality Pillar # 3: Quality Is about Pride in What You Do and a Passion for Goodness

There are various and famous definitions for quality in literature. Juran, for example, defined it as the fitness for use (Juran and Godfrey, 1999). Crosby spoke about zero defects (Crosby, 1979). Garvin introduced important dimensions of quality (Garvin, 1988). In addition, it is well accepted by many authors that quality is about satisfaction of customer needs, conformance to standards, and exceeding customer expectations.

In recent years, the following meaning of quality is becoming more evident: ***Quality is about being proud of what a person does. It is a***

***passion for goodness to deliver value to all society, to make the lives
of workers, customers, and all people more enjoyable. It is about
finding meaning in what one does and the sense of self-reward
through helping others.***

Deming's views on quality, demonstrated in his 14 points of management,
clearly challenged the status quo (Montgomery, 2001). One of these points
was concerned with instilling pride in what workers do, and not to depriv-
ing them of it. At a time when many manufacturing facilities focused on
quantity only and threatened their workers with getting fired if they did not
meet individual production targets, Deming strongly opposed the setup of
quotas or quantified targets that treated workers as machines or slaves. He
noticed that workers who operated under such circumstances became less
motivated and did not focus on quality at all.

Deming's point mentioned here might be considered as contradicting the
principle of using performance measurement as a way to improve processes
(see Section 3.1). Thus, it is important to point out that it is well agreed
nowadays that targets remain very important in enabling improvement, but
they need to be smartly and positively used to motivate employees, not the
opposite.

Quality is about the sense of goodness to carry out the best practices and
to help others, internal or external to any organization, by serving them well
and providing them with almost perfect services or products, which make
their lives more comfortable and enjoyable. It is about feeling proud of the
achieved work, which can only happen when it is perfected. It is also about
understanding the meaning of the services provided and the benefits of the
use of the products made. To help one's team understand the meaning of
their work, it is essential to make it clear to them how their work impacts
customers' lives. This can be achieved by inviting some customers to talk
about how the products made by the employees are used to save lives, as
in the example of the medical industry. Sometimes, employees need to be
taken to visit customers to enable them to see how their products make a
difference in customers' lives. This connection, although sounding basic,
does help instill pride and self-satisfaction in those employees, so they
become more motivated and focused on quality and improvement. They
often come back from such visits with more ideas for improvement, after
they observe how customers use their products. This experience enables
them to empathize more with their customers, which helps them design and
make better products. Also, this pillar is aligned with the Japanese concept
of employee self-discipline (see Section 10.2), which implies a high level of

maturity in understanding what quality is about and committing to prevent the passing of any defect to the next step in the process (Imai, 2012).

3.4 Quality Pillar # 4: Quality Does Pay for Itself and Thus Costs Nothing

The gap between the baseline performance level for a key performance indicator (KPI) and its ideal performance level (which is almost impossible to achieve) is equivalent to the COPQ. Han and Lee (2002) claimed that the COPQ is anywhere between 20% and 40% of the total organization revenue, which makes it a very essential concept. The American Society for Quality (ASQ) recognized four categories for COPQ, which consist of appraisal cost, prevention cost, and internal and external failures cost (Sower *et al.*, 2007). The following is an explanation of these four categories for COPQ (Devor *et al.*, 1992; Montgomery, 2001):

a. Internal defects: Failures discovered inside an organization prior to delivery, in the form of a waste of scrap or rework. They occur when one employee or department allows a defect to pass to the next department (or the next internal customer). In transactional (nonmanufacturing) processes, this failure can simply mean missing, late, or incorrect information. The process is stopped until a correction or rework takes place. Dr. Ishikawa famously stated that the next process step is the customer, referring to internal customers within the same company. The importance of the internal customer view implies that departments within the same firm shall not operate in separated silos. For example, the maintenance department needs to view and support the operation team as their own customer by ensuring all equipment is readily available and not treat them with a poor attitude or provide them with low-quality service.

b. External defects: Discovered by the customer after delivery and result in higher losses (than internal defects) such as product recalls, warranty issues, and reputation damage.

c. Prevention cost: Includes the cost of setting up a quality assurance department to take initiatives such as the setup of training programs focused on enhancing the capabilities of employees to produce quality products. It also includes the cost of efforts in design and manufacturing, done to prevent nonconformities. An important subcategory of it is quality planning and engineering, which are the costs associated with the generation of a quality plan and its related communication procedures, inspection plan, reliability plan, the data system, all specialized plans and activities of the quality assurance function, and the costs of auditing systems.

d. Appraisal cost: Includes costs of measuring, inspecting, and auditing products and components to ensure their conformance to quality specifications, which "ideally" shall not be required. In an ideal process, these programs do not add value, as an ideal process is done right the first time and every time. However, the goal of any audit shall be to find gaps, learn about them, and improve the process using corrective and preventive actions. These actions are implemented to ensure the process comes under control and to reduce the risks associated with those gaps. Thus, the audit goal is for those gaps not to appear again in the future. So, even if another audit is done, it will not reveal the same gaps anymore.

However, prevention costs such as quality planning and capability studies are not always considered as part of COPQ. These costs stay even after the status of *zero defects* is achieved.

Within the LSS project and the ISO approach, the corrective action process includes the following steps: identify the problem, contain it, identify the cause as well as the solution to prevent problem recurrence, verify the implementation, and validate its effectiveness. In addition, the preventive action approach includes the following steps: analyze the process to identify potential failures or process deficiencies, improve the process by enhancing its procedure using error-proofing methods, and validate the effectiveness of the preventive action (Farmer and Duffy, 2017).

The language of business managers is dollars. Every decision made needs to be based on feasibility studies to justify any investment, by taking into account its rate of return. In the 1970s, Bill Crosby wrote a book titled *Quality Is Free* (see Crosby, 1979). However, if quality has a cost, then how could it be free? Well, quality is free in the sense that it pays for itself. It is true that various companies spend much money to set up quality assurance programs involving process improvement teams. However, these programs typically result in successful initiatives that can be measured in terms of financially tangible savings, in the order of millions of dollars. Actually, these savings are often used to justify budget approvals that result in expanding these programs and sometimes investing in automation software packages that can further enhance processes, such as the use of robotic process automation (RPA) or process management applications (Sohini, 2020). It was Jack Welch, who publicized the importance of such programs like Six Sigma, which resulted in millions of dollars of savings for General Electric (GE). His announcement led to many companies embracing Six Sigma as an approach for process improvement and financial savings. This reported success has helped spread this methodology (Raisinghani *et al.*, 2005). Welch's commitment was essential to the success of Six Sigma deployment, as its effective implementation depends heavily on how passionate the leadership is in its support (Antony, 2006).

Typically, process improvement projects utilizing approaches like LSS aim to enhance the current performance of a process to a higher targeted level based on a benchmark of a best-in-class level. This gap is equivalent to the targeted financial savings, which can be either cost reduction savings or incremental margin (profit) resulting from additional revenue. Companies shall take into account a long-term view of quality when evaluating their relationship with their stakeholders such as customers, suppliers, own employees, and the society at large. They shall abstain from focusing on short-term gains, which may negatively affect their long-term stakeholder relationship and, hence, the sustainability of their business performance. Categories of project financial benefits include direct cost savings, incremental margin, lower carrying cost or working capital, cost avoidance, and other payable-time improvements (Martin, 2007). Financial project savings can be classified into the following:

a. Soft savings: Related to partial-time savings (and, hence, cost savings) of employees' working time, as well as any working capital savings or cash balance enhancements related to faster collection of dues or accounts receivable, and the reduction of inventory amounts.

b. Hard savings: Related to additional profit (resulting from smart initiatives to enhance revenue) as well as the absolute removal of spending against historical spending run rates (recurring payments or bills) as a result of introducing smart alternatives, not cost slashing. Hard savings also include head count–related savings (if a full-time person who is no longer required for the simplified process is relocated to another preapproved vacant position or has retired without replacement). It is important to note that the goal of continuous improvement (CI) cannot be to fire employees, as no one will become interested in CI anymore.

Typically, the gap between the current performance level and the ideal performance level is equivalent to COPQ. A portion of that is considered as the targeted savings,, which is estimated as the difference between the current performance baseline and the targeted performance level. The estimated savings in any project include hard and soft savings, as depicted in Figure 3.4. Also, Figure 3.5 shows a number of examples of soft and hard savings (or profit), based on smartly increased revenue and operational cost reduction initiatives. This can serve as a guide to calculate the impact of improvement projects, as an estimate at the beginning of projects and as an

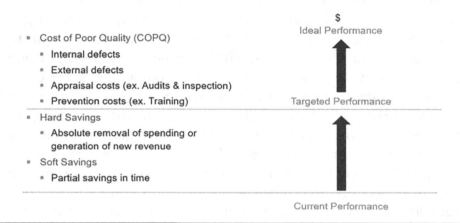

Figure 3.4   COPQ and estimated savings.

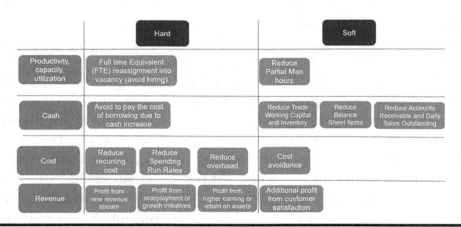

Figure 3.5   Classification of operational expenses savings and additional profit typically resulting from Lean Six Sigma (process improvement) projects.

actual sum at the end of projects. A clear connection has to be established, linking improvement actions directly with the resulting change in performance. Proper evidence is usually sought to demonstrate where the numbers used in the analysis came from. This can be in the form of copies of quotations, contracts, emails, *etc.*

To determine the actual savings or net financial impact of an LSS project, a cost and benefit analysis is performed usually in the improve phase. This analysis is mainly about estimating both the incurred costs as related to the solution implemented and the benefits or the costs avoided. The cost of the implemented actions may include design, labor, equipment, material, transport, controls, development of software, communication, and security. These costs need to be compared to the benefits of the avoided cost, such as the cost of scrap, rework, nonconformities, accidents, regulatory violations, repairs, recalls, and reinstallation. The payback period is the duration elapsing before recovering the investment spent during a project. It is noted that some costs are difficult to estimate, such as customer dissatisfaction (Farmer and Duffy, 2017).

An illustration of the calculation of savings will now be presented. In a warranty department, if a team manages to simplify the process of reviewing a warranty claim and reduce the processing time by an hour every day, then given that the average cost of an employee in that department is $20 per hour, an annual soft saving can be calculated as follows (Typically, savings are tracked for one year only. Not that they won't occur in future years, but simply in order for improvement teams to move ahead and focus on other novel opportunities.):

$$\text{Soft savings} = 1 \text{ hour/working day} \times \$20/\text{hour} \times 250$$
$$\text{working days/year} = \$5,000 \text{ per year}$$

Also, if the same team manages to completely solve the root cause of a major warranty complaint that is frequently occurring (10 times per working day) and causing a loss of $10 per occurrence, then the annual hard savings can be calculated as follows (assuming that the data comparison of the "before" and "after" improvement situations clearly indicates a statistically significant difference):

$$\text{Hard savings} = (10 \text{ occurrences per working day before improvement} - 0$$
$$\text{occurrences per working day after improvement}) \times \$10 \text{ per}$$
$$\text{occurrence} \times 250 \text{ working days/year} = \$25,000 \text{ per year}$$

A significant improvement in customer satisfaction can lead to additional sales, revenue, and profit. However, it is often challenging to link such improvement directly to the enhancement of profit and thus may only be considered as a soft saving. With time, more of the soft savings will eventually be converted into hard or more tangible savings.

Other categories of savings include the reduction in capital expenses within projects' execution compared to their approved budgets; savings from merger and acquisition projects based on synergies or elimination of duplicated functions; and savings from procurement based on negotiation of prices, claims, and variations. These can be typically considered as part of the soft savings category, although some companies consider some of them as hard savings.

Regarding savings validation and the role of the finance department, there are mainly two stages in any process improvement project when a finance team is required to help:

a. At the beginning of the project, to calculate and confirm the method used for estimating the financial impact of the project.
b. At the end of the project, to validate if the resulted savings are real, tangibly achieved (impacting the bottom line or the financial profit and loss statement of the company), and directly linked to the improvement actions.

Moreover, it is important to plan the efforts of process improvement and have annual targets set. These targets are "gradually" increased year over year toward achieving the best-in-class benchmarks, which are known in the industry. One key measure used to assess the CI efforts at an organization is the ratio of realized dollars of savings to the total amount of revenue dollars. For different organizations, this ratio can vary from 0.2% to 4.5%, as shown in Table 3.1.

In a study conducted by Pulakanam (2012), the execution of Six Sigma projects contributed an amount of savings, which was equivalent to about 1.7% of the total revenue over the duration of deployment. It was also equivalent to more than double the dollars invested.

Another important measure to keep in mind is the count of trained employees on CI methodologies like Lean Six Sigma, compared to the total head count of the organization. Pyzdek (2019) described the expected number of Six Sigma trained belts per 1,000 employees in a mature organization, as depicted in Table 3.2. It is recommended to increase the total count

Table 3.1 Ratio of Savings of Six Sigma Programs to Revenue by Different Organizations

Organization	Year	Savings as a percentage of revenue
Motorola	1986–2001	4.5%
Allied Signal	1998	3.3%
General Electric	1996–1999	1.2%
Honeywell	1998–2000	2.4%
Ford	2000–2002	2.3%

Source: Adapted from Cyger (2022)

Table 3.2 Count of Six Sigma Belts per 1,000 Employees at a Mature Organization

Count of employees	1,000
Count of Master Black Belts	1
Count of Black Belts	10
Count of Green Belts	50

Source: Adapted from Pyzdek (2019)

of trained employees gradually, year over year. It is recommended that all employees be put through a basic training of Yellow Belt, so they are familiar with the basics of the LSS methodology, and they can speak the same language of quality improvement to help the Green and Black Belts within their functional teams.

3.5 Quality Pillar # 5: Do It Right the First Time and Every Time

There is nothing worse than producing something to less than completion or even perfection, especially when one is capable of doing so. While this has to be balanced with a bias for speed and action, the implication for not doing the right thing at the right time in service or manufacturing is incurring additional cost that could have been avoided. The earlier an error or a defect is discovered, the cheaper it is to fix it. Obviously, external defects discovered by customers are much more expensive to fix than internal defects discovered before reaching the customer. Ideally, organizations strive to achieve zero COPQ, including zero defects.

It is the responsibility of every employee working through the value stream chain not to allow defects to be passed from one stage to another. Inputs shall be defect-free and so shall be the outputs. Every employee is responsible for quality. It is neither the manager's sole responsibility nor the quality assurance department's responsibility. This understanding is an essential part of any organizational culture that aims at high levels of excellence and sustainability.

Also, quality is about working in a "smart" manner, not necessarily a "hard" manner. It is about making sure the right things get done first in the order of priority, by the right people equipped with the right tool. Much effort is wasted when teams do not pay enough attention to choosing the right team members or the right tools. In order to overcome change resistance in any project, the right selection of representatives from various sections of the value stream chain (who are affected by the process change) is vital. Similarly, using an improper tool to fix the process ends up not only in wasting time and effort but also in possible safety issues or even the loss of life in some cases.

It is not enough to do the right thing once. Consistency in doing so is a must, or else, the customer will be at the mercy of variation. Variation can be classified into two types: common and special. Not much can be done about common variation, which is naturally inherent in the process, such as the randomly embedded differences in raw material batches and the uncontrollable variation in environmental factors. For special causes, assignable root causes are sought in order to eliminate them. Bringing the process into stability is one of the first steps in process improvement. Having a better control over the process behavior enables process owners to shift the process average closer to the specified target, in order to enhance the capability of the process to satisfy its customers.

Attention shall be drawn to explore the sources of variation. In addition to sources related to measurement devices and methods, variation within the parts themselves, variation between the different sampled parts, and variation happening over time are all important to investigate. A multi-vari analysis can help pinpoint the source of variation. Decreasing variation in the process's intended function can help minimize the opportunities for defects to happen.

When throwing darts, the objective is to ideally hit the bull's eye every time. However, this is almost impossible to achieve for every single trial. If all the darts fall close to each other in a concentrated area, it means they were precisely thrown with less variation. On the other hand, if they are scattered evenly around the target, it means they are accurate but not consistent or precise. The objective in any process is to achieve both (high precision and high accuracy) so that the process is done right every time.

3.6 Quality Pillar # 6: Quality Loss Is a Cost to the Whole Society

A popular story that explains Taguchi's concept of quality loss to society is the following one, which is adapted from Sullivan (1988). A Japanese manufacturer of vinyl sheets, which are used by farmers to protect agricultural crops from storms, had the sheets' thickness well under control, in terms of the average and variation. The process was stable and predictable under the control of the common causes of variation. When compared to the thickness specifications dictated by a Japanese industrial standard, issued by the regulatory authorities, the sheets' thicknesses were well within the specifications.

Motivated by the potential for additional profit, the manufacturer decided to aim for a lesser thickness than the nominal target, by centering the narrow distribution closer to the lower specification limit, producing a very uniform sheet barely above the lower tolerance limit. This was justified by the manufacturer, as the produced sheets' thicknesses were still falling within the specification limits. Aiming for a lesser thickness enabled the manufacturer to produce longer sheets and increase profitability. However, it did entail some additional risk of some sheets falling much closer to the minimum specification limit.

Unfortunately, that year witnessed a severe storm that these sheets did not endure. This resulted in three losses: the loss in the vinyl itself, as the product got destroyed and could not withstand the wind; the loss to farmers in crop damages; and the loss to society, in terms of prices rising due to supply shortages. This also led to a huge loss of agricultural crops, forcing the Japanese government to use taxpayers' money to import crops to compensate for the lost volume. Thus, the loss to the society is much greater than the manufacturer's gain. The standards were later changed to specify a new average for all manufacturers to use as a nominal.

As explained, Ginichi Taguchi's fabulous principle of quality, loss to society can be well demonstrated through this story. The whole society may suffer due to one manufacturer getting greedy. So it is very important to reflect on quality in the broad sense, as it affects everyone within the society—*i.e.*, all stakeholders, and not just a single manufacturer or customer. Indeed, this is a great concept that Taguchi came up with, not only emphasizing quality but also sustainability.

When it comes to quality, variation is the enemy. The moment a KPI measured value deviates from the target, there is a higher risk for defects to occur, and thus additional cost is incurred per Taguchi's view of the COPQ. Unlike the traditional way of looking at quality loss, where the cost function is a step function incurring a positive value for the COPQ only when exceeding the specification limits, Taguchi's view of the COPQ is quadratic, where cost is incurred in an increasing manner the moment deviation from the nominal target occurs, as in a parabola (Taguchi *et al.*, 1989). The loss starts to occur as the measured KPI approaches closer and closer to one of the specified limits. The traditional view (common in the West), on the other hand, indicates that as long as the measured values are within the specified limits, no loss is incurred at all. Obviously, Taguchi's approach is more proactive, as it emphasizes that the average of measured values shall be as close as possible to the target. A shift in the process would cause the tail of the distribution to extend further beyond the closer specified limit, with more opportunities for defective items to appear (see Figure 2.4 in Section 2.16, which depicts the difference between the two models or functions for the cost of quality).

The difference between the step-loss function and Taguchi's quality loss function (QLF) can be explained by the following example (see Figure 3.6). In the 1980s, Ford Motor Co. outsourced a major subassembly to a Japanese firm as well as to one of Ford's US plants. Overtime, complaints and warrantee claims from the customers using the US-built subassembly far exceeded the other one. Ford collected samples from both firms' subassemblies, disassembled their parts and measured them. It was found that while both had zero defects (when compared to the specifications), the Japanese subassemblies had much less variation. The loss to society in the US firm case is

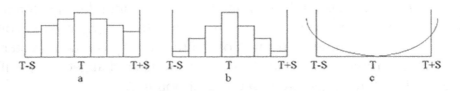

Figure 3.6 Illustrations for the inadequacy of the zero-defect model as adapted from Gunter (1988). (a) US-built, (b) Japanese built, and (c) quadratic, typical, and reasonably approximate QLF.

much higher, and they also incurred higher inspection costs. Figures 3.6(a) and 3.6(b) explain how the data looks like in the cases of the US-built and Japanese built subassemblies, respectively. Figure 3.6(c) shows the quadratic, typical, and reasonably approximate QLF (Gunter, 1988).

The QLF defines quality as the "uniformity around a target value", with the specification limits being irrelevant in this context, as the overall loss caused by a product increases if the product deviates more and more from the target, regardless of whether it is within the specification limits or not. Products manufactured closer to the targets function well and are easily assembled together. The concept of conformance to specifications can become a barrier to quality improvement (QI), as seen earlier from the vinyl example. QLF can help justify spending money to improve the capability of a process even when it is already capable. It has the unique advantage of overcoming the system of "cost control", which is an internal company inhibitor to QI. Most US companies impose financial payback guidelines, which must be met by improvement actions, but these guidelines often prevent QI. QLF helps in prioritizing QI initiatives. An example from Nippondenso, a Japanese company that uses QLF in project prioritization, showed that out of 43 characteristics in nine processes, the top priority was for a process with a Ten Sigma capability, and not for other processes with lower sigma values. A US company would never assign a priority to a process with Ten Sigma capability. US companies need to use Taguchi's QLF to translate the idea of process and product design optimization, in order to improve cost and quality (Sullivan, 1988).

Here is another example to further illustrate Taguchi's concept. Comparing two identical televisions manufactured by two of Sony's facilities: one in the United States and another in Japan. The color density for the televisions made in Japan was more preferred by customers, as it followed a normal distribution, not a uniform one. Overall, a much higher portion of Sony-Japan's televisions received a higher grade (Phadke, 1989). Another popular example is for cars made by a Japanese auto-manufacturer: one at a factory in a Western country and another in Japan. It was noticed that the cars assembled in the Western country failed more often than the ones assembled in Japan. The investigation revealed that one of the main reasons for these mechanical failures was related to the difference in the way the QLF was viewed. For the parts manufactured in the Western country, where the manufacturer mainly aimed at respecting the upper and lower specification limits (without focusing on the variation level or the target itself as in the Japanese factory's case), the assembly failures were related to parts that were either too loose or too tight when assembled together, which caused them to fail more frequently.

3.7 Quality Pillar # 7: Build Quality into the Process Design Itself Starting from The Early Stages

Quality evolution started with individual craftsmen perfecting their work and building quality into it. After that, the focus somewhat shifted to production quantity. Inspectors were hired to inspect quality past production, which is not considered proactive. Eventually, quality control (QC) emerged to help monitor quality "during" production. After that, the approach of quality assurance (QA) was introduced to build quality into the design of the product and the process, by focusing on quality in the early stages of production. This QA approach is obviously more proactive and less costly despite its initial cost. The reactive approach of using a cure is more expensive, as it comes late in the process.

The pursuit of pure water requires searching for the origin of the spring. As water flows, it will carry value down the stream toward customers in the valley. If the water is not pure to start with, it will only get worse down the stream. The longer teams wait to fix a problem, the more costly it will become, as they consume much more resources, energy, material, and time; hence, the famous saying that states that "prevention is better than cure".

In addition, tools like mistake-proofing, Kano model, and quality function deployment (QFD), which are often used as part of the design for Six Sigma (DFSS) approach, can be well suited for such a scope of QA. QFD and the Kano model can enable customer service teams to better understand the voice of the customer and the critical customer requirements so that the product characteristics can be properly matched with them (for more information, see Sections 11.3, 11.8, and 11.9).

International Organization for Standardization (ISO) systems, such as the popular ISO 9001 quality management system (QMS), require investigating for any nonconformities to find short-term corrective actions and long-term preventive actions. This approach helps eliminate or at least mitigate the associated risks. ISO systems can help, if implemented properly, in establishing standard management systems based on best-known practices, which are essential for QA.

3.8 Quality Pillar # 8: Start with the Low-Hanging Fruits, Quick-Fixes, or Just-Do-Its

Once a comprehensive study is conducted for any process, using the framework of a value stream map (VSM), for example, a list of opportunities are typically identified. These opportunities can be generally classified based on the level of complexity in resolving them.

Why start with complicated problems when someone has plenty of "low-pain" opportunities that would result in "high gains"?

It is recommended to focus on what will generate more financial savings, in a short period of time, and with the least investment of time, effort, or resources. An example that is often used by quality practitioners is that if someone is standing under an apple tree, the first type of opportunities to tackle shall be the low-hanging ones, within the reach of their hands. These are quick wins or often called "just-do-its". They are typically under the practitioners' own control, do not require cross-functional intervention, and their solutions are already known in many cases. Being easy to get does not mean they will result in modest savings. Actually, some of them may result in millions of dollars of savings. An example of that can be better clarified through the following story.

Few years ago, a Black Belt worked for a company that subscribed to a program that provided various benefits to its employees. This program provided various levels of cards that gave various discounts and benefits to the holders. One of the key benefits was related to the financing facility for buying new cars, which was a huge program cost incurred by the company. Led by the Black Belt, a team was tasked to look into potential cost savings. They found that the advantage for using that particular card with that feature was negligible, as employees that benefited from that feature were less than a handful. The act of improvement was simply to opt out of it and only use the basic card with the basic benefits. This resulted in reducing the extra annual amounts paid, which was in the order of hundreds of thousands of dollars.

Right above those quick opportunities on the scale are the medium ones. These are medium in terms of their complexity and difficulty to tackle. They are more suitable for the use of a Lean approach, utilizing Lean tools for process improvement. These opportunities are the ones typically arising after using the Lean VSM exercise, which highlights various gaps and opportunities for Kaizen events.

On the top of the apple tree, the more complex type is prevalent. These opportunities are more suitable for the Six Sigma statistical methods and simulation tools. They may take a few months to be resolved, and the solutions require extensive analysis, as they are not known from the beginning.

3.9 Quality Pillar # 9: Seek Continuous Improvement. Maintain Continuity and Totality of Quality

Improvement is a journey that has a start but never stops. Thus, it is continuous in nature, where every improved situation becomes the new norm, which then gets challenged again to seek further improvement. There is no such thing as a perfect process. However, practitioners always strive toward it. That is why they typically think of an ideal state, which powerfully enables them to envision a future state, which, in its turn, will take them a step closer to that ideal state. Between the successive improvement stages, it is essential to standardize and maintain the improved status so as not to fall back to the old ways of doing things. This is where the "control" phase of DMAIC plays a key role, including the use of tools like mistake-proofing and risk control plans. Standardization is a key part of the Kaizen Gemba approach as described by Masaki Imai (Imai, 2012). Companies that take the time to ensure all improvement actions and best practices are captured and documented are way faster in achieving a steep curve of improvement than other companies that have to start all over from scratch every time they start an improvement project (see Section 6.4 for more information about this particular idea of holding the gains and maintaining process control). Standardization allows teams to build upon historical achievements, which turns the wheels of improvement much faster (see Section 11.1 for more information about standardization).

The totality of QM is about focusing on all aspects of QI, including people, processes, and products (*i.e.*, the three Ps) (Lemonis, 2021). It is about a comprehensive vision that takes into account all activities of running and improving the business processes.

As Juran stated, improvement can be achieved through projects, which are continuously executed, one at a time (Montgomery, 2010). Essentially, this is the role of the process improvement practitioners, such as the Lean Six Sigma (LSS) Green and Black Belts, who lead various improvement projects across their organizations. Each project aims at breakthrough improvement resulting in tangible savings, which contribute collectively to the financial status of the organization.

3.10 Quality Pillar # 10: Imagine the Ideal State. Seek Perfection with a Bias for Action

Envisioning the ideal state of a process requires teams to innovate, think "outside the box", and anticipate future needs of customers by challenging the norms and imagining the impossible.

A sheet of paper can be faxed easily, but can a physical product be transmitted instantly? Ideally, if a customer would like to get a product, it shall somehow appear at his/her doorstep. While this sounds too ideal and too good to be true, 3D printing is already used by various organizations to exactly do that. As a matter of fact, organizations now can "print" products at their premises using 3D printers. This is a disruptive innovation that proves how important it is to empathize with customers and envision the ideal or even the impossible.

Seeking perfection is the ultimate goal and a key principle in Lean management. However, it is often narrated that "perfection is the enemy of progress". One of the key characteristics of a successful company that maintains its leading position in the market is being biased for action. It is great to strive toward perfecting ones' work. However, this shall not be exaggerated to take much more time than logical, which will make the whole operation economically unfeasible. For example, if a team took a month to prepare a noncritical design, which is "95% ready", they shall not hold on to it and spend another month trying to get to 99% or so. Also, "bias for action" means no delays are tolerated due to bureaucratic procedures or multiple checks or approvals. It also means that employees are high performers, ready to respond at any time and eager to support and collaborate with others. If a meeting can be conducted in a day or two, then there is no reason why it should be scheduled after a week or two.

3.11 Quality Pillar # 11: Innovation Is about Empathy, Collaboration, and Tolerance for Failure

Empathize with your customers. Do not undermine any simple idea, as it might be transformed into a radical innovative product through proper team collaboration. Accept the fact you may sometimes fail, but never give up the chance to try again.

Innovation is about the creation of something new. It is about a change that starts with creativity, which is the ability to generate different and useful ideas that are typically radical. In any organization, creativity depends on the way of interaction and behavior of its employees. Invention is the creation of a new or different combination of needs and means. It is the first step in innovation. The inventor is not necessarily an entrepreneur, as the success of an invention requires resources and expertise. Also, not all people are inventors, but anyone may come up with an idea that other people may collaborate and build upon. It can then be put into effective use via a full cycle of innovation methodology. For example, in 1907, Spangler, who was a janitor, sold his vacuum machine invention to Hoover, who was an entrepreneur (Tidd and Bessant, 2013).

The word "innovate" is derived from the Latin word, "innovare", which means "to make something new". Innovation is to bring, develop, and exploit a new creative idea, opportunity, solution, process, technology, position, view, market, paradigm, or mental model to a widespread, practical, and effective use by designing, manufacturing, managing, forming a new organization, opening a new market, or launching a new product or service (Tidd and Bessant, 2013).

Innovation is about empathy, through which organizations can outthink their competitors. It is about tapping into the most recent trends that are changing customers' behaviors. It is also a significant driver of organizational growth and profitability. Ingenious products, services, solutions, and processes create new value and exceptional customer experiences. Moreover, innovation is a key enabler for any organization to exceed customers' increasing expectations. It is about new ideas that may have not existed in the past or a modification or a new application of an existing idea. The idea can be very simple, but its strength might be in the collaboration of teams to build on it so as to come up with a creative solution. It is about cooperative competition.

Innovation is associated with future foresight, which depends on narratives and various indicators gathered from recent communication trends, including certain ideas of interest to different groups of people. The more interesting a certain idea is, the more attention it will get, and the more likely it will be developed into reality.

A key consideration in innovation is to put one's self in the place of the customer or to watch the customer while receiving a service or using a product. What do they think? How do they feel? What difficulties do they face? What do they prefer? How can their experience be made more delighting?

Innovation requires reformed values, flexible culture, infrastructure, and tools. It requires training of employees on creativity techniques so that they challenge absolutes, understand the customers' needs, harness new trends, leverage resources, use metaphors, reverse their approach, change their perspective, and look for alternatives. They need to modify, synthesize, and adapt their approaches. Innovation is much more than science, as scientific discoveries predate commercial products. It is difficult to find a consistent definition or understanding of innovation (Ng, 2009). According to Ng (2004), innovation is an everyday engagement and not an accidental happening. Here are some definitions of innovation from the literature:

■ Innovation is a strategy used by companies to deliver value to customers (Ng, 2009).
■ Innovation is the intentional introduction of significantly beneficial ideas, processes, products, or procedures within an organization (West and Farr, 1990).
■ It is the "successful implementation of creative ideas within an organization" (Amabile, 1998).
■ According to McAdam *et al.* (1998), innovation is the process of realizing new ideas that are made attractive to customers. It is the continuous renewal of quality by all employees.

There are two common types of innovation:

■ Incremental or continuous enhancements to existing technologies: It is about doing what is regularly done, but in a better way. An example of that is the introduction of "Sony Walkman" based on the fading, basic, and handy tape-recording device after the addition of headphones.
■ Radical or discontinuous enhancements, which transform the way someone thinks about or uses a product: It is about doing what someone does, but differently or by changing the rules of the game. It is about the enhancements to new technologies causing dramatic shifts (Tushman and Anderson, 2004). An example of it is the introduction of "iPods", which replaced compact disk (CD) players and transformed the music industry. It is much more difficult to bring a structured methodology to the nonstructured approach of radical innovation.

Also, another classification for innovation is the incremental or architectural system of innovation versus component innovation. The innovation pattern starts with a highly uncertain phase of open possibilities until reaching the later stages of gradual maturity and focusing on incremental innovation, described in Abernathy and Utterback's model (Tidd and Bessant, 2013) as follows:

1. A fluid phase, including experimentation, exploration, uncertainty, and flexibility, which are about changing the rules of the game by introducing a new technology or a new market. This is called creative, destructive, disruptive, or discontinuous innovation with an accelerated effect of improvement.
2. A transitional phase, including dominant design, outside which it is difficult to explore, with a room mainly allowing for imitation and development.
3. A specific phase, including standardization and integration, and moving from radical to incremental innovation, while focusing on cost, reliability, quality, productivity, and functionality.

Innovation is a continuous cycle that keeps repeating itself with every disruption. As some products reach maturity in the market, no new investment into those products may bring favorable return. This motivates a new wave of innovation, but it may still happen at any time.

According to (Francis and Bessant, 2005), the innovation scope has four Ps, which are product, process, paradigm, and positioning. Rothwell (1994) came up with five generations' framework for the chronological development of innovation. Additionally, there are two innovation process models (Tidd and Bessant, 2013):

A. An innovation process model under steady-state conditions (repeated, continuous, incremental, and well defined in terms of space or scope):

- Search, or find opportunities for change: Legal, market, technology, competitor actions, *etc.*
- Select what to do and why: Inputs include signals about possible opportunities and current knowledge base in the firm but may seek external expertise and the fit to its strategy.
- Implement: Acquire the knowledge, commit, execute under uncertain conditions or unexpected difficulties, sustain, finalize, obtain feedback, check, and act while anticipating market friction.
- Capture: Get the benefits (commercial market share and cost improvement), change the world as in social innovation, get patency or license, and obtain complementary assets that are hard for others to duplicate.

B. An innovation process model under unsteady-state conditions, which are harder to define and learn, as innovation happens occasionally and radically under discontinuous state or under unclearly defined space or scope. This model needs a different set of routines, tolerance for uncertainty, flexibility, and learning through failure, in addition to the ones developed for the steady-state conditions model.

The introduction of innovation as an improvement and survival methodology is getting more popular due to the collapse of various companies. These companies lost their market share to other companies, which, in their turn, introduced unexpected, value-adding, and innovative products. Thus, applying CI alone is not sufficient, especially as mature and automated processes reach a saturation stage in terms of improvement opportunities. On the other hand, applying an innovation approach alone has its limitations. The combination of Lean Six Sigma (LSS) and innovation leads to achieving CI and business success, utilizing both, incremental and radical breakthrough improvement. A program that engages the entire organization can be created by combining the two methodologies. Drawing on the principles, tools, and philosophies of both methodologies enables companies to produce breakthrough improvements that can result in profound business results (Salah, 2017).[1]

In addition to many external resources, employees are a main source for innovative ideas. In order to transform the organizational culture into an innovative and value-adding culture, these employees need to receive an effective and relevant training program. This program shall include key topics, such as change acceptance, creativity techniques, and team collaboration. It also needs to include the flexibility to substitute, modify, eliminate, combine, or create new ideas. The criteria used in evaluating the new ideas gathered from employees can be based on business need, financial impact, implementation cost, business sustainability, originality of idea (connection of concepts or distinct ideas to create new solutions), ease of implementation, and feasibility of implementation. Awards for creative employees and the recognition of teams play a key role in motivating the whole organization toward more success. Finally, it is important to remember to be tolerant and accepting of failure when trying new initiatives. Innovation requires investing money and effort, trying new ideas, analyzing pilot studies, and experimenting with product launches, which may succeed or fail. A company where no one is allowed to experiment and fail trying new ways will not succeed in innovation.

Note

1. Section 3.11 is mainly prepared based on my published work: Salah, S. (2017). Lean Six Sigma and innovation: Comparison and relationship. *International Journal of Business Excellence, 13*(4), 479–493.

Chapter 4

Fundamental Pillars Related to Change Management

4.1 Quality Pillar # 12: Blame the Process, Not the People, and Do Not Shoot the Messenger

When a problem happens or a complaint is received, it is unfortunate that some managers unprofessionally start looking for someone to blame. They engage in what is called a "blame dance". They might blame their own subordinates, colleagues, or even their own managers. They may never take responsibility or demonstrate effective leadership. If they choose to blame the person who brought the problem to their attention, it will be the last time that person (or any other person from their team) steps out to talk about any problem. This will unfortunately spread a culture where employees hide the problems rather than raise them to seek solutions. They will do so for fear of being blamed for a problem they did not cause.

Also, when a problem happens or a complaint is received, some managers insist on introducing more checks and approvals into the process instead of dealing with the root cause of the problem to eliminate it. Introducing one more step into the process is not just about the few seconds spent on reviewing and signing a document or approving it (even if done using a workflow through a software system) but about the hours, if not days, wasted in waiting for that step to happen.

Edwards Deming indicated that the majority of problems are due to systems of processes, not people (Deming, 1986). No normal person will show up at work with the intention to cause damage to a process. On the

DOI: 10.4324/9781032688374-6

contrary, every employee seeks to do a good job, where their boss thanks them, pats them on the shoulder, and says something like: "You've done a great job today". This simple gesture of a few words of appreciation can go a long way to motivate an employee. It is interesting to ask a group of people when the last time they received or gave such a compliment at work was.

Effective managers attentively listen to complaints and properly investigate the root causes of problems. They spend more time in the Gemba and listen humbly, while encouraging their teams to speak up about their challenges. They work with them to proactively fix the problems they face.

4.2 Quality Pillar # 13: The Root Cause of Many Problems Lies in Miscommunication

Similar to the approach depicted in the theory of inventive problem solving (TIPS, or TRIZ, based on its Russian name), where solving a new problem requires analyzing the way inventors managed to solve comparable problems (Cavallucci, 2017), a simple study was conducted by a Six Sigma Master Black Belt to analyze many Six Sigma projects led by various Green and Black Belts at one North American company. The goal of the study was to find out what the categories of breakthrough improvement in each of those projects were about. The analysis showed that the issue of "communication" was the most frequent category for the types of improvement actions implemented. The majority of root causes were easily traced down to "miscommunication". Here are a few examples of some of the common improvement counteractions implemented within those studied projects:

- A new process had to be created.
- A standard best practice had to be captured.
- Employees had to be trained to follow a standard procedure.
- Employees had to be trained to collaborate as a team even if they were from different departments.
- Employees had to be trained to better understand their roles and responsibilities.
- A standard procedure had to be posted at a work cell.
- A root cause related to why wrong information was provided had to be rectified.

■ A root cause related to why the necessary information was missed had to be rectified.
■ A root cause related to why the required information was delayed had to be rectified.

So, before searching for answers to a complicated problem, it is important to ensure that the basic solutions relevant to effective communication are implemented.

As inspired by the famous sayings of Dewey, "[A] problem well stated is half solved", and of Aristotle, "[W]ell begun is half done", clear communication leads to better understanding and effective solutions.

Much can be learned from ants in terms of effective communication. Ants use their antennas to sense important messages as their legs spray a pheromone, which helps other ants find the shortest path from the nest to the food source. When more ants use one route, the chemical smells stronger, and the optimal route emerges. Scientists studied the ants' behavior and used it to come up with algorithms to help solve practical mathematical problems, such as ant colony optimization.

Here are some interesting points related to communication:

■ Listening dilemma: Humans can reach a 150-words-per-minute rate of talking. However, they can reach a 1,000-words-per-minute rate for listening, making it a tough task not to be distracted while listening (Garber, 2008).
■ The span of attention for an adult had fallen from 12 seconds in 2000 to 8 seconds in 2015 (Statisticbrain, 2021).
■ A person typically loses 50% of communicated information right after an event and another 25% in two days (Lee and Hatesohl, 1993).
■ The Chinese language symbol (注意 means "to pay attention") for listening has ears, eyes for contact, and a heart for attention.
■ In emails, people use a limited portion of their ability to communicate. In calls, they use more of that ability (mainly with the voice tone). In face-to-face communication, they use way more of their ability, as they utilize their full body language. Bohns (2017) suggested that requests done by face-to-face interaction are 34 times more successful than when sent by emails. Thus, face-to-face communication is important when sensitive messages are to be communicated.

■ Effectiveness of communication depends on the sender's abilities and the receiver's abilities as well. Thus, it is important to clarify the message and to confirm the understanding of that message.

So, why is effective internal communication important? What is the risk of doing nothing different?

To answer these two questions, here are some interesting points from the literature:

1. Companies with effective internal communications have a higher market value and deliver 29.5% higher shareholder return than others (Watson Wyatt Worldwide, 2004).
2. An estimated $37 billion is lost annually in various UK- and US-based enterprises, due to employee misunderstanding, as per an IDC research white paper published in 2008 (Grossman, 2012).
3. On average, employee misunderstanding costs a 100,000-employee company $62 million per year (Grossman, 2012).
4. The cost of poor communication was estimated at $26,041 per knowledge worker per year for small and medium-sized companies, as per SIS International Research for Siemens Communication (Grossman, 2012).
5. Employees who rate their companies' effective internal communication as "world class" are more committed to remaining at their jobs than those who rate it as "neutral or poor" (Grossman, 2012).

Finally, internal communication is the management of interactions and relationships between all stakeholders within an organization. It is about establishing a dialogue or a two-way communication. Communication can be direct and verbal or indirect through body language or posters. It can also be vertical or horizontal and business or social. One great way of communication is using visual tools that can guide people with the least effort. Other ways are written reports, instructions, magazines, campaigns, *etc*. Challenges in communication can be various barriers such as languages, cultural, emotional, and personal.

One technique often used in effective communication is called the "sandwich" technique. This technique is attributed to Marshall Rosenberg, who is considered the father of nonviolent communication (Rosenberg, 2003). When a person needs to communicate a somewhat negative message reflecting a request for change, they can sandwich it using two positive statements where they start and end with positive notes. This way, the recipient of the carefully stated negative message will be more accepting to cooperate rather than taking a defensive or personal attack attitude.

Another commonly advisable technique when communicating a frustration or disappointment about something is to focus on describing one's own feeling rather than blaming others. Thus, instead of saying to another employee, "You delivered the report very late, your work was incomplete, and you missed many key points", one could say, "[T]he report seems to have taken a lot of effort, which I highly appreciate. However, I am surprised that it is missing some important points. Let us work on it together". One last key advice about communication is to never write when angry so as not to let emotions dictate one's language. One needs to calm down first and then reply after rephrasing properly.

4.3 Quality Pillar # 14: Show the Gap, Involve, and Then Execute the Change Plan

One of the main barriers in CI is employees' resistance to change.[1] Thus, for any organization, the proper approach for change management is important. A major problem experienced in many CI initiatives has been the failure to implement change (Gunasekaran, 2006).

Employees may resist to try new methods of work due to different reasons, such as fear of the unknown; limitation of time and resources; difficulty of breaking habits; unwillingness to delegate authority; denial of problems; lack of proper communication about problems; lack of skills; lack of performance metrics; and the focus on narrow departmental goals, not the customer's goals. People differ in terms of their reaction to change. Some may resist it, while others may support it or simply choose to be neutral by waiting and checking, and then deciding whether to support it or oppose it. It is important to note the difference in one's own team's perception to change in order to modify one's approach accordingly. All team members need to be supported accordingly. A good leader will listen carefully, communicate transparently, and support all members even if they oppose change. Some tactics may include giving some ownership and leadership role to some key resistors and assuring the team of endless support (Six Sigma Training, personal communication, 2008).

A time-and-motion study was once conducted by a Six Sigma Black Belt for the utilization of big loaders to handle logs and bundles of lumber. These loaders were worth several hundreds of thousands of dollars in addition to their running cost, in terms of maintenance, fuel, and associated labor. This was identified as a considerable area for improvement at various lumber factories at a time when the Canadian dollar value was soaring close to the US dollar value, eroding a considerable portion of the profit and making it tougher for Canadian factories to survive.

The Black Belt's supervisor kicked off that project at each factory. He ensured that all the members of the team affected by the study were present and started explaining to them the reason why the study was taking place and its importance to the very survival of the factory and the jobs of all workers. He assured the team that nobody would lose his/her job because of this study. However, he explained that some changes might be required to the way work is organized, by relocating some workers to ensure adding value. He went on explaining the steps of the study so that they didn't get surprised to see the Black Belt sitting in a truck in the yard observing the operation and assessing how they spent their time. Finally, after answering all their questions and concerns, the meeting was over, and a future meeting was agreed upon to discuss the progress as well as the results.

After that, the Black Belt started the study by gathering data through task observation to measure and record the time each trip took in the yard between various locations. Typically, after a few hours, the same numbers were repeated, indicating a sufficient sample. After that, he would turn back into the office and plug in all the data into Excel sheets. In addition, based on the factory data, he calculated the average volume of logs fed into the factory within each shift taking into account the different categories of logs and the variation in volume from one shift to another. Knowing the average volume carried by each loader per trip, he simply managed to calculate how many trips were required per shift. Also, based on the average cycle time per trip, he was able to calculate the total time required (ideal productive time based on ideal cycle time) per shift and divide it by the total time scheduled (available time or actual cycle time) per shift, to finally find the percentage of utilization for each loader. This is referred to as the performance percentage, which is part of the overall equipment effectiveness (OEE) calculation (Pyzdek and Keller, 2019). See Equation 3.2 in Chapter 3 for more details on OEE.

This was done based on average numbers, as well as minimum and maximum numbers, to show all scenarios. Finally, here are some examples of the improvements identified and implemented by the team as a result of these projects:

- Elimination of an old loader.
- Replacement of two old loaders with one slightly bigger loader.
- Introducing staggered shifts to cover peak times with more loaders.
- Shifting differently categorized log-piles' locations to better account for the frequency of trips (most frequently loaded types are stored closer to minimize waste of motion).

These recommendations were all implemented and, hence, resulted in huge savings for the applicable factories in the order of millions of dollars. The loader operators who no longer were required to work in the yard were all accommodated in other vacancies where they could add value to the business. Actually, for some of them, it was used as a promotion to take charge of other responsibilities.

One important lesson learned from this study and these time-and-motion projects was related to leading change. Change leadership is not only about the technical aspects of executing a project, but also about managing people during the project. Sitting with all the team members affected by the project prior to starting it and showing them the gap and the reason for it is crucial to success. This step is the first step that addresses their concerns and explains to them why this project is important and how it may positively affect them. It is about getting them out of their comfort zone and motivating them to embrace change. The second step is to involve them, so they feel they are part of the change (*i.e.*, the improvement project) and that it is not forced upon them. This can be achieved by inviting them to progress meetings, engaging them in discussions, asking for their ideas, and effectively communicating with them to address any concerns they might have. The third and final step is simply about mobilizing the team to execute the change. In sum, there are various models available in the literature about change management, such as Kotter's model (Kotter, 2012). However, the three simple steps that can be commonly agreed upon and recommended for change management are as follows: show the gap, involve the people, and execute the change.

Finally, here are some important notes for effective change management (Salah and Rahim, 2019):

- Continuously share the benefit, gap, and reason for change across the organization.
- Clarify the urgency of the change initiative.
- Recognize the differences in receptiveness to change, and explain the resulting benefits for people.

■ Share the vision, spread change without forcing it, make it last, and monitor its progress.

■ Use evolutionary (not revolutionary) and strategy-based tactics to transform the organizational culture from a bureaucratic one to a quality culture, and plan for continuous and systematic change.

■ Eliminate fear and stress, treat problems as opportunities, and blame the processes, not the employees.

■ Educate employees about flexibility to change across all levels of the organization; train employees in all needed disciplines, including health and safety; empower teams to implement change; involve all employees; spread a culture of learning; adopt best practices; standardize the procedures; and refine the culture continuously.

■ Establish an information system and a visual MS to support change.

■ Build MSs with the objectives of QC, quality assurance, and respect for humanity.

■ Instill passion and commitment to change and CI in the leadership.

■ Instill passion for quality and teamwork values across the organization.

■ Encourage acceptable behavior, and align it with the successful implementation of performance measures, incentives, and symbolic rewards.

■ Align the organization's needs with the operation and culture.

■ Install a horizontal structure in addition to the commonly used vertical structure, and encourage process thinking.

■ Use facts and two-way communication when making decisions, and ensure effective asking and listening to achieve consensus among team members.

■ Use a standard approach to prioritize, measure, stabilize, control, streamline, improve, document, and certify the different processes.

■ Build a daily MS based on understanding problems and performance measurements.

■ Perform constructive evaluation, and build a relationship of trust and win-win.

■ Partner with the best few suppliers, and focus on what pleases the customers.

■ Empower people, and assign them to new responsibilities to help drive new behaviors and boost their attitude and morale.

■ Focus in a balanced way on both financial or technical aspects and human values.

■ Use a common language, proper resources, and cross-functional teams to mobilize change.

- Consider using external coaches for facilitation, and focus on both soft and hard factors.
- Focus on leadership role, strategic and operational issues, people contribution, project management, and process management approach.
- Choose qualified change leaders.
- Create short-term wins to help provide evidence that sacrifice is worth it, recognize change agents, fine-tune the vision, neutralize critics and resistors, keep leadership on board, and build momentum.

4.4 Quality Pillar # 15: People Are the Weakest Link in Any Improvement Chain or Project Execution Stages

You may have the best program, methodology, tool, or solution, but you always need people to buy in or accept change and see what is in it for them in order to enable improvement to happen.

It is relatively easy to learn about a new improvement technique and its implementation. Dealing with knowledge and equipment can sometimes be challenging. However, it can be considered easy when compared to dealing with humans. Indeed, humans are complex creatures with a mix of thoughts and emotions that influence their behaviors. Often described as creatures of habit, they prefer to stick to what they already know or what they are used to. Also, adult humans would rather learn by seeing than by being told.

Showing one's team a simple video for a high-performing facility can make it much more easier for them to comprehend what type of change the team leader is trying to influence. In response to change, it is not always easy to anticipate how people may react. People love to change but hate to be changed. Obviously, some people resist change in a way that is stronger than others.

So, while preparing to roll out any improvement program, it is very important not only to reflect on the technical aspects of the introduced changes but also to equally focus (in parallel) on the soft and social aspects of how people will be affected and may choose to respond to such a program.

Involving people is crucial to succeed in securing their buy-in (or approval) to what a change or improvement program is aiming to achieve. They need to see the gap and the benefit of the program, so they can better empathize with it. This engagement of employees in a change program is a key ingredient to achieve and sustain high performance levels.

While Six Sigma methodology started with a heavy focus on individuals like the Green and Black Belts, Lean methodology has always been focused on team engagement and mobilization using the Kaizen Gemba approach. The Six Sigma methodology was heavily focused on what would get the Green or Black Belt certified as individuals at the end of their projects. A decade or so ago, Six Sigma programs started injecting modules for soft aspects of project management, including team dynamics and change management. The realization that Green and Black Belts needed to understand these aspects made it necessary to be included in the Six Sigma (or Lean Six Sigma) body of knowledge.

PI is a team-based approach. Teams can be of various types such as project teams, work teams, and sports teams. Even a family is considered a team. At the same time, individuals can be part of various teams where they have to manage different relationships in every direction. Thus, they need to manage their superiors at work in relation to their demand, expectation, and authority. They also need to manage those who report to them, in order to guide them, delegate responsibilities to them, and hold them accountable for achieving targets. In addition, it is important to manage customers, both internal and external to the department, as they hold significant power in sustaining business operations and rely on services or products provided by the individual. Horizontally, cooperative relationships with colleagues are governed by mutual influence to create a constructive environment and facilitate the successful completion of tasks. Thus, in a PI project, it is important to understand who the various stakeholders are and to manage their expectations for a project to succeed. Team members need to be aware of team dynamics and roles, clear on their goal and accepted behaviors, kept informed through effective communication, aware of team decision basis, and committed to maintaining a balanced participation of all members of the team. Overall, team members require the support of the management in terms of coaching, training, and provision of constructive and candid feedback.

Whether it is a CI team, self-managed team, or cross-functional team, a team passes through the following stages: forming, storming (frustration and resistance to the allocated task), norming (reconciling responsibilities and loyalties), performing, and adjourning. A project team approach is one of the best structures for two companies to partner in providing services. A self-directed or self-managed team approach is suitable in equally sharing leadership and responsibility among all team members. High-performing teams are authorized to make decisions about the situations they face. A virtual team approach is used when people from different locations need to meet regularly using teleconference and internet tools. This setup reduces costs and ensures real-time data updating. Cross-functional teams are typically deployed to study and enhance a difficult process that involves various departments within an organization (Farmer and Duffy, 2017). The life cycle for any team consists of the following stages that describe the dynamics of teams (Bens, 2000; Pyzdek and Keller, 2019):

- The first stage is team forming, where the team members are typically excited, nervous, and polite. Team leaders need to develop a team charter, including basic information about the project objectives, team members, roles, and sponsors.
- The second stage is storming, where conflicts start to arise among anxious team members, as they typically defend their ideas and opinions related to the assigned task. Sometimes, these conflicts lead to frustration, which can cause some members to withdraw from the team. In this stage, the team leaders should help the team members discuss their differences openly and facilitate their collaboration toward accomplishing the assigned tasks.
- In the third stage of norming, the members start to reconcile their differences and accept the team rules while growing a sense of respect and support toward all other team members.
- Now that the team members are settled, they can start the fourth stage of performing, where the team members demonstrate characteristics of high performance such as unity of purpose, empowerment, flexibility, bias for action, effective communication, and high morale.
- Finally, the team adjourns as recognition takes place to celebrate success and shares the best practices or lessons learned.

Not only is it natural for conflicts to arise within teams, it is also beneficial, as it enhances the quality of ideas and actions taken by the team. Differences in opinion can often be attributed to incomplete sharing of information or lack of effective communication. However, a skilled and neutral facilitator is often required to ensure the team members avoid arguments and stay flexible to achieve consensus. Also, the facilitator ensures that a win-win relation is dominant instead of a win-lose relation among team members. In order to avoid failure in team work, a skilled facilitator will ensure that the team remains focused on facts and data, not opinions or accusations. He or she will listen actively, focus on a written agenda, and insist on achieving consensus and balanced participation in the discussion. This way, no single individual will dominate the discussion or impose their opinion upon others (Pyzdek and Keller, 2019).

4.5 Quality Pillar # 16: Empower Your Subordinates, and Hold Them Accountable by Measuring Their Performance. Do Not Underestimate What They Are Capable of

Rather than micromanaging his or her subordinates and insisting on inspecting and approving every single document or transaction done by them, a capable leader adopts an engaging style of management. This style is about empowering subordinates to take responsibility in making decisions and be accountable for them. Preparing employees for such responsibilities is the mission of the leader, and it is achieved through training, coaching, and mentoring. A humble leader, as emphasized in Japanese quality approaches, is willing to patiently listen to subordinates to find out what obstacles they face and what prevents them from executing their tasks successfully. Smart leaders work toward a zero-defects status. They train their subordinates so that even when they check their work, they will not find any mistake. Thus, they gradually will inspect lesser amounts of their work, until they decide that they can fully empower them with the tasks they are assigned to perform. This empowerment instills a lot of trust and motivation into each subordinate and typically results in much simpler procedures as well as great time and cost savings. Empowering subordinates does not mean leaving them alone completely, without balancing that with a set of smartly established measures of performance to help hold them accountable to the new responsibilities assigned to them. If an employee struggles to achieve the assigned targets, the leader steps in to find out the reasons for that. The leader positively works with the employee to correct the situation. The targeted performance measure shall be set smartly. Targets need to be specific, measurable, action oriented or achievable, realistic or relevant, and time constrained or time bound (or SMART). They need to be used in a positive way to motivate employees (Rouillard, 2009). The opposite of that would match what Deming warned against in his famous 14 points of management, where he advocated the removal of targets due to their negative influence on quality and people (Deming, 1986). This is well agreeable if targets are not set or used properly.

Some managers unfortunately underestimate what employees in their teams can do. Perhaps because of some negative incidents that happened in the past, they have drawn the conclusion that they must check all the work themselves and not delegate tasks to anyone else. Imagine how much lost productivity and wasted time exist in various companies because of this. That is why the Japanese named one of the types of waste (or Muda) as the waste of "human resources". This type of waste highlights the huge loss of potential productivity that could have been otherwise realized had managers empowered their subordinates and trusted that they could do more. One commonly heard story is about a typical person who was often unnoticed at work but shined when given a chance and surprised everyone with the good work he or she was able to accomplish. Another inspiring story is the one in 1907 by Spangler, who was a janitor suffering from asthma due to dust. He came up with the magnificent idea of the first simple vacuum machine—an invention he sold to Hoover, who was an entrepreneur who introduced it as a commercial product known even today (Tidd and Bessant, 2013).

On the other hand, how do customers feel when a retail store worker refuses their request and tells them to wait for management decision on a refund? How many customers are lost due to such an attitude and lack of empowerment? On the other hand, consider the example of Walmart stores, where returned goods are handled with the utmost ease and care to customers; this is a positive example of employee empowerment. While there is a cost incurred in this process by the retailer (although mostly covered by the suppliers themselves), it will definitely pay off, by ensuring those customers stay satisfied, loyal to the brand, and always shop at the stores of that retailer.

4.6 Quality Pillar # 17: When Employees Come Up with a Solution, They Are More Likely to Implement It and Hold It in Place

Forcing employees to perform tasks and implement improvements can generate results in the short term. However, it may not last over the long term. While solutions or the reasons for decisions may be crystal clear and logically convincing to managers, there might still be much resistance by employees, as they cannot see the reason, benefit, or impact of those decisions, especially upon them. Skilled leaders can influence their subordinates to seek the right direction by simply challenging and asking them the right questions. These leaders do not offer the solutions directly, even if they know what is best, but rather, influence their subordinates to arrive at the conclusion themselves. Asking the right questions can help stimulate thinking and influence the team members to generate bright ideas, even better than what leaders themselves may have known or expected. Besides leaders, process improvement practitioners sometimes fall into the same problem of dictating what the improvement actions shall be (based on their previous experience of similar challenges). However, it is much better to listen more patiently and ask the right questions to get the whole team to think creatively until they reach a solution on their own. This way, they are more likely to embrace change and ensure the gains are held in place over the long term.

Once again, humans are creatures of habit, and it is hard for them to change, especially if they do not see the benefit of change. As young kids, people listen, in general, to what they are told to do. However, that is not applicable in the case of adults. Adults learn by seeing and doing. Thus, one of the best ways to get team members to understand the necessity for any improvement or change a leader is leading is to take them on a benchmarking trip to see how other people (who already got solutions implemented for similar challenges) operate. This way, they can appreciate better how the proposed change is going to positively affect them and their jobs. Throwing in a motivating challenge to the team will bring their competitive energy to high levels and will eventually get them to adopt and innovate new solutions.

4.7 Quality Pillar # 18: Engagement Leads to More Productivity, and It Is Not Necessarily about a Salary Increase

For any organization, employees (often referred to as the human capital) are valuable assets. They affect the outcome of their organization by the decisions they make and the way they act. If employees are well treated by their organization and if they interact among each other in a positive and healthy manner, their actions will be positive, and hence, the organization overall will be successful.

While this seems to be a very basic and acceptable idea, many organizations do not get it right. As per Gallup (2021), research had shown that 85% of employees globally are not engaged. Imagine how much is lost due to employees showing up to work but not being properly engaged.

There are various reasons why employees may not be engaged, such as the loss of the meaning of work, the lack of attention to the good work they do, not being thanked or recognized enough, being deprived from having pride in what they do, their income not covering their basic needs, not being fairly compensated for their work, and not being provided with a clear career plan or opportunity to grow.

It is to be noted that the aforementioned issues are not all about money or salary increase. If such issues are well taken care of, then employees can easily become engaged. This will result in a great enhancement in various aspects of performance, which can result in a huge financial impact for the organization.

For example, Gallup's recent analysis showed that engaged employees outperformed others by 10% in customer loyalty, 18% in turnover, 23% in profitability, 14% in productivity, 64% in safety incidents, 81% in absenteeism, and 66% in well-being (Robison, 2020).

Being engaged means waking up every day with a positive attitude toward work, enjoying the hours spent at work, being passionate and motivated about one's own work, and always thinking of how to enhance its outcome. A great example that can illustrate the importance of engagement is the example of the founder of a dairy products company. This businessman decided to offer all his 2,000 employees a great gift by granting them stock shares, equivalent to 10% of the company's value. The amounts were based on their contribution and years of service at the company (Storm, 2016). Some employees got shares equivalent to $1 million and broke into tears, which was captured by a documented news report. The owner addressed them stating that they were no longer employees but partners. What a great way to motivate employees.

This joy does match with what Deming called "joy at work" (Juran and Godfrey, 1999). Indeed, engagement is about partnership, where the business is treated as one's own. Enabling employees to feel that way is a shared responsibility with the leaders of the company. However, money is not necessarily the only way to engage employees. A simple "thank you" can go a long way to lift the spirit of an employee. Simple gestures can bring happiness to employees, brighten their days, instill trust and motivation, and spread a culture of cooperation and team collaboration. Some organizations are already setting up departments of "employee happiness" within their own human capital divisions. Investing in training employees to become highly engaged and to be better at engaging others is another key factor for successful companies. In any organization, process improvement (PI) is everyone's job. PI culture encourages every employee to be always eager to collaborate with PI teams, ready to respond and support PI teams, respectful of others, and motivated as a team player.

4.8 Quality Pillar # 19: Cross-Train, Empower, Support, and Reward with Incentives

TQM depends on the effectiveness of how an organization manages its human resources (Morrison and Rahim, 1993). Out of the different aspects of individual human resources management (HRM) that were evaluated, Yang (2006) found that "training" was among the key factors that had the most impact on TQM.

A Black Belt once worked on a CI project at a facility where houses were built in modules and shipped and assembled at construction sites. These houses required employees who mastered different trades, such as carpenters, plumbers, electricians, and carpet installers. The project goal was to find a way to evaluate the skills of employees and put up a plan to enhance those skills, which would not only improve production but also employee motivation. A Kaizen team was assembled to achieve this goal in five days. The team started by creating a list of all employees and plugging it into a

Table 4.1 Cross-training Matrix, Showing the Corresponding Trade Level, Out of Four Levels (by Each Employee by Each Trade)

Name	Carpenter		Plumber		Electrician		Carpet installer	
A. B.	Level 1		Level 1	Level 2	Level 1		Level 1	
			Level 3					
C. D.			Level 1	Level 2	Level 1	Level 2		
					Level 3	Level 4		
E. F.			Level 1	Level 2	Level 1			

Note: Gray color indicates training plan.

matrix showing all the relevant trades and classifying them into four levels each. This included meeting with all the experienced employees to properly define what each trade level covered in terms of its body of knowledge and skill set. After that, an assessment was performed for each employee to determine what trade level truly represented their abilities. The matrix was simply divided into four squares for each trade, and then a number of squares were changed from white to black color to indicate the trade level that corresponded to each employee. Moreover, a gray color indicated the next trade level's planned training for the corresponding employee. This matrix can be referred to as a cross-training matrix (see Table 4.1). It made it easier to notice that some employees had demonstrated good capabilities in more than one trade. This created a competitive environment, where employees started to show more interest in pursuing the next level of training in their trade. Some even started to learn about other trades. It also made it easier to define a clear career path for ambitious employees. It helped them become more motivated. They became so proud of what they were able to achieve. It also enabled managers to trust and empower employees with more responsibilities, based on their level of experience. It also helped managers and supervisors plan better to utilize the time of their team members and collaborate with other teams' supervisors to speed up work execution while maintaining a high-quality standard. If one employee is not available, it becomes easier to assign another capable employee to a particular job, using this cross-training matrix. Finally, with more progress in mastering the various trades and their levels, recognition closes the cycle, where high achievers get promoted and their achievements get celebrated.

Note

1. Section 4.3 is partially prepared based on my literature review from my thesis titled: "Total company-wide management system: A framework for Six Sigma and continuous quality improvement", 2009, available at the library of the University of New Brunswick.

Chapter 5

Fundamental Pillars Related to Strategic Quality Management and Company-Wide Management Systems

5.1 Quality Pillar # 20: Share the Vision and Ensure Transparency

Determining the vision, mission, objectives, and associated factors of success is a collective effort headed by managers with the participation of all staff. This is achieved through open communication and is seen as a best practice (Kaye and Anderson, 1999).

Indeed, setting up a clear vision is a key element of success for any organization. A participative approach is essential to come up with a vision that inspires all employees and stays active in their minds all the time. Such a vision is what is needed to achieve strategic alignment of all efforts in an organization toward one common goal.

A vision is about what an organization is aiming to become in the future. It is about what a team is trying to grow into or achieve. Transparency of the vision is important so that all employees are clear about the current situation, what the targeted future would look like, and the direction of the company. Sometimes, companies withhold certain confidential plans for logical business reasons to ensure the best deals are reached. However, they need to be clear about that with their employees

 DOI: 10.4324/9781032688374-7

by communicating continuously and effectively about their progress toward their goals. This way, their employees will not feel left out and, hence, disengaged.

Transparency in all aspects of management leads to trust and spreads an atmosphere of fairness, equality, and clarity. Human resources teams play a critical role at ensuring all employees are clear about their future career plans and are given equal opportunities to grow and excel. This means that employees would feel as part of the future of the organization. They will take the lead in shaping that future and not sit passively in the back seat waiting for it to happen on its own.

Balanced score cards (BSCs) are based on strategies that translate the leadership vision into operational metrics. They provide key performance indicators (KPIs) in four areas: customer, financial, internal processes, and learning or resources growth. It is balanced such that improving cycle times and reducing cost are not achieved at the expense of quality (Pyzdek, 2004). BSCs consider both monetary and nonmonetary objectives in a balanced way, where those objectives can be linked with each other using cause-and-effect matrices (Pfeifer *et al.*, 2004).

5.2 Quality Pillar # 21: Align All Employees toward the Same Goals

For a team of rowers to win at the Olympics, they have to paddle faster than other teams. Moreover, all team members have to paddle at the same pace, rhythm, and speed. If one is paddling slower or even faster than others in the team, it won't help them at all. Actually, this rower may impede the team and cause them to lose a lot of energy and momentum. Similarly, in a process setup, if one step is not balanced with the other steps, it will only create more waste of time or inventory of documents or subassemblies waiting to be processed at the next step or bottleneck. By rewarding locally enhanced efficiencies, all that managers would be doing is rewarding them for making their colleagues working at the next stations look bad while the external customer won't feel any improvement.

Balancing the service line or production line is crucial to ensure all steps are aligned and governed by one goal, which is to satisfy the customer demand or takt time (for more information, see Section 9.8). All steps shall operate at a speed equivalent to, or synchronized with, the rate of customer demand.

So, like the team of rowers, successful teams need to be aligned with one vision and one mission. This will optimize their efforts, time, and energy and maximize their chances to beat the competition and delight their customers.

Obviously, the role of the process owner or team leader is critical in bringing the team together, to overcome any obstacles preventing them from achieving their goals. This is also complementary to the role of the Lean Six Sigma Green Belt or Black Belt, who leads the team through the structured improvement approach of define-measure-analyze-improve-control (DMAIC). These project leaders need to ensure that teams understand the importance of working in alignment with the organization strategy and the customers' requirements.

5.3 Quality Pillar # 22: Do Not Start a Quality Program without Management Commitment

Even with the best methodologies in place, numerous studies pointed out that most industries are failing in their QI efforts (*e.g.*, Devane, 2004; Bhasin and Burcher, 2006). It is widely agreed by many researchers and quality practitioners that management commitment is a key success factor for any QI or CI program. Several references in the literature emphasized how critical management commitment is (*e.g.*, Chapman and Hyland, 1997; Kaye and Anderson, 1999; Hoerl, 2004; Yang, 2004; Anderson *et al.*, 2006; Antony, 2006; Martin, 2007; Crump, 2008). Various quality improvement programs failed due to management teams not believing in them. Employees naturally will resist change unless they see a clear commitment by their management teams indicating that improvement programs are there to stay and not to fade as a temporary flavor of the day. If managers are not walking the talk, or are not convinced themselves of the quality improvement program, then it will be very difficult for it to succeed.

This puts great emphasis on the importance for quality practitioners to work closely with managers and ensure they are fully supportive of such programs. The commitment needs to be cascaded down from top management to middle management and so on. Before offering relevant training to employees, managers need to be trained themselves in order to understand why these programs are required, what they are about, who will be affected by them, and what their role in them is about.

5.4 Quality Pillar # 23: Have a Strategic Approach to Improvement Utilizing an Integrated Company-Wide Management System (ICWMS)

ICWMS, proposed in detail by Salah and Rahim (2019),[1] can be considered a comprehensive system that aims at aligning employees in the same strategic direction of the organization. ICWMS promotes a total quality culture, which is engaging and motivating to all employees. ICWMS mainly draws on 5MSs, and the tools used within these components are generally acknowledged. However, the grouping and connection of these components with each other represents the novelty of this system. These five components are strategic quality management, quality project management, daily (operation) quality management, process management, and quality performance management. A brief description of these components is provided next. For a thorough understanding of ICWMS, Salah and Rahim (2019) provided a detailed review of these components and an explanation of how they fit within ICWMS.

5.4.1 Strategic Quality Management

Strategic management is about developing achievable strategic plans and implementing them to ensure the proper alignment of the industrial organization as a whole (Kaplan and Norton, 2004). The strategic management approach, promoted by ICWMS, is a participative approach, which can encourage employees to express their ideas and concerns. It starts by forming a cross-functional team; benchmarking against competitors; performing PEST (*i.e.*, political, economic, social, and technological) analysis; performing SWOT (strengths, weaknesses, opportunities, and threats) analysis; using quality function deployment (QFD) to identify enabling strategies; establishing a vision, mission, and strategic goals; linking the strategic goals to the BSC using KPIs; identifying obstacles; and developing initiatives to overcome these obstacles using the Hoshin planning X-matrix (Hoshin Kanri or policy deployment) and assigning them to teams. These initiatives are managed as part of the second component of ICWMS, which is quality project management (Salah and Rahim, 2019).

5.4.2 Quality Project Management

Initiative or project management is about managing the execution of the strategy, and it mainly depends on clear accountability (Kaplan and Norton,

2006). The evaluation of initiatives includes continuous reviews of progress against plan, using feedback systems (Friday-Stroud and Sutterfield, 2007). It starts by selecting initiatives and teams, empowering and training the team members, clarifying roles and measurable targets, monitoring progress, focusing on the technical and social aspects of change, and capturing knowledge (Salah and Rahim, 2019).

5.4.3 Daily Quality Management (or Operation Quality Management)

Daily or operations management is about following up with the employees who execute the assigned tasks on a regular basis. It ensures that they understand how their daily activities contribute to the satisfaction of the strategic goals of the organization (Yang, 2004). Deming highlighted the importance of daily CI (Walton, 1990). The focus of daily management is the *check-act* part of the Deming cycle (*i.e.*, plan-do-check-act, or PDCA), which is about evaluating the results, understanding the reasons for any deviations from targets, and taking corrective actions. It is based on understanding problems, measuring performance, and people involvement. It starts by following up with the people who execute tasks, ensuring they understand how their work affects the strategic goals, using a communication plan and reporting system, including KPIs, visual management, agendas, actions, and variances from targets (Salah and Rahim, 2019).

5.4.4 Process Management

Most activities performed in an organization can be thought of as processes connected to form a system of work (Snee, 2004). These processes and their variations must be measured before they can be controlled. Also, processes should be looked at from the perspective of the customer. Process management is about a group of practices that provide better stewardship of business processes, using metrics, tools, and documentation (Motwani *et al.*, 2004). Process management is a method for managers to select, organize, and manage the design, standardization, stabilization, and improvement of processes. Risk management can be thought of as part of process management and documentation of best practices. In ICWMS, process mapping utilizes a five-tier process for documentation, which is based on the process classification framework (PCF) published by the American Productivity & Quality Center (2018). Process management starts by assigning process owners, defining operating polices, selecting prioritized processes that affect customers and strategic goals and improving them, and developing standardized procedures (Salah and Rahim, 2019).

5.4.5 *Quality Performance Management*

Quality performance management is concerned with defining employees' roles, linking the individual performance to the organizational goals, and appraisal of performance. Out of various aspects of human resources management, Yang (2006) noticed that employee training, incentives, and development had the greatest impact on TQM.

Performance management starts by defining job responsibilities and measurable objectives, defining a performance-based incentive program for better motivation, conducting interim and year-end performance reviews against objectives to build up development plans, and developing the organization's capabilities. Finally, ICWMS provides a solid foundation for managing and improving all activities of a business, to ensure proper alignment and enhance the performance of an industrial enterprise (Salah and Rahim, 2019).

5.5 Quality Pillar # 24: Have a Strategic Approach to Drive Sustainability

In 2007, a lumber production enterprise commemorated the successful reaping of the initial cohort of trees sown five decades prior. The company had implemented a strategy since 1957, whereby they planted approximately three trees for each tree harvested annually, showcasing their commitment to responsible and ethical practices. This plan exemplifies a laudable and sustainable approach toward business and environmental conservation, ensuring the well-being of future generations.

The expensive seeds are carefully selected from the best trees, with the highest-quality features. A nursery operation helped prepare millions of tree seedlings during the winter, in order to be planted in the summer in the areas where the tree-cutting took place. The cost of running this operation was, to a great extent, deductible from the taxable income of the company, as encouraged by the government. This shows how government policies encourage partnership with the private sector to achieve the goals of sustainability, which can be beneficial to the whole society. One LSS Master

Black Belt (MBB) stated, "[I]t took us fifty years to grow one tree and hence we hold a huge responsibility to optimize the output as we decide how to slice it in few seconds".

In a project related to the seeding process, one designed experiment aimed at finding the optimal settings of the seeding machine to ensure that one seed falls into each tray cavity. It cost money to miss a cavity or to have two or three seeds in one cavity which required rework or thinning.

Sustainability is mainly concerned with economic, social, and environmental aspects. For any business to be successful in the future, it has to be profitable so that it can sustain itself and its employees. It also has to be socially sustainable, where all its employees, their families, and the community at large can benefit from the existence of that business. This does intersect with corporate social responsibility (CSR) as an important part of social sustainability. In addition, environmental sustainability is crucial to the survival of any business. This includes aspects of raw material sourcing, waste disposal, pollution, and aftermarket recycling.

Sustainability is important to maintain the benefits and quality of the multidimensional and competitive ecosystem surrounding any organization. Quality management helps organizations ensure they meet the social needs of their customers, the community, and their own employees; the financial needs of the stakeholders; and the environmental needs of the whole society. All these aspects need to be balanced in order to achieve sustainability.

Sustainability of business requires a culture to be changed into a quality culture: each employee's job has to be motivating, enriching, satisfying, and interesting. Also, bureaucratic hierarchy levels need to be reduced and flattened to allow for more commitment, flexibility, empowerment, delegation of authority, friendly and open interpersonal relationship among all employees, and supportive environment with rewards and recognition driving positive behavior.

Employees may resist executing sustainability initiatives if they do not understand the objectives and the importance of these initiatives for any organization. All relevant efforts in an organization need to ensure that alignment exists between the organization's culture and the pursued quality culture. Hence, all initiatives become collectively aligned toward the achievement of sustainable quality. Employees need to take such initiatives seriously, or else they may not be successful. In addition, measurement of progress against goals is critical to drive sustainability of performance.

Also, critical factors to sustainability from EFQM and MBNQA perspectives include focusing on leadership commitment, strategic planning, policies, information, data analysis, customers, partners, employees, processes, and waste.

Here are the eight qualities for highly successful, excellent, and sustainable organizations (Peters and Waterman, 1982):

1. A bias for action: A preference for doing something or accomplishing anything (rather than sending a question that goes through cycles of reviews and approvals or sharing useless reports).
2. Close to the customer: Learning their preferences and catering to them.
3. Autonomy and entrepreneurship: Breaking the corporation into small companies and encouraging them to think independently and competitively.
4. Productivity through people: Instilling (in the minds of all employees) the awareness that their best efforts are essential for the company's success and that they will be rewarded for that success.
5. Hands-on, value driven: Insisting that corporate executives keep in touch with the firm's essential business.
6. Stick to the knitting: Remaining focused on the business the company knows best.
7. Simple form and lean staff: Few administrative layers and few people at the upper levels of the organization.
8. Simultaneous loose-tight properties: Fostering a climate where there is dedication to the central values of the company, combined with tolerance for all employees who accept those values.

These eight qualities need to be maintained in order for any business to remain successful.

The use of quality and management system models such as Lean, Six Sigma, LSS, ISO 9001, MBNQA, EFQM, and ICWMS is essential to transform a business into becoming sustainable.

According to Sinclair and Zairi (1995), Zairi and Liburd (2001), and McDonald *et al.* (2002), and based on studies of the winners of various quality model awards over a few years, TQM sustainability is mainly dependent on the following:

■ A series of transformational change models.
■ The existence of a number of significant factors related to TQM.
■ The establishment of a culture of CI, learning, and innovation so as to have in place a sustainable environment of growth.
■ An emphasis on measurement using a balanced perspective.

Zairi and Liburd (2001) explained that sustainability is about how organizations adapt to surrounding changes in the business environment and how they capture best practices and achieve competitive performance. Thus, sustainability can be considered as follows:

■ A fundamental concept that should be an important aspect of all further policy developments.
■ A development that is based on a perceived need to address environmental deterioration and maintain the vital functions of natural systems for the well-being of present and future generations.
■ An ability of a company to adapt to the changes in the business environment, capture the current best practices, and maintain competitive performance.
■ A development that meets the current needs without compromising the ability of future generations and organizations to meet their own needs.
■ An approach to achieve a steady state, where both people and nature thrive.

The reasons for targeting sustainability include ethical considerations, intergenerational equity, survival aspects, and various organizational advantages and risks. In order to succeed in the pursuit of sustainability, a global management process for sustainable development is needed. Management processes are needed on the personal, organizational, and societal levels. Sustainability is critical to the performance and competitiveness of any company. The proper assessment of the organization's vision and mission statements is the foundation of a sustainable and effective performance measurement system. The achievement of sustainable development is based on the triangle of "person-organization-society". One approach for realizing that is to redefine the priorities of stakeholders. TQM effectiveness and organizational performance can be evaluated using a self-assessment model of quality management, such as the European Quality Award (*i.e.*, EFQM), Deming Prize, and the Malcolm Baldrige National Quality Award (MBNQA). Sustainability of TQM in an organization is achieved by the successful implementation of critical success factors (CSFs) as intended by the awards criteria (Zairi, 2002a, 2002b).

The TQM Sustainability model has Six Sigma at its core and consists of 12 components (Zairi, 2002a):

1. Process management.
2. Policy deployment.

3. Benchmarking.
4. Innovation.
5. Teamwork.
6. Learning.
7. Creative culture.
8. Self-assessment.
9. Excellence.
10. Six Sigma.
11. People development and involvement.
12. Performance measurement.

TQM Sustainability depends on a series of transformations by the business, where the focus shifts toward continuous process improvement (Zairi, 2002a). Transformational models to achieve sustainability include Lean, Six Sigma, Lean Six Sigma, EFQM, and MBNQA.

5.6 Quality Pillar # 25: Adopt a Self-Assessment Quality Model as a Foundation for Comprehensive Quality Improvement

For any organization, excellence models are important for success. Excellence models are structured approaches applied to improve quality across various functions in an organization. By tradition, different models are implemented in various companies across different countries, with each proposing its own strength. Recently, many models have gained attention, as they form a critical foundation for improving and controlling the operational systems to achieve strategic alignment toward excellence and sustainability of performance.

One of these well-known models is the Malcolm Baldrige National Quality Award (MBNQA) in the United States. The MBNQA was launched by the Department of Commerce's National Institute of Standards and Technology (NIST) and the American Society for Quality (ASQ) in 1987. The award's important objective is to improve the effectiveness of US organizations. It includes seven main criteria: leadership, strategic planning, customer focus, measurement, analysis, knowledge management, workforce focus, operation focus, and results (Lee and Lee, 2013).

The European Foundation for Quality Management (EFQM) was established in 1988 by a team of managers from European organizations to promote operational excellence, based on MBNQA. The EFQM model has nine main criteria, which are divided into two parts—the organizational enablers criteria: leadership, people, strategy, partnership and resources, and processes, products, and services; and the achieved results criteria: people, customer, society, and performance (Lee and Lee, 2013). EFQM facilitates the implementation of TQM principles and transforms the organizational culture into a TQM culture. The assessment process begins with an award submission in a narrative style, followed by a visit led by certified assessors who analyze the documentation and conduct interviews to appraise the organization's processes definition, implementation, and understanding. Then a feedback report is created including the excellence point ranking for all categories, based on the EFQM award criteria and the radar methodology (Ahrens, 2013).

MBNQA stimulates an understanding of the requirements for operational excellence and competitiveness as well as the sharing of information about successful performance strategies. EFQM shifts the attention of employees to performance excellence, motivates them to develop improvement initiatives, and demonstrates achievable results across the organization. EFQM self-assessment is a comprehensive, systematic, and regular appraisal of an organization's activities and results against the excellence model. The self-assessment process assists the organization in identifying its strengths and actions of improvements, which can then be planned, implemented, and monitored for progress (Dale *et al.*, 2016).

In the UAE, the fourth generation of the Government Excellence System (GES) was launched in 2015 as an evolution for the various quality award programs in the country. These programs first started with the launching of the Dubai Quality Award (DQA) in 1994, which was mainly based on the EFQM (GES, 2015). In 2009, and in a step to have an excellence award at the national (federal) level, the UAE Award for Government Excellence was introduced under the Sheikh Khalifa Government Excellence Program (SKGEP), based on a decree issued in 2006. Then, in 2015, the Mohammed bin Rashid Award for Excellence in Government Performance was launched based on GES (SKGEP, 2019). GES was initiated to unite the various awards across the UAE and was customized to the requirements of the government sector. Eventually, GES was implemented to drive improvements across government institutions in Dubai and Abu Dhabi and to replace the previous versions of the Dubai Government Excellence Program (DGEP) and Abu Dhabi Award for Excellence in Government Performance (ADAEP), respectively, with modified versions while maintaining the same award names.

The Abu Dhabi version of GES included 12 criteria instead of 9 as in Dubai (modified from the EFQM criteria), and they included main criteria and sub-criteria. Those criteria fall under three pillars of focus: vision achievement and digital government, innovation and future shaping, and organizational enablers or support. For DGEP, the 9 criteria are vision achievement (seven-star services and smart government), innovation and future shaping, and enablers (GES, 2015; DGEP, 2019). The objective of GES is not only about winning the awards in various categories but, more importantly, to enhance the improvement efforts by identifying strengths and bridging the opportunities in management and service delivery (Salah and Salah, 2020).[2] Salah and Rahim (2019) listed the main practices of ICWMS and other quality awards and MS models.

Here are some of the most important reasons why organizations start self-assessment programs (Dale *et al.*, 2016):

- Identify opportunities for improvement.
- Create a focus on TQM, based on model criteria.
- Direct the improvement approach.
- Motivate employees for the improvement process.
- Manage the business operation.

Also, Dale *et al.* (2016) listed the following benefits of using self-assessment models:

1. Provide a definition for TQM that enhances awareness and ownership among managers.
2. Enable measurement to be made in a structured approach.
3. Enhance, and regularly evaluate the rate of improvement.
4. Challenge teams to reflect on the basic elements of their operation.
5. Provide an objective and a measurement system.
6. Share the best practices, and facilitate learning.
7. Enhance awareness about the basic principles of TQM.
8. Create a more interconnected environment at work.

Moreover, in order for a self-assessment exercise to be successful, the following factors are important (Ritchie and Dale, 2000):

- Management commitment and employees' support to allocate proper resources.

- Executing actions obtained from previous self-assessments.
- Ability to use the selected model as a measurement tool.
- Staff training to properly execute self-assessments, know where to start, and realize the need for documented evidence.
- Adoption of self-assessment outcomes into the business plan at every business unit level in a timely manner and the integration of functions across departments.
- Not letting this program be added to employees' current workload, as it requires much time and may become a burden that causes loss of motivation.
- Establishing a framework for performance management and progress monitoring, such as an excellence maturity assessment matrix.

Finally, Table 5.1 provides a summary for some criteria that can be used in pursuit of excellence, along with a clarification for how excellence maturity can be evaluated for an organization.

Table 5.1   Excellence Criteria, along with Examples of Aspects to Monitor and Consider for Maturity Evaluation

	Excellence criteria	*Examples of aspects to monitor and consider for maturity evaluation*
1	Strategy execution and performance management	Leadership involvement in vision, mission, and strategic initiatives deployment, the use of balanced scorecards, stakeholders' management, and achievement of financial targets.
2	Production and service excellence	Plan for process digitalization, processes digitalization status, digitalization KPIs, and customer satisfaction.
3	Process management	Documenting and reviewing processes, KPI monitoring, managing nonconformities and opportunities from ISO audits, Lean Sigma training plan, and evidence of improvement in KPIs.
4	Digitalization and automation	Plan for process digitalization and its execution progress.
5	Excellence road map	Excellence road map plan, benchmarking plan, best-in-class targets for KPIs, best practices implemented, awards won.
6	Sustainability	Environmental, economic, and social sustainability plans and progress measurement.

	Excellence criteria	Examples of aspects to monitor and consider for maturity evaluation
7	Innovation	Participation of managers in identifying challenges, participation of external stakeholders and employees in generating ideas and innovation activities, ideas evaluation, ideas implementation, and ideas savings .
8	Employee satisfaction and engagement	Wellness and happiness initiatives, employee recognition, training plan, attrition rate, and employee satisfaction.
9	Risk management and governance	Corporate governance, regulations and compliance, risk management plan, business continuity and crisis management, and information security.
10	Tracked improvement projects	Excellence road map plans and their progress measurement.

5.7 Quality Pillar # 26: Effectively Lead a Sustainable Quality Culture to Achieve Performance Excellence

It is well agreed today that effective leadership is very essential for any organization that aims at high levels of excellence in its performance. Sustaining excellence in future performance is critical in order to stay competitive and ensure survival. Leadership is about the creation of a work environment that motivates and engages employees as well as the creation of a culture that is conducive to quality. Figure 5.1 shows various characteristics that describe what a quality culture is about. It takes patience and commitment to set up such a culture. From the fundamentals of quality management, leaders can draw on various principles, which define how to lead in the modern world of the 21st century. From being ethical and humble to being transparent and accountable, charismatic leaders need to demonstrate high standards of morals to lead by example and be looked up to, or even admired, while getting the job done. Leaders of the future need to focus equally on hard and soft aspects of management, striking a balance between the Western focus on numbers and the Eastern focus on people. It is about being confident and brave to share the gaps, admit mistakes, and welcome help. It is about encouraging people to think differently and dare to try new, improved ways, while acknowledging that it is acceptable to expect failure from time to time. It is about living up to universal human values that eliminate any

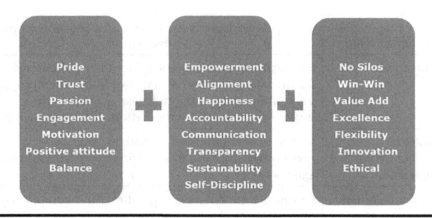

Figure 5.1   Characteristics of quality culture.

contradiction or negativity in the hearts and minds of employees (or follow-ers). It is also about treating people not as employees but rather as partners. It is about social responsibility toward the whole society, environment, and future generations.

Finally, great leaders share the following traits:

- Empower their teams to execute delegated tasks of different levels of challenge while supporting them to achieve their goals and holding them accountable through the continuous measurement of progress against targets.
- Engage their teams and instill in them a sense of pride in what they do. They enable them to see the vision and how they can achieve that vision.
- Motivate their team and influence them with a continuous flow of posi-tive energy that lifts their morale and spirit to achieve high levels of excellence.
- Make other people aspire to become like them. They are role models and can spark a positive attitude as a result of all of their interactions.
- Communicate continuously and exemplify transparency.
- Are humble and respectful of others.
- Are focused on winning and getting their teams to win as well.

Every employee shall aspire to be a great leader, influencing others through positive attitude!

Notes

1. Section 5.4 is mainly prepared based on my work in my thesis titled: "Total company-wide management system: A framework for Six Sigma and continuous quality improvement", 2009, available at the library of the University of New Brunswick, as well as our work: Salah, S. and Rahim, A. (2019). *An integrated company-wide management system: Combining Lean Six Sigma with process improvement*. Cham, Switzerland: Springer Nature.
2. Section 5.6 is mainly prepared based on our work: Salah, S. and Salah, D. (2020). Comparison between the UAE Government Excellence System, Malcolm Baldrige National Quality Award and European Foundation for Quality Management model: Implications for excellence models. *International Journal of Quality and Innovation*, 4(3–4), 121–131.

THE METHODOLOGY OF SIX SIGMA

Chapter 6

Fundamental Pillars Related to Six Sigma

6.1 Quality Pillar # 27: Use a Structured Approach for Improvement Like the Integrated Lean Six Sigma (LSS) Five Phases of Define-Measure-Analyze-Improve-Control (DMAIC)

As a quality practitioner, when approaching managers and their teams with a proposal for studying and improving their processes, the answer is often negative, indicating that they already are confident of how good their processes are and that they are already working on various improvement initiatives. However, the key difference in their approach and a Lean Six Sigma Master Black Belt approach is the use of a "structured" approach. This approach starts with the proper selection of processes and teams to perform studies, following a well-proven methodology of specified steps that, if done properly, will deliver higher rates of improvement.

Walter Shewhart was the first to introduce the plan-do-check-act (PDCA) cycle for problem solving and work improvement (Breyfogle, 2003). It was later publicized by Edwards Deming, who changed the reactive "check" part with a more proactive "study" part. The Japanese approach of Kaizen Gemba is focused on the PDCA cycle of efforts led by management, which is followed by the plan-do-standardize-act, or PDSA, cycle of efforts led by the operations' teams to maintain the improved ways of operation (Imai, 2012). This is the core of daily quality or operation management part of

DOI: 10.4324/9781032688374-9

ICWMS, as introduced in Chapter 5, where progress is checked against targets, and variation is highlighted for investigation and improvement.

The PDCA cycle of improvement consists of the following steps (Farmer and Duffy, 2017):

■ Plan: Select project, define problem, set target, and identify recommendations.
■ Do: Collect data, prioritize, and analyze; test potential causes, determine and test solutions, and evaluate cost and benefits.
■ Check: Consolidate ideas, select next potential project, and obtain management approval.
■ Act: Plan implementation and training, standardize, and maintain improvement.

Motorola first introduced Six Sigma in the mid-1980s when Bill Smith (Devane, 2004; Kumar *et al.*, 2008) and Mike Harry (Harry and Schroeder, 2000) put together a new framework for improvement. At General Electric (GE), this framework was enhanced (similar to Deming's PDCA cycle) and called MAIC (measure-analyze-improve-control) (Dahlgaard and Dahlgaard-Park, 2006). This framework cleverly packaged and grouped various management tools and quality tools (graphical and statistical) into each of the four phases of the Six Sigma methodology. It was later that the define phase was added to that framework, which became famously known as DMAIC. Other companies later added a recognize phase at the beginning of any project to help identify and select projects or added a validate phase after the control phase to further emphasize the financial savings validation as a result of the enhancement of poor quality.

It is partially attributed to Jack Welch, the former CEO of General Electric, that Six Sigma spread widely in North America and eventually globally, when he announced that GE managed to save hundreds of millions of dollars by implementing the Six Sigma methodology (Raisinghani *et al.*, 2005). The most unique feature about Six Sigma is that it is a structured and highly disciplined approach. It has become so mature that each phase has a clear road map with a detailed checklist used as a tollgate, with requirements to fulfill, in order to proceed from one phase to another.

Prior to Six Sigma, total quality management (TQM) had widely spread as a process improvement approach, utilizing quality circles and the seven basic quality tools. However, it was purely recognized as a philosophy, which did not achieve the same results as Six Sigma. This was mainly attributed to the lack of a robust and structured approach in TQM. Nevertheless, TQM is considered the umbrella for all quality improvement efforts, and Six Sigma is an extension of it, as it evolved to become widely used. They both share many common aspects and goals (Salah *et al.*, 2009a).

The modern approach of Lean Six Sigma kept using the same structured phases of DMAIC after both methodologies got integrated. Both Lean and Six Sigma can be considered as toolboxes that include various tools to select from. The selection of a suitable tool depends on the nature of the problem faced.

The weakest level of control in a process lies in the use of verbal instructions, which can be easily forgotten or misunderstood. It is well agreed that standardized approaches, such as standard operating procedures, best-in-class practices, and other structured methodologies are much better than nonstandardized approaches. The moment somebody deviates from following the standard approach, there is a higher risk of crossing the specified tolerances (upper or lower specification limits) and thus resulting in higher amount of defects. However, standard procedures are not created to remain unchallenged or to limit the innovative creativity of teams. On the contrary, the moment a better procedure is identified, the team can proceed to adopt it (see Chapter 5 to read more about the relevant topic of process maturity, which was discussed as part of the process management component of ICWMS).

One important note to pay attention to is that standardized procedures shall not be created for the sole purpose of satisfying an ISO certification. If taken seriously, standardized procedures, which are created by the experienced teams who do the work themselves, can be of great benefit for any organization seeking to achieve optimal levels of quality, cost, and delivery. Actually, the use of the ISO internal audits can result in great enhancements to any procedure, where teams get challenged to ensure that they are using a simplified, cost-effective, quality-focused, and measurement-based approach to help them manage their processes.

The use of DMAIC enables a Green Belt to be much more confident to lead his or her team with a clear step-by-step road map. By leading a Six Sigma project, a Green Belt learns firsthand how DMAIC can be followed to achieve successful project results. Each phase has an important purpose and smoothly flows into the next one. Each phase builds upon what was done in the previous phase, and once all its requirements are fulfilled, it logically leads into being ready to start the next phase. Here is an explanation for each of the five phases of the integrated LSS DMAIC approach (Salah *et al.*, 2010):

1. Define: Understand TQM and LSS methodologies and tools, select the proper project and team members, develop the project charter indicating the problem and objective, set up a timeline and change management plan, evaluate the COPQ and waste, understand the voice of the customer (VOC) and the critical-to-quality (CTQ) characteristics using the supplier-input-process-output-customer (SIPOC) diagram and the quality function deployment (QFD) tool.

2. Measure: Establish the baseline performance using a data collection plan; use control charts, capability charts, graphical tools, and descriptive statistics to measure the central location and variability of the data; map the current-state VSM; identify waste and time metrics; use a Kaizen event approach to implement quick improvements; use a measurement system analysis (MSA) to validate the reliability of the data; use a cause-and-effect diagram and failure mode and effect analysis (FMEA) to brainstorm potential causes.

3. Analyze: Implement quick improvement actions; create a data collection plan to verify the critical causes; use graphical tools to investigate the reasons for variation; develop hypotheses related to the sources of variation and strength of relationships; analyze the current-state VSM in terms of unnecessary steps, the flow of products and information, and the lead time, and rework; and create a future-state VSM design to implement in next phase.

4. Improve: Optimize the settings of the critical inputs; improve processes (using tools like benchmarking, regression, simulation, and control charts); document the standard operating procedures and best practices; create an improvement action plan; use Kaizen events to implement improvements, such as single-piece flow, cell design, total productive maintenance (TPM), and quick changeover (see Chapters 10 and 11 for more information on these topics).

5. Control: Validate the FMEA, MSA, process capability, sigma level, and control charts; design a control plan using mistake-proofing approach; hand over the responsibility to process owners who monitor the performance metrics to ensure they are in control; and reconfirm the financial analysis.

As per Farmer and Duffy (2017), it is important to note that there are different roles played by employees within any LSS program deployment in any organization. Yellow Belts (YBs) are trained to understand the basics about LSS and its statistical tools. They are not fully allocated to work on improvement projects, but they can play a key role in supporting improvement teams as team members, process owners, or managers. Black Belts (BBs) are leaders of the LSS program, who are responsible for executing projects and achieving the targeted results of improvement. They help in selecting team members, allocating resources, providing knowledge, monitoring progress, managing changes, managing risks, and sustaining results. BBs utilize selected Green Belts (GBs) to lead project teams through DMAIC phases. In addition, project sponsors are typically managers, who support improvement teams by allocating resources and removing obstacles.

Finally, some of the key metrics used to evaluate the progress and success of a Lean Six Sigma program at any organization include the following:

1. Actual hard and soft savings achieved by LSS projects.
2. Count of LSS projects.
3. Count of trained YBs, GBs, and BBs.
4. Savings achieved per project.
5. Average time to complete an LSS project.
6. Defects per million opportunities (DPMO), defects per unit (DPU), and rolled throughput yield (RTY).

6.2 Quality Pillar # 28: Use a Proper Project Selection Approach

There are various reasons that trigger the selection of improvement projects. For example, these projects are usually done to free up capacity required for future expansion, increase revenue and profit, reduce costs, enhance productivity, and solve a chronic issue related to customer satisfaction or to eliminate a risk or defect (Salah, 2015).[1] A simple way to prioritize the selection of PI projects would be to consider how easy they are to implement and how great their benefit will be to the customers and stakeholders. Salah (2015) and Salah and Rahim (2019) listed some recommendations for how the framework for project selection and prioritization is developed: it needs to be aligned with the organization's strategy; needs a project accumulator (collecting ideas based on customer complaints, strategy, brainstorming, BSC KPIs, financial KPIs); and a prioritization matrix, including five to eight weighted factors (like cost of implementation, profit impact, capacity, growth, resources, availability of data, change difficulty, risks, probability for success, customer issues, and employee issues); and a mechanism to assign the next project to the next available resource. Organizations can conduct a strategic planning session involving all employees to brainstorm the barriers preventing them from achieving the vision of their organization. Based on the top voted barriers, potential projects are then identified and added into the project accumulator. The weighted prioritization factors are then used by the team collectively to calculate the overall rank of each project. The project with the highest rank is then assigned to the next available and suitable team.

6.3 Quality Pillar # 29: Strive to Achieve a Higher Sigma Level (Lower DPMO), but Remember That It May Not Always Be Feasible

The goal for any process is to eliminate defects. Defects are costly to any company, and they are divided into either internal defects (typically discovered prior to shipping to customers) or external defects (typically discovered after shipping to the customer). Obviously, external defects are much more expensive to rectify. Not only do they affect cost but also the brand's reputation. The answer for the defects challenge lies in quality assurance and designing quality into the product so that it is done right the first time and every time (as usually targeted). Defects are also one of the types of Lean waste or Muda. They are part of the COPQ, as discussed earlier in this book, particularly in Section 3.4.

As a methodology, Six Sigma strives to eliminate variation and stabilize the process. By aiming at the target while reducing variation, there will be fewer chances to exceed the specification limits and generate defects. In a Six Sigma process, fitting a process distribution well within the tolerances will result in a defectives level of only two parts per billion opportunities. In the long term, the famous number for a process operating at a Six Sigma level capability is 3.4 defective parts per million opportunities. The latter level is what Motorola came up with, due to the perceived wear and tear causing the means of their processes to shift by 1.5 sigma. This is a fact that Motorola is often criticized for and is not well accepted to be generalized (Sheehy *et al.*, 2002; Raisinghani *et al.*, 2005).

Sigma level is a measure of the capability of a process to satisfy customers. Most companies operate at a three sigma level, which corresponds to a defectives level of 0.27% or 2,700 parts per million opportunities (Kwak and Anbari, 2004). So, for companies starting their journey of process improvement, the baseline performance measured by sigma level can be evaluated. If the sigma level is found to be at one sigma, then obviously, the goal would be to target the next level, which is two sigma, and so on. When reaching the common benchmark of three sigma, companies need to consider, if feasible, to proceed to higher sigma levels or not. Sometimes, it can be very costly and may require a considerable investment in resources, such as people skills, advanced equipment, or expensive automation.

6.4 Quality Pillar # 30: Hold the Gains, and Control the Process (See Section 11.1 for More Information on Standardization)

It is no wonder that the fifth phase in any Six Sigma or Lean Six Sigma project is the "control" phase. This phase is very important to ensure that improvements are held in place so that people do not fall back to the old ways of running their processes. The following is a real example to illustrate the importance of this phase. When an improvement team of BBs did not pay attention to the importance of this phase, they got caught by surprise. After being improved, various processes did gradually change back into the old ways. Hence, the team decided to conduct an audit for all applicable projects, in order to investigate the reasons for such a failure to hold the gains. The auditors needed to ensure that the control plans, which are typically handed over to the process owners, are well prepared and robust enough to ensure the gains are held in place.

Control plans are used in the LSS control phase to present a structured approach for identifying and implementing value-added control methods for the entire system. They ensure to establish the proper monitoring, measurement (including detailed explanation), analysis of control subjects (using control charts), and rules of implementation of improvement actions to restore the process. This can be established using a dynamic control plan (DCP), which combines all the key information in the form of FMEA, standard operating procedures (SOPs) (living documents updated to reflect any process change while describing detailed instructions to perform the process steps consistently, before getting controlled and communicated), gauge control plan (including maintenance, calibration, and proper management of the instruments for safety, quality, accuracy, minimum variation, and corrective actions), and quality planning sheets (QPSs) (Farmer and Duffy, 2017).

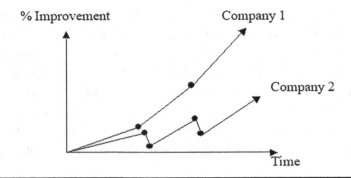

Figure 6.1   Examples of a company that uses a structured PI approach (company 1) and another that does not (company 2).

The effect of the control phase is similar to the effect of a wedge that keeps a big rock, pushed up a hill, from rolling back to the bottom of the valley, where it was first found. The wedge is what locks the achievement in its place to ensure that the next step will be building further improvement, in addition to what was achieved earlier.

Comparing two companies in the way they handle improvement can further explain this principle. A company that uses proper control plans will be successful in building upon earlier achievements, whereas a company that does not use proper control plans will always restart from scratch after every improvement project, since its results do not get maintained. This can be the difference between winning companies and other low-performing companies. It is exactly for this reason why the Japanese Kaizen Gemba approach emphasizes the use of PDSA after the use of PDCA, to ensure the new, improved ways are standardized and maintained. Figure 6.1 shows the rate of improvement for a company that follows a properly structured DMAIC approach versus another one that does not. For Company "2", there is a decline in the rate of improvement right after every project is done due to the lack of proper controls, which are emphasized as part of the control phase of DMAIC.

6.5 Quality Pillar # 31: Learn from Other DMAIC Six Sigma Projects, and Replicate Elsewhere to Maximize the Benefits

As per the principles of project management, it is important to take the time after finishing every project, to reflect on the key lessons learned from that project. This way mistakes can be avoided in the future, and benefits can be replicated as well.

One of the benefits of following a structured approach of improvement is the sharing of such best practices of one project to generate similar results and savings in other departments and locations.

Here are some examples for a successful implementation of an LSS DMAIC project and expanding its benefits to other locations: reduction of fuel cost in one company branch as a result of using a different supplier or a new efficient equipment, reduction of energy bill in one building as a result of the use of solar systems, introduction of a new service at one location, introduction of a new technology in one division, *etc*. Therefore, every project report needs to have a section that explains the leverageability of the benefits of the project and where else might these benefits be applicable.

Note

1. Section 6.2 is mainly prepared based on my published work: Salah, S. (2015). A project selection, prioritisation and classification approach for organisations managing continuous improvement (CI). *International Journal of Project Organisation and Management*, 7(1), 1–13.

Chapter 7

Fundamental Pillars Related to the Use of Basic Quality Tools (Utilized in Six Sigma Projects)

7.1 Quality Pillar # 32: It Is Powerful to Have Data. Dive Deep into What Your Data Tells You, Using a Histogram and Statistical Parameters to Analyze Your Data Statistically and Graphically

So, when it comes to data, where do you start? How useful is it to start with a histogram?

To the famous saying: "In God we trust. For everyone else, show me the data", one may add: "Show me the numbers". Data provides an important piece of evidence to support any business decision. Moreover, since the language of business is dollars, one can even add: "Show me the money", per the well-known phrase by the movie character, Jerry Maguire. Indeed, data can prove someone right or wrong. Anyone can be more powerful when equipped with data. There is a huge difference between managing a business traditionally by feelings (or hunch) versus managing it by facts.

Descriptive statistics provide a visual of what the process output looks like. Using a collected sample of data from a process, quality practitioners can create graphs and calculate descriptive statistics, which will enable them

DOI: 10.4324/9781032688374-10

to understand the shape or pattern of the distribution of the population (the appropriate statistical distribution needed to predict the behavior of the population), the average output and how centered it is compared to the target, the actual variation in the process, and how widely the data is spread. Figure 7.1 shows three important characteristics for describing variable data.

A team of quality practitioners had selected a certain KPI that required examination. This KPI had been tracked daily for the last three months, and its data was populated in one column of an Excel database. First, they need to ensure the data is authentic and resulting from a reliable measurement system (see Section 3.1 for more on MSA). Then they need to examine the data to see if any numbers or entries look suspicious, have missing information, or are incorrect. After that, they need to look at the shape of the data distribution. One of the most commonly dealt with distributions in nature is the Gaussian bell curve or normal distribution. The basic quality tool that can help them understand the shape of the data distribution is the histogram. Many tools and hypotheses can be easily examined if the data is normally distributed, making it easier to deal with. The histogram can indicate whether the data is normal or not, but a normality test using a normal probability plot is still required for a more accurate judgment. Statistical software packages like Minitab can help test whether the data is normal or not. These packages can help fit a bell curve nicely into the histogram itself for shape evaluation. They can also help run a probability check for normality using hypothesis testing where a p-value is examined based on a typical

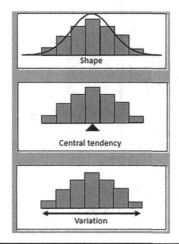

Figure 7.1   Three important characteristics for describing variable data as adapted from Six Sigma Training, personal communication (2008).

5% probability threshold. The statements of hypotheses for a normality test are as follows:

Null hypothesis (Ho): Data is normal (*i.e.*, the null is "dull", and there is no difference expected).

Alternative hypothesis or assumption (Ha): Data is not normal.

Based on the statistical test conducted, if the resulting value of p is less than or equal to 0.05 (*i.e.*, $p \le 0.05$), the null hypothesis is rejected in favor of the alternative, as there is enough proof or statistically significant evidence that the data is not normal (if the p is low, the null must go).

If the data is normal, then the observations will act according to the normal distribution and its applicable characteristics. Most data points (around 68%) are clustered around the average of the KPI sample, within an equivalent distance of one standard deviation on both sides of the average. Similarly, 95% of the data lie within two standard deviations from the average, and 99.73% lie within three standard deviations from the average. This is graphically demonstrated in Figure 7.2, which shows (through a generic example) the area under a normal distribution curve, corresponding to

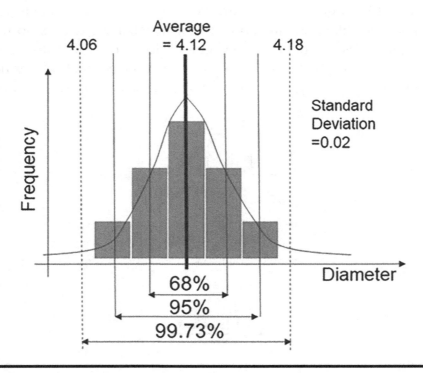

Figure 7.2   A generic example of a normally distributed sample of cylinders (diameters in mm) as adapted from Six Sigma Training, personal communication (2008).

different distances from the mean. These ratios (for the area under the normal curve) will help estimate process capability. This is done after ensuring the process is stable, using statistical control charts (see Section 7.5).

Generally, statistics related to statistical parameters, such as the average (*xbar*) and the standard deviation (*s*), are calculated based on the studied data to make inferences about the whole population's mean (μ, or mu) and standard deviation (σ, or sigma).

The average is compared to the target to see if there is a shift in the process mean and in which direction. The goal in process improvement is to ensure the process average is as close as possible to the specified target. The moment it deviates from that target, a loss of quality is generated.

Thus, it is essential to examine the measures of central tendency of data. Statistics such as the average, median, or mode are evaluated. These statistical parameters all indicate around which values all data points tend to be clustered. Averages are equal to the sum of all data points divided by their count. The median is the value that falls exactly in the middle when arranging all data points in an ascending or descending order. The mode is the value that is repeated the most.

If the data is not normally distributed, then the median is a better indicator of central tendency than the average. To illustrate that, here is a story of a couple that was looking for a house to buy. Their budget was $110,000, while the average house price in the neighborhood they were interested in was $150,000. So, based on an initial assessment, the couple did not seem to have enough money to afford buying a house in that neighborhood. However, when they examined the historical price distribution for all houses per the municipality records, it did not look normally distributed. It was skewed to the left (toward the lower-cost houses). Apparently, a few luxurious houses were priced way higher than many of the houses in that area, which caused the average to look too high. When the couple examined the median for the same data set, the median value was $110,000, which fell well within their budget. It meant that there were many affordable houses in that area.

It is not enough to look at the average of a KPI behavior compared to the target in order to ensure a process is successful in delivering what customers want. What one needs to be also careful about is the variation in the process, which has an impact on its capability to satisfy customers. It is those moments that customers won't forget as negative incidents, particularly when variation is high and providers fail to satisfy targets. Consider the example of a train occasionally arriving later than the targeted time, causing customers to miss an important connection. Customers will forget all the good days when the train arrived on time and only remember the rare incidents of variation. Thus, the measures of variation are importantly examined. Statistics such as the standard deviation, variance, and range are evaluated to understand the way a certain KPI or the process itself behaves. Lower variation is favorable, as it leads to more consistency, higher customer satisfaction, and less rework.

The range is calculated by subtracting the minimum value in a sample from the highest value in that sample. The standard deviation (*s*) is equal to the square root of the sum of squared deviations of all data values from the average (*xbar*), divided by the sample size (*n*) after being adjusted to (*n* − 1) (for reversing the effect of underestimation, due to the use of *xbar*) (see Equation 7.1). The variance is equal to the squared value of the standard deviation.

$$s = \sqrt{\frac{\sum (x - xbar)^2}{n-1}} \tag{7.1}$$

One final note relevant to the measures of variation, is that as the sample size (*n*) grows larger, the standard deviation becomes a much more reliable measure for variation than the range. The range takes into account only two values of the whole sample. To help illustrate that, see Figure 7.3. Two samples of six items each are plotted using dot diagrams, which clearly show more dispersion in data points' locations for the first supplier (sample A) than for the second supplier (sample B). While the ranges are equal, the standard deviation for sample A indicates a much higher variability than

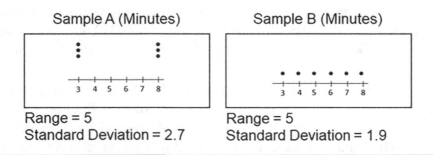

Figure 7.3 Comparison of the calculated values for the standard deviation and the range for two suppliers' delivery times as adapted from Six Sigma Training, personal communication (2008).

sample B, which confirms that the standard deviation is a better indicator of variation than the range, especially when starting to use larger samples.

The standard deviation is used to evaluate how steady and consistent the process is. For any process, the lower the range or the standard deviation, the better it is. This will later be compared to the upper and lower specification limits, which will help to evaluate the capability of the process to satisfy customers' specifications. This comparison can take place once the process is declared stable, based on its dominant type of variation (see Section 7.2 for more information).

The central limit theorem is essential for many statistical analysis approaches, such as the calculation of confidence intervals for a sample mean (Breyfogle, 2003). It indicates that the sum of independently distributed random variables is approximately normal (Montgomery, 2001). Regardless of the distribution of the individual observations or data points, the distribution of the sample averages themselves for samples taken from the same population would tend to be normally distributed. This theory makes it easier to deal with data sets, as explained earlier. An example of that would be the use of X-bar charts (see Figure 7.4).

A histogram is one of the basic quality tools that can be used to summarize and display data graphically. It can be thought of as a snapshot or a picture taken at a moment of time, which depicts all the history of the selected KPI, up to that particular moment when the picture was taken. It can effectively show what the baseline performance looks like, and it can

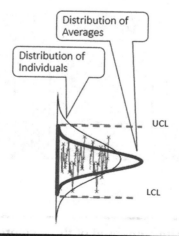

Figure 7.4 An X-bar Control chart which is constructed based on the normality assumption as adapted from Six Sigma Training, personal communication (2008).

help understand the central tendency, amount of variation, and the behavior of the process being examined. The shape of the population depicted in a histogram is important, as it indicates the appropriate statistical distribution that needs to be considered to gain a better understanding of the population being dealt with. When a histogram has a "bell" shape, the normal distribution theory and applicable characteristics are used to make predictions about the population. Multiple peaks (in a multimodal distribution) indicate that something has been altered, which is often uncovered by the collected data itself.

The bimodal distribution has a shape similar to the back of a two-humped camel. It occurs when combining (into one set of data) the output of two machines or processes that have different distributions. It is often revealed by the use of data stratification (Farmer and Duffy, 2017).

A histogram can sort data into categories and reveal valuable information about different suppliers or departments, as depicted in Figure 7.5. Their performance can be easily compared to conclude who is leading with the best practices in place and who might be facing challenges. In Figure 7.5, if the specified target is five units, then the supplier in the middle is preferred to deal with than the others, as the average coincides with the target, and the

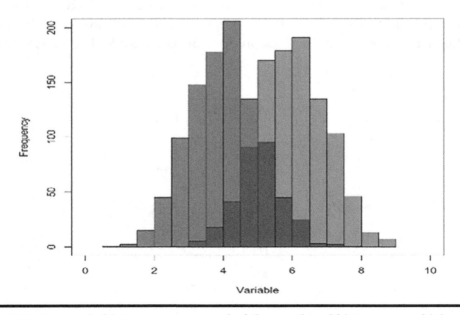

Figure 7.5   A generic histogram composed of three colored histograms, which sort data into three categories as adapted from Six Sigma Training, personal communication (2008).

range of observations (difference between maximum and minimum) appears to be slightly narrower than the other two suppliers.

In another context, suppliers who appear to abide by the lower and upper specification limits while rejecting a high number of defects might be charging their clients more than they should pay (to compensate for their losses of poor quality and rework). This behavior can be seen in Figure 7.6, which shows what the supplier sees on the left-hand side of the graph and what a customer sees on the right-hand side, when analyzing samples of the received products.

In another case of comparing the distributions (shown in Figure 7.7) for two suppliers of industrial tubes, it can be easily noted that both of them equally operate at an average of 4.12 mm. Thus, in terms of central tendency and regardless of the targeted inner diameter value, none of them stands out as a better supplier. Also, both demonstrate a somewhat normally distributed behavior. However, when looking at their variation, it can be noted that supplier A is superior, because of the lesser range over which the sample data is spread. Suppose that the target was 4.12 mm and the acceptable tolerance

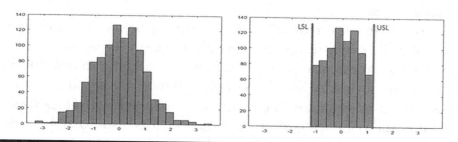

Figure 7.6   A histogram from a costly operation which got force-fitted into the acceptable range of specification by rejecting defectives.

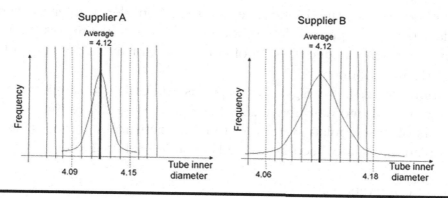

Figure 7.7   Comparison of two suppliers of tubes.

around it was ±0.02 mm. Then, it can be concluded that supplier A is more capable than supplier B.

7.2 Quality Pillar # 33: Understand Sampling and the Use of a Proper Sample Size

Sampling is a key technique that helps in capturing data about the process under investigation. This data is required for analysis and has to be representative of the population under consideration, without any bias. Good data will help ensure a good conclusion and statistical inference.

However, cost considerations in sampling are very important. In order to know the true values of the key statistical parameters of a population correctly, one has to take a 100% sample where every item in the population is measured. This is typically not practical, expensive, time consuming, and sometimes can be in the form of a destructive test. Thus, sampling is a reasonable choice that can provide reasonable and acceptable results despite some risks of errors.

According to (Pyzdek and Keller, 2019), one important aspect of sampling is the use of point estimate versus interval estimation. Typically, the studied statistics (which are calculated from a sample) include the sample mean, the sample standard deviation, and the sample variance. These sample statistics are known as point estimators, because they are individual values used to represent the true parameters of the population. It is also possible to create an interval spanning around each of these statistics. This interval has a preestablished probability of including the true value for the selected population parameter. This interval is referred to as a confidence interval. An alternative to point estimation that provides a better idea of the amount of the sampling error is called interval estimation. Confidence intervals can be one-sided, using an upper or lower bound that would encompass the value of a parameter with a specific level of confidence, or two-sided, using both upper and lower bounds.

In various practical Six Sigma applications, the collected sample data is usually converted into descriptive statistics that are used to estimate the parameters of the population in order to make statistical inferences about that population. Data collection methods include (Keller, 2005):

- Direct observations.
- Manual data collection using check sheets.

- Automatic data collection using automated systems, sensors, and other tools.
- Experiments.
- Surveys of various types.
- Interviews.
- Focus groups.
- Research studies.

Here are some relevant definitions of data sampling and data analysis, which are important to understand (Keller, 2005; Pries, 2009; Pyzdek and Keller, 2019):

- A population is a group of all items of interest to a statistics practitioner or the totality of items.
- A parameter is a descriptive measure of a population.
- A sample is a subset of data drawn from a population.
- A statistic is a descriptive measure of a sample.
- Statistical inferencing is the process of making an estimate, prediction, or decision about a population based on sample data.
- Discrete data is attribute data that represents a set of integers or whole values, which can be counted, as in the case of tracking the number of defects.
- Continuous data is variable data that represents a set of real values measured on a continuous scale. They are continuous in the mathematical sense, and they are infinitely divisible.
- A point estimate is a single value (such as the sample average or the variance), which is used to represent a population parameter (such as the mean or the variance).
- Interval estimate of a parameter is the interval between two statistics, which include the true value of the parameter. This interval is associated with some probability or risk related to an alpha value (α), which represents the risk of rejecting the null hypothesis when it is true.
- The p-value is the smallest level of significance in a hypothesis testing process, which would lead to the rejection of the null hypothesis (Ho).
- Type I error or alpha (α) is the producer's risk of rejecting the null hypothesis when it is true.
- Type II error or beta (β) is the supplier's risk of failing to reject the null hypothesis when it is false.

- ■ Power of test (1 − beta or 1 − β) is about correctly rejecting the null hypothesis. It is about how well the test performs to report accurately. It is about the probability that will lead to the rejection of the null hypothesis when it is false. Beta (β) is the probability of failing to reject the false null hypothesis.

Many statistical software packages provide power and sample size calculations. Minitab's "Power and Sample Size" option in the "Stat" menu can help estimate these for a variety of test formats. Generally, the power of a statistical test is improved when:

- ■ there is a large difference between the null and alternative conditions;
- ■ the population standard deviation is small;
- ■ the sample size is large; and
- ■ the significance level alpha (α) value is large.

The drawn conclusions and estimates are not always going to be correct. Thus, two measures of reliability for statistical inferences are typically introduced, which are called confidence level and significance level. Confidence level is the proportion of times that an estimating procedure would be right, if a sampling procedure was repeated many times. Confidence level equals to 1 − α. On the other hand, significance level measures how frequently the conclusion about the population will be incorrect in the long run (Keller, 2005; Pries, 2009).

Data is also classified as per the measurement scale into interval data arranged in intervals, nominal data indicating frequency of occurrence, and ordinal data indicating a ranking or hierarchy (Pries, 2009).

As generally perceived, the larger the sample size, the better the accuracy of the results obtained based on that sample. However, this is not an accurate statement. As indicated by (Juran and Godfrey, 1999), doubling the sample size does not result in doubling the precision of estimates. The precision depends on the absolute sample size rather than the size expressed as a percentage of the size of the population. A smaller percentage of a larger sample might be more precise than a larger percentage of a smaller population. Also, the cost of sampling is an essential factor to be optimized, when aiming for an increase in precision.

Using a sample of data, a range can be obtained for the confidence interval located around a selected parameter, such as the mean. When sampling, it is necessary to decide to what level of accuracy (or tolerance) the parameter needs to be estimated.

As depicted in Equation 7.2, the sample size n is a function of the following (Pries, 2009):

- the standard deviation s;
- the tolerance units t; and
- the variable value z, which depends on the confidence level,

where:

$$n = \left(\frac{z * s}{t} \right)^2 \tag{7.2}$$

The value of s is usually obtained by research, expert knowledge, or pilot testing. The tolerance t is assumed, and z is commonly chosen as 1.96, which corresponds to a confidence level of 95%. Additionally, the sample size n can be calculated using software packages like Minitab.

Here are some examples of appropriate sampling strategies (Pries, 2009):

- Random sampling, which ensures each member of the population has an equal chance of being included in the sample.
- Stratified sampling, where the population is first divided into subpopulations (strata) and random sampling is then conducted within each stratum.
- Systematic sampling is a sampling method in which samples are taken at specified points in time.

Acceptance sampling is one of oldest aspects of quality, which is concerned with inspection. Based on acceptance sampling, a decision is made whether to accept or reject a sample. Acceptance sampling plans may vary from single to multiple sampling plans, where the decisions might be to accept, reject, or even take a second sample (Pries, 2009). Aspects to consider when deciding on a sampling plan include cost of inspection, destructive testing, measurement system analysis (MSA), liability to clients, and history of suppliers. Sampling, in general, needs to be random, representative, and rational without any bias.

Data can be qualitative or quantitative. Qualitative data is obtained from reliable sources such as interviews, which can be expensive. It can be in the form of categorical groups of data described in words (like tall and short or customer satisfaction levels or product types or colors). On the other hand, quantitative data is obtained from product data, corrective actions, cost data, and service delivery. Quantitative data is either variable or attribute. Variable data is obtained from measurements done on a continuous scale. Attribute data is discrete data obtained by counting the occurrence of events. Data collection tools include flowcharts, interviews, surveys (used to inexpensively obtain large samples but sometimes may have low response rates, translate customer opinion into quantitative numbers, and quickly provide inputs), electronic surveys (which are structured, interactive, convenient, likely to have high response rates, faster, instantly analyzed, less costly, and better at targeting specific audience), a checklist with standard questions about a service or maintenance issues, focus groups (which require skilled facilitators and are used to gain direct and unbiased feedback, perceptions, thoughts, and opinions about a service or product), brainstorming, check sheets, automatic data capturing (which is accurate and timely;, lowers risks in finance, health care, and security; is expensive to set up; requires software and hardware interface with the data source), cause-and-effect diagram, and force-field analysis diagram (which is used to review forces favoring or countering an issue or decision).

A data collection plan includes a description of the sampling approach of measurement, covering "what" to measure, "how" to measure, "where" to perform the measurement, "when" to perform the measurement, and "who" will perform the measurement. It is usually initiated in the measure phase of an LSS project (Farmer and Duffy, 2017).

Sampling plan is about the lot size, sample size, rejection criteria, or acceptance number. These plans can be based on the use of statistical tables, such as Dodge-Romig sampling plans and operating characteristic (OC) curves, or the use of statistical software packages like Minitab, to help with the selection of sample sizes and the power of sampling. Finally, there are two data types to consider when sampling (Pries, 2009):

1. Variable or continuous data, measured on a continuous scale that is indefinitely divisible, such as measurements of time and length.
2. Attribute data, which is typically counted, such as the number of defects per unit.

Considering the types of available data, Table 7.1 shows some corresponding examples and common graphs that can be used to better understand the

Table 7.1 Common Graphs Associated with Variable and Attribute Data

Type of data	Examples	Common graphs
Variable measurements (taken on a continuous scale)	☐ Time (in hours) ☐ Dimension (in mm) ☐ Weight (in grams) ☐ Cost (in $)	☐ Histogram ☐ Box plot ☐ Dot plot ☐ Scatter plot ☐ Control chart
Attribute (obtained by counting): —Binomial (tracking defectives, where only two outcomes are possible (pass or fail)) —Poisson (tracking defects, where many categorical outcomes are possible)	☐ Number of invoices with one or more errors ☐ Number of errors in each invoice	☐ Line graph ☐ Control chart (*P*-Chart) ☐ Line graph ☐ Pareto chart ☐ Pie chart ☐ Concentration chart ☐ Control chart (*C*-chart and *U*-chart)

Source: Adapted from Six Sigma Training, personal communication (2008)

data and obtain useful information, before conducting further data analysis using other statistical tools.

7.3 Quality Pillar # 34: Use an Appropriate Distribution That Fits Your Data, in Order to Properly Conduct Your Analysis

Random variables are described by their probability distributions, which, in their turn, are described by statistical parameters, such as the mean and standard deviation. Distributions are either continuous or discrete. A continuous distribution is a distribution of a variable, which is measured on a continuous scale. A discrete distribution is a distribution of a measured parameter, which particularly takes whole values. An estimator for an unknown parameter is defined as a statistic corresponding to that parameter, in the form of a point or an interval. Hypothesis testing statements are often made about the values of the parameters of probability distributions (Montgomery, 2001).

The most commonly encountered distribution in Six Sigma work is the normal distribution, which is a continuous distribution. Sometimes the process itself produces an approximately normal distribution. Other times, a normal distribution can be obtained by performing a mathematical transformation on the data or by using the averages distribution as per the central limit theory (Montgomery, 2001).

By the use of the *z*-transformation, any normal distribution can be converted into a standard normal distribution with a mean of 0 and a standard deviation of 1. Thus, a typical normal distribution table can be used to find the probabilities or corresponding areas under the normal curve (Pyzdek and Keller, 2019). This can also be easily done using statistical software packages, like Minitab. Statistical techniques, such as *t*-tests, *z*-tests, analysis of variance (ANOVA), and many other tests, assume that the data are at least approximately normal. This assumption is easily tested using various statistical software packages, like Minitab. There are typically two approaches used for testing normality (Pries, 2009; Pyzdek and Keller, 2019):

■ graphical: as in the use of histograms and normal curve; and
■ statistical: through the calculation of a "goodness-of-fit" statistic and a *p*-value. This gives a clear acceptance measure. Usually, the researcher or practitioner rejects the normality assumption if $p \leq 0.05$.

Beside the normal distribution, here is a brief explanation of other commonly used distributions in Six Sigma and practical process improvement methodologies (Keller, 2005; Pries, 2009; Pyzdek and Keller, 2019):

■ A chi-square test is a statistical tool used to find whether dependence (goodness-of-fit) exists (or not) between random variables taken from different populations. A chi-square test could also be used for testing the goodness-of-fit between an "observed" frequency distribution and an "expected" frequency distribution.
■ Student's *t*-distribution is a distribution defined in terms of the normal distribution. As *k* (or the degrees of freedom) approaches infinity, the *t*-distribution approaches the standard normal distribution. Here are the three common uses for this distribution:
  – One-sample *t*-test is used to compare the mean to a targeted value.
  – Two-sample *t*-test is used to compare the means of two samples (before and after improvement or between two suppliers, two branches, *etc.*).

- Paired-sample *t*-test is used to compare the means of two samples when the data is dependent (*i.e.*, each value in the first sample has a corresponding value in the second one).

■ *F*-distribution is a distribution defined in terms of the normal distribution and is practically useful for making inferences about the variances of two normal distributions that one is interested in comparing. It is noted that the chi-square, Student's *t*, and *F*-distributions are all used commonly to create confidence intervals, test hypotheses, and calculate statistical control limits.

■ Two distributions often used for examining attribute or discrete data are binomial and Poisson distributions. In a binomial distribution, data is acquired by counting the number of defective items (proportion defective or defective parts per million opportunities). Whereas in a Poisson distribution, it is obtained by counting the number of defects or errors per unit of work, unit of time, *etc*. Binomial data can be examined for stability and statistical control, using *P*-charts, whereas *C*-charts and *U*-charts are used for examining Poisson data (*C*-chart is used when the sample size is constant).

7.4 Quality Pillar # 35: Use Hypothesis Testing to Confirm if the "Potential" Causes Brainstormed or Identified by an Improvement Project Team Are Indeed "Critical" Causes of Negative Effects in Order to Counteract Them

Statistical inference is necessary to help answer the questions raised about data. Initially, a scientific hypothesis is formulated. Once certain rules are applied to the data, the scientific hypothesis is either rejected or not. In proper tests of hypotheses, a null hypothesis and an alternative hypothesis are formulated. They are mutually exclusive and exhaustive (Pyzdek, 2003; Pries, 2009).

A statistical hypothesis is a statistical statement about the values of the parameters of a probability distribution. It can help answer questions such as the following:

■ Is the data normally distributed?
■ Is the process capable of satisfying customer specifications?
■ Is the mean for retail branch A equal to the mean of retail branch B?

■ Is the standard deviation in the first sample equal to the standard deviation of the second sample?
■ Is the proportion of defects in first sample equal to that of the second sample?

This verification helps practitioners to check the conformity of process parameters to their specified values and to conduct comparisons by looking for evidence of improvement, before and after the implementation of corrective actions or best practices.

In addition, a hypothesis is a claim or a statement that is related to a property of a population, such as the mean, the variance, or a certain proportion (Kiernan, 2014). It is a tentative explanation that accounts for a set of facts and can be tested by further investigation. It is also considered a test that aims to discover if the observed difference is real or not. The null hypothesis represents the "status quo", where no claim is made for anything special or different. The alternate hypothesis (or research hypothesis) is the claim that is being studied. The data must demonstrate beyond a reasonable doubt that the research hypothesis is true. The null hypothesis and alternative hypothesis are mutually exclusive and complementary. The choice of test depends on the type and distribution of the data, as well as the kind of comparison that is being made. Table 7.2 shows some common hypothesis tests and their corresponding application. Also, Table 7.3 shows a couple of examples of hypothesis testing.

Here are various situations, which are common and applicable for hypothesis testing:

■ Testing the equality of population mean to a specific value.
■ Testing the equality of means from two populations.

Table 7.2 Common Hypothesis Tests and Their Corresponding Applications

Hypothesis test	Usage
t-test z-test	to compare population means
f-test Levene's test	to compare population variances
proportion tests chi-squared test	to compare population proportions or percentages

Source: Adapted from Six Sigma Training, personal communication (2008)

Table 7.3   Example of Hypothesis Tests

Claim	Null and alternative hypotheses
There is a difference between the average cycle time from the two teams.	Ho: All means are equal (There is no difference between the average cycle times for team A and team B.) Ha: The means are not equal (There is a difference).
There is a difference between the proportions of lost sales leads between the two branches.	Ho: All proportions are equal (There is no difference in proportions for the sales leads for branch A and branch B.) Ha: The proportions are not equal (There is a difference).

Source: Adapted from Six Sigma Training, personal communication (2008)

- Testing the equality of means from more than two populations.
- Testing the equality of variances.
- Testing the equality of population proportions (Binomial data).
- Testing the equality of population defect rates (Poisson data).
- Testing for association and relationship.

The sample size is typically chosen based on the desired "power" of the hypothesis test and the difference needed to be detected (Good, 1994). The number of samples needed (or sample size) depends on the following:

- The cost and difficulty of obtaining samples.
- The size of the difference that needs to be detected.
- The importance of avoiding errors of type I (which has a probability of α) or type II (which has a probability of β).

When all other terms are constant (Bullard, 2022):

- As the significance level α increases, the power increases.
- As the standard deviation s of the population increases, the power decreases.
- As the size of the difference (needed to be detected) decreases, the power decreases.
- As sample size increases, the power increases. However, the sample size increase is typically associated with a cost increase.

Other examples of using hypothesis testing include the comparison of means of normal distributions (when variance is known or unknown), comparison of variances of normal distributions, and the use of nonparametric tests when dealing with nonnormal distributions. Statistical inference within hypothesis testing generally involves the following steps (Pries, 2009):

■ Formulate a hypothesis about the population or a "state of nature", and choose a test statistic (*t*-statistic, *f*-statistic, *etc.*) depending on the challenge faced or the required investigation, as well as the nature of the data distribution.
■ Choose an alpha (*α*) risk value, and define the pass or fail criterion. A significance level of *α* = 0.05 is typically selected.
■ Collect a representative sample of observations from the population.
■ Calculate the statistics (selected earlier) based on the sample.
■ Either accept or reject the hypothesis based on the predetermined acceptance criterion, and come up with a practical conclusion.

Moreover, there are two types of error related to statistical inference (Pries, 2009):

■ Type I (*α* error): The probability that a hypothesis will be rejected, when it is actually true. The value of *α* is referred to as the significance level of the test.
■ Type II (*β* error): The probability that a hypothesis will be accepted, when it is actually false.

Besides hypothesis testing, another method typically used in statistical inference to make conclusions about populations of data and to verify the causes of undesirable effects is the estimations and confidence intervals method. When an average is calculated based on a sample, it is used as a point estimate to make a prediction about the true mean of the population. This mean is unknown unless every single item in a population is measured, which is an expensive and impractical procedure. A point estimate has a probability of not being correct. Thus, an estimation interval is considered to provide a range of values that is likely to include the true value with a typical level of 95% confidence. To illustrate the estimation of a population mean, the example of a team that wants to verify if a supplier is providing the specified average thickness of a metal component at 2 mm is considered. A sample of 64 components is randomly selected, based on which both the average and standard deviation were calculated as 1.915 mm and 0.133 mm, respectively. This means that 1.915 mm is the point estimate for the true mean of the population. However, a margin of error can be estimated as the difference between the observed sample average and the true value of the population mean. This margin is estimated based on the assumption of normality. For a confidence level of 95%, the risk level alpha (α) is 5%, which corresponds to critical limits of the interval being located at standard normal z values of 1.96 and −1.96. Therefore, it can be concluded that the true mean of the population of components is anywhere between 1.882 and 1.948 mm. As it does not include the target of 2 mm, it is concluded the supplier is not abiding by the required nominal thickness. For small samples that are fewer than 30 items in size (unless the standard deviation is known), the Student's t-distribution is used in place of the z-distribution (standard normal distribution) to make inferences about the population mean. As the sample size grows larger, the shape of the t-distribution approaches the shape of the z-distribution. Another typical example to investigate would be to find if there is a significant statistical difference between the averages of two suppliers. This can also be applicable when comparing two populations, before and after the implementation of an improvement. A two-sample t-test can be used to investigate the same. Typically, if the confidence interval of the difference between the two compared averages contains a "zero", it is still possible they might be equal. Similarly, a proportion of defectives can be compared to a certain target value (not to be exceeded), using a one-proportion test. Also, a two-proportion test can be used to compare two proportions from two populations to check if they are the same or statistically different (Six Sigma Training, personal communication, 2008).

Analysis of variance (ANOVA) is one of the commonly used tools that utilizes hypothesis testing. For an ANOVA test to be properly conducted, the observations are assumed to be random samples drawn from normally distributed populations, with equal variances. The ANOVA test is typically performed using the following steps (Pyzdek, 2003; Pries, 2009):

1. Formulate both the null and alternative hypotheses, for example, as follows:
   - Ho (All means are equal) versus
   - Ha (At least two of the means are different).
2. Decide on the level of significance. For a typical analysis, a significance level of $\alpha = 0.05$ can be selected.

3. Calculate the *F*-statistic, which is the ratio of the mean-square between groups to the mean-square within groups. The critical value of *F* is typically found in standard tables (or provided by statistical software), including the degrees of freedom required for the calculation.
4. If the calculated *F* value is greater than $F_{1-\alpha}$ (or if the *p*-value is typically lower than 0.05), then the null hypothesis is rejected in favor of the alternative hypothesis. Otherwise, the examiner fails to reject the null hypothesis, and thus, it remains valid. It is noted that statistical software packages, like Minitab, enable conducting an ANOVA test easily with a few clicks (for additional information on ANOVA, see Section 8.3).

If the data is not normally distributed, nonparametric tests can be used to test various hypotheses as follows (Pries, 2009):

■ Levene's test uses the *F*-statistic to test the equality of variances of different samples, as an alternative to Bartlett's test in the case of normally distributed data.
■ One-sample Wicoxon test is used to compare the median of a sample to a specific targeted value. It is used as an alternative to the one-sample *t*-test.
■ Kruskal-Wallis test is used to compare the medians of three or more samples, as an alternative to the ANOVA test.
■ Mann-Whitney test is used to compare the medians of different samples, as an alternative for the two-sample *t*-test of means (for additional information on the Mann-Whitney test, see Section 8.3).

7.5 Quality Pillar # 36: Achieve "Stability" of the Process First; Then Seek to Accomplish "Capability" to Meet Customer Specifications. Do Not Confuse the Calculated Control Limits Used in Statistical Control Charts with the Customer-Set Specification Limits Used in Capability Analysis Charts

Life won't be possible without variation. Variation provides possibilities for collaboration, integration, and cooperation. People of different skills need each other to survive and function. However, in the business and industrial world, variation is the enemy. The moment one deviates from a standard way of performance, there is a risk of facing possible losses or defects of some kind as a result. Unexpected levels of service that fail to meet customer expectations will result in dissatisfaction. So, while it is part of the world's nature to have variation in everything around us, it is not welcomed in service delivery or goods manufacturing. Ideally, all goods shall have the same consistent level of quality. Lower levels cause failures to happen. Even higher levels of quality may come at a high cost and may not necessarily be required by the customer (*i.e.*, the customer is not willing to pay for extra amounts or features or high tolerances).

However, it shall be also noted that variation is what sparks innovation. Sometimes, it is that new variation in the way of operation that reveals a better way, which can become the new adopted standard or best practice.

For a process to be consistent and under control, its key performance indicators (KPIs) need to be monitored to ensure they are stable and, thus, predictable. This can be manually achieved by a simple collection of data or, even better, by the use of a software to plot the data using a statistical process control chart. Variation is naturally expected in any process. However, variation shall be due to inherent, random, and natural causes, which are embedded in the process, not special or assignable causes.

Random causes include those related to environmental conditions or differences in raw material, which are generally difficult to control. On the other hand, special causes are the root causes usually discovered using various quality tools, such as fish-bone diagrams or other statistical tools. These root causes are eliminated in order to bring the process back under statistical control, which means it would behave as per the normal causes of variation governed by the common characteristics of the normal distribution. This means that the process behavior can be predictable in the future.

If a histogram is a picture frozen at a moment of time, then a control chart is a video recording for the historical behavior of the process over time. It is a statistical chart that depicts the voice of the process itself in the form of a trend that serves as a record of the health of the process in terms of stability. Historical data can be used to generate charts that show the voice of the process and its historical baseline. This is important at the beginning of any process improvement project in order to understand the gap between current performance and the targeted performance. Control charts are composed of the average line, upper and lower bounding control limits that are calculated (not specified), and the trend of data points over time. The horizontal axis is always the time variable, tracked in units

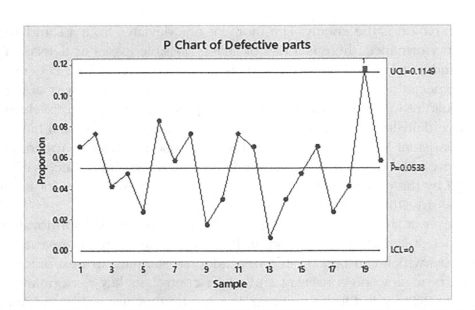

Figure 7.8 An example of a statistical process control chart for the proportion of defectives, based on weekly collected samples as generated by Minitab software.

of minutes, hours, days, weeks, *etc.* The control limits are calculated based on the variation in the data values themselves. Various software packages can be easily used to construct such graphs for the data of various types of KPIs. Figure 7.8 shows an example of a control chart for the proportion of defectives or nonconformities called the "*P*-chart". For an item within a sample to be considered defective, it takes at least one type of defect to be present in it.

The out-of-control conditions are based on the unlikely behavior of the process, where a certain point falls in a location that has a very low probability of occurring normally. For example, the probability of an individual point to fall outside the control limits is only 0.27%, or 0.135% on either side (*i.e.*, the upper limit or the lower limit side), which is very low, although still possible. The action to take in such a case would be to investigate if there are any special causes, which can be eliminated to bring the process back into stable behavior. This probability is based on the characteristics of the normal distribution, where 68% (approximately) of the data points fall within one standard deviation from the average, 95% within two standard deviations, and 99.73% within three standard deviations. Since the upper and lower control limits are calculated based on three standard deviations from the average, there is a low chance for a point to fall outside these limits naturally (*i.e.*, 100% − 99.73% = 0.27%). Similarly, the probability for a data point to fall on either side of the average is 50%. Hence, the probability for seven successive points to fall on one side of the average is ($(0.5)^7$ = 0.78%), which is very low. Software packages like Minitab can perform up to eight different checks for suspected out-of-control conditions, based on their likelihood of occurrence. Figure 7.9 shows a sample of some of these tests of suspected special-cause variation.

There are various types of control charts that can be used depending on the type of data being tracked. For variable data measured on a continuous scale, averages and ranges (*X*-bar and *R*) charts as well as the individual moving range (IMR) charts are commonly used. When the sample size is increased, the chart of the samples' calculated standard deviations (*S*-chart) is favorably used to replace the use of the ranges chart (*R*-chart). For a typical *X*-bar chart, a sample size *n* (ranging from 4 to 6) is used to detect process shifts of two sigma or larger. For smaller shifts, a larger sample size is needed, or other types of control charts can be used, such as the cumulative sum or exponentially weighted moving average (Montgomery, 2001). For attribute data such as data related to defectives percentages or count, a *P*-chart is used when dealing with defectives percentages following a binomial distribution, and a *C*-chart or *U*-chart is used when dealing with count of defects per unit following a Poisson distribution. For more information on how to construct such charts, see Devor *et al.* (1992), Montgomery (2001), Breyfogle (2003), and Keller (2005).

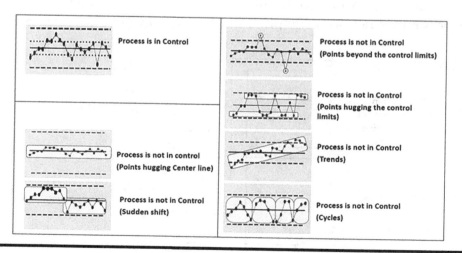

Figure 7.9 **An approximate illustration for an example of an "in-control" condition versus a few examples of "out-of-control" conditions suspected for special cause variation, as adapted from Six Sigma Training, personal communication (2008).**

On the other hand, the capability of the process cannot be examined unless the process in stable. Otherwise, it will have no practical meaning. Capability analysis is a quality tool that enables people to find how capable a process is to satisfy customers' requirements. These requirements are typically specified by customers themselves, experts, consultants, or by a government body. This body can be an authority for standardization and metrology, which is specialized in determining safe and acceptable standards and tolerance levels (specification limits). Various statistical software packages can help people easily create the charts for process stability and capability.

The goal for any process improvement project shall be to ensure the process is both stable and capable. This means that the average for the KPI under focus is coinciding with the target and that the variation is reduced for better stability and capability.

A process sigma level is an indicator for process capability. As a matter of fact, Six Sigma methodology focuses on minimizing defects, which is the same as aiming for higher capability. Once again, this cannot be achieved except after stabilizing the process so that it has less variation and better predictability. For an illustration of the meaning of stability for a process under statistical control, see Figure 7.10, which shows a stable process behavior versus an unstable process behavior.

To explain the concept of process capability, the process of parking a car in a home garage can be considered. The walls of the garage represent the upper and the lower specification limits, which are dictated by a customer or homeowner, for example. Also, the width of the car is considered

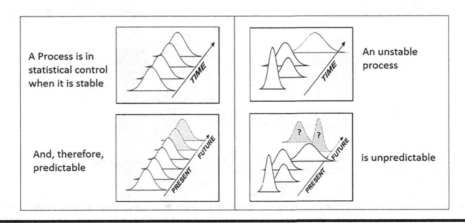

Figure 7.10   Understanding statistical process control as adapted from Six Sigma Training, personal communication (2008).

to be equivalent to the value of one standard deviation. The more consistent the process is, the lesser the width of the car. A defect in the process would happen when the car hits one of the walls, during parking attempts. This would cause a damage to the car, since its side exceeded one of the specification limits. In a six sigma level process, 12 cars of the same width (equivalent to the value of one standard deviation) are parked next to one another, filling and fitting exactly the whole range between the two walls of the garage (*i.e.*, the USL and LSL). In this process, with the mentioned six sigma level of capability, the capability index (C_p) is equal to 2. The chance for a car to hit any of the two walls is two times out of a billion parking attempts or opportunities (the famous number is 3.4 defective parts per million opportunities or ppm, due to the 1.5 sigma shift in the process mean as found in the long term by Motorola, although later found to not be always applicable). However, many companies operate at a three sigma level, which is equivalent to a 0.27% defect rate, or 2,700 defects per million (Kwak and Anbari, 2004). This means that the process is "just" capable, with a capability index of 1. For more information on how construct a capability chart, see Devor *et al.* (1992), Montgomery (2001), and Breyfogle (2003). The capability index C_p is calculated per Equation 7.3, by dividing the specification tolerance range over the process's natural range of variation, where *s* stands for the standard deviation:

$$C_p = \frac{(USL - LSL)}{6 * s} \tag{7.3}$$

Figure 7.11 shows three examples of capability charts. Figure 7.11(a) shows a case where the variation in the process exceeds the specification limits, causing the process to produce many defects. Thus, it is not considered a capable process. Figure 7.11(b) shows a process that has less variation than the previous one. The width of the curve does not appear to cross the thresholds. Thus, the process is considered a just-capable process (*i.e.*, $C_p = 1$). Figure 7.11(c) shows a six sigma level process, which is very capable. In general, a process needs to achieve a C_p value of 1.33 or higher to be considered capable. The three parts of the figure can be thought of as an illustration for the performance of three different suppliers or for one supplier at three different stages of improvement.

Companies typically spend huge amounts of money in order to resolve their problems. These amounts typically range from 25% to 40% of their sales revenue. For example, when GE teams started their Six Sigma program

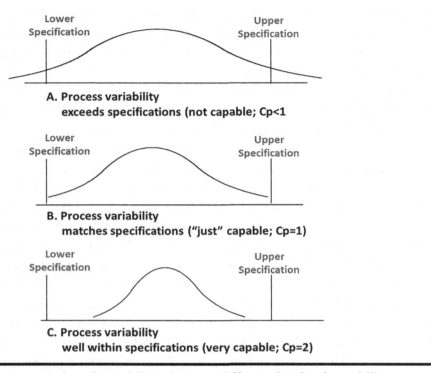

Figure 7.11   Three examples of capability charts at different levels of capability.

in 1995, they estimated that their sigma level was 3.5 and that the COPQ gap was costing them billions of dollars every year (Harry and Schroeder, 2000). Major use of data based on capability analysis, includes the following (Montgomery, 2001):

- Prediction of how well the process will hold tolerances.
- Assisting designers in modifying a process.
- Enabling a procurement team to select the best vendor from various competing vendors.
- Reduction of process variability.
- The use of histograms to show an immediate view of the process performance, which requires typically 100 or more observations for a reasonable and reliable study of capability.

Poor capability shows poor centering of the mean of the process and an excess of variability. However, it is based on normality assumption. Else, the data may need to be transformed into becoming normal (Montgomery, 2001).

Once the process is stable, the potential capability index (C_p), as well as the actual capability index (C_{pk}), can be used to assess the capability of the process in meeting customer specifications. They are both equal when the process is centered, where the average of the samples taken coincides with the specified target. However, when the distribution is not centered on target, C_{pk} becomes the actual measure of capability, because it takes into account the shift that happened in the process. This shift causes more defective parts to result, as the tail of the normal distribution extends beyond the closer specification limit.

If the sampled data is not under control (*i.e.*, not stable), then C_p or C_{pk} shall not be used, as they both ignore the "between" subgroup variation. In that case, the capability performance index (P_p) or the capability performance centering index (P_{pk}) may be used to assess capability but only as a snapshot within the short time when the sample was taken. This is not a reliable way of assessing capability but may be used due to the limited data availability in some cases.

If the sampled data is not normally distributed, then one first needs to find a suitable distribution that fits the sampled data. Statistical software packages can provide a variety of distributions to check our data against for the best fit. After that, a capability analysis can be conducted, based on that particular distribution. However, it is still important to ensure that the process is stable. This can be achieved using an X-bar control chart, because the distribution of averages will tend to be normal, regardless of the distribution of individual points, per the central limit theory. Another important point is the need to ensure that the data is derived from a single source or stream rather than from different sources. An example of that would be when dealing with different suppliers, machines, department teams, *etc.* Otherwise, it is required to separate the data and assess each stream (on its own) for normality, stability, and capability. However, if the data is attribute data (not variable), then the average proportion of defectives (typically observed in a *P*-chart), can be simply used as an indicator for the capability of the process.

7.6 Quality Pillar # 37: Evaluate the Relationship between Potential Causes (or Input Factors) and an Output Variable, Using Tools Such as Scatter Plots. Remember That a Relationship Does Not Necessarily Imply Causation

A scatter plot or scatter diagram is considered a simple tool often used in regression analysis. A scatter diagram is a plot of one variable called the independent variable (x), which is usually shown on the horizontal axis versus another variable called the dependent variable (Y), which is usually shown on the vertical axis. Correlation and regression analysis are two important tools often used in Six Sigma methodology. Correlation analysis is about the study of the strength of the linear relationships among variables. Regression analysis is about modeling and understanding the relationship between a dependent variable (Y) and one or more independent variables (x or x's). A simple linear regression (SLR) analyzes the relationship between one x and a Y. A regression problem considers the frequency distribution of one variable when another is held fixed at each of the various levels. A correlation problem considers the joint variation of two variables, without being restricted by the experimenter (Pyzdek and Keller, 2019).

Thus, in order to study the relationship between two variables and to find whether they are proportionally related to each other or not, scatter plots can be used to graphically evaluate that relationship. Obviously, a more accurate way would be to calculate a correlation coefficient to establish how strong the relationship is. A set of points that slopes upward indicates that the relationship between the two variables is positive. This means that as one variable increases, the other variable will also increase. On the other hand, a set of points sloping downward indicates a negative relationship between the two variables, which is inversely proportional. This means that as one variable increases, the other variable will decrease. A diagram with a cluster of points, which makes it difficult to determine whether the trend is sloping upward or downward, indicates that there is no linear relationship between the two variables. Nevertheless, there might be other types of relationship between them, such as quadratic or cubic relations.

In addition, a regression model can assist in finding the best-fitted line and its formula, which, in its turn, can be used to predict the corresponding output or dependent variable, given any known value for the independent or input variable. Figure 7.12 shows an example of a scatter diagram and a fitted line. Sometimes there might not be a strong correlation linearly, which may trigger testing the data for a curvilinear (*e.g.*, quadratic or cubic) relationship. In addition, it is always advisable not to consider that the relationship necessarily implies causation, since other inputs or factors may have a more direct impact on the output than the one tested. What one can be sure about is the degree of association between the two variables being studied, which can be calculated in the form of a coefficient of correlation (r). Figure 7.13 shows various examples of scatter plots along with their corresponding values for the coefficient of correlation, as adapted from Pyzdek

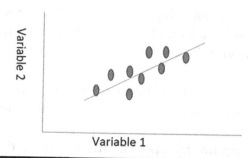

Figure 7.12   An example of a scatter diagram and a fitted line.

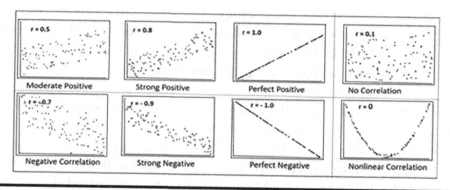

Figure 7.13   Examples of various scatter plots along with their corresponding values of the correlation coefficient (r), as adapted from Pyzdek and Keller (2019) and Six Sigma Training, personal communication (2008).

and Keller (2019). Also, the relationship between one output variable and various input variables can be analyzed, using tools like multiple regression, where one additional input can be added to the model at a time, in a step-by-step approach. Moreover, the use of design of experiments (DOE) is favorable in such cases, as it takes into account both main factors effects and their interaction effects.

Regression equations (or mathematical models) are used to predict the values of the dependent variable Y for given values of the independent variables (*i.e.*, the x's). Before using a mathematical model to make predictions, this model should be checked for adequacy. For this purpose, a number of tests exist in different statistical software packages, such as the "lack of fit" test and the "analysis of residuals".

The general purpose of multiple regression is to learn more about the relationship between several independent variables (or x's) and a dependent

(Y) variable. When this relationship is known, critical x's are identified, and their operating levels can be chosen. Regression is more useful when dealing with observational data rather than data obtained from a designed experiment.

There are some key steps to be followed when analyzing the relationship between two variables (Six Sigma Training, personal communication, 2008):

- Draw a scatter diagram, interpret it, and calculate the correlation coefficient (r), to determine if the two variables are correlated.
- Perform simple linear regression analysis (SLRA), and interpret the regression equation.
- Calculate, and interpret the coefficient of determination (R^2) and the relevant probability values (p-values) to determine the adequacy of the mathematical model (*i.e.*, the regression equation).
- Make predictions using that mathematical model.

To obtain data, the historical data or real-time data can be gathered, or an experiment can be designed to try certain settings and check their effects on the output variable or the KPI of interest. Obviously, the experimental approach has a better chance of producing a good predictive model.

A scatter plot provides a graphical representation of paired data. It is particularly suitable for use when the relationship between two sets of data, which are suspected to correspond to each other, is investigated. Any two variables are considered correlated when they relate to each other in a certain way. In order to statistically measure the strength of the linear relationship between them, the correlation coefficient r is used. This coefficient ranges from a value of −1 to 1. A correlation coefficient r, which is near a value of 1 or −1 signifies that the two variables have a strong linear correlation. When r is near 0, no linear relationship exists. To avoid reaching a wrong conclusion about correlation, quality practitioners need to examine the data itself as well as the scatter plot. In the case of an outlier, they need to find out its root cause, counteract its effect, eliminate that outlier, and repeat the correlation analysis.

In SLR, they seek to obtain the graph and the equation of the straight line, which best represents the relationship between two variables. The coefficient of determination R^2 indicates the amount of the variation in Y, which is explained by the equation of the regression line.

The strength of the relationship between two corresponding variables can be determined by plotting a scatter diagram and by computing the correlation coefficient r. When a cluster of points in a scatter diagram appears to form a detectable direction, it is possible that a correlation may be present. The less scattered the points away from each other, the stronger the correlation.

Thus, regression analysis helps in finding a model for the relationship between pairs of numerical data. The variables are plotted graphically in a scatter diagram to provide a visual pattern, which enables one to find out if there is a linear relationship. The relationship is depicted using an equation that identifies the best-fitting straight line, which passes through the data within the scatter plot. The best line is identified using the least-square method, which aims at minimizing the total squared error values, between the observed values and their predicted values from the fitted line. The coefficient of determination R^2 is a number between 0 and 1, which measures how well the data fit the line, indicating the proportion of variation in the output as explained by the regression line. The fit is strongest when data hug the line perfectly, where R^2 is equal to 1 (Farmer and Duffy, 2017).

7.7 Quality Pillar # 38: Learn about the Use of Various Team Tools for Decision-Making

Brainstorming is a technique often used in process improvement, which helps teams identify, sort, and rank various ideas. This technique may allow for a round of discussion to influence a better understanding of the advantages and disadvantages of each idea, before making a final decision on the selection and prioritization of these ideas. However, team members can use various decision-making tools, such as direct brainstorming, where they share and develop volumes of ideas openly and verbally. It is a powerful approach to solicit ideas in the different stages of any project. It generally requires a skilled facilitator who encourages divergent thinking, to explore various possible causes and solutions of a problem. It starts with a creative phase to generate many ideas and ends with an evaluation phase to select the most useful and applicable ones. If members feel safer contributing ideas anonymously as in the case of controversial or emotional topics, the brain-writing tool can be used to encourage participation. Brain-writing is a nonverbal form of brainstorming, which is suitable for members who think better in silence, and can be used for ideas that require a detailed explanation. Team members write their ideas and share them with each other to allow for collaboration. It encourages every member to participate and prevents few members from dominating the discussion. On the other hand, multi-voting enables the team to recognize an item that is not the top choice of any of them, in order to be selected as a top choice if favored by all team members (Farmer and Duffy, 2017). Multi-voting is a decision-making tool used by teams to sort a large list of possibilities, issues, or root causes and summarize them into a smaller list of top-priority items for final selection (Breyfogle, 2003).

It is important for improvement teams to understand various decision-making tools, such as nominal group technique (NGT) and multi-voting. Every team needs a well-defined procedure for decision-making and clear ground rules for how meetings shall be conducted. Sometimes, opinion polls might be required. On other occasions, consensus may be important. Team members need to be aware of the tackled problem, alternative solutions, and their consequences. Then they need to agree on an approach (PDCA, DMAIC, 8D standardized problem-solving technique, decision tree, *etc.*) to select solutions, implement them, and evaluate their impact. There will always be a probability for errors in decision-making, like type I and type II errors in hypothesis testing. However, improvement teams may use a scientific data-based approach, DOE, and other statistical and hypothesis tests for verification and decision-making. A decision tree is a graphical tool, which integrates (for a defined problem) both uncertainties and cost with the available alternatives in order to decide on the best alternative (Breyfogle, 2003).

NGT is a tool used by teams to select the main choices from different acceptable choices in a structured manner. It helps in identifying and ranking the main problems that require attention. It also helps in identifying the main strengths of a division or making decisions regarding problem solutions by consensus (Farmer and Duffy, 2017). NGT is one of the seven basic management and planning tools. It helps speed up team consensus on the relative importance of various issues or root causes. First, all issues raised from a brainstorming session are listed in front of the team members. Then the list is narrowed down after removing any duplication and assigning a letter to each issue. After that, each team member assigns a rank in the form of a number to each raised issue. The most important issue gets a value equal to the total number of items, and the least important gets a value of 1. Finally, a total prioritization number is calculated based on all individual scores gathered from the team. However, voting procedure may vary due to team preferences and the nature of the present situation (Breyfogle, 2003).

Root cause analysis tools include the eight disciplines (8D) problem-solving methodology using corrective and preventive actions, cause-and-effect diagrams and matrices using the five whys, drill deep and wide (DDW), tree diagrams, waste and value analysis in VSMs, failure mode and effects analysis (FMEA), change analysis (assessing the potential effects of a change on an outcome), barrier analysis (prevention errors related to reasons why prevention activities fail to identify defects), and prediction analysis (reasons for failure to predict errors) (Farmer and Duffy, 2017).

7.8 Quality Pillar # 39: Ask Why Several Times before Identifying the Root Causes of the Problem

In the measure phase of Six Sigma, various knowledge tools are used to help identify the critical pain points of a process, such as a fish-bone diagram, cause-and-effect matrix, failure mode and effect analysis (FMEA), and current-state map or flowchart.

To create a fish-bone diagram, a proper brainstorming session needs to be effectively led by a trained facilitator. Proper planning for the session is required, in order to ensure that all selected team members are clear about the problem. The key question in the brainstorming session is mainly focusing on finding why a certain KPI behaves the way it does (based on its historical data or baseline measurements). For example, when the KPI under investigation is the production line efficiency, the question can simply be "Why has our production line efficiency been averaging a low value of 67%?" Asking "why" more than one time ensures drilling down to the root causes so that the team members can vote and select the key issues. These issues obviously are considered as "potential causes". They are mainly confirmed to be "critical" once the data is examined and tested. If the data is not available easily, it may simply be confirmed by relying on the team votes captured earlier during the brainstorming session. However, one needs to keep in mind that voting is the weakest authentication method, as it mainly depends on employees' opinions.

The fish-bone diagram, created by Ishikawa, is a graphical tool that can show all the potential causes of a problem, which are brainstormed by the team. Typically, the graph has six branches, which are sometimes called the 6Ms (machine, material, manpower, method, measurement, and mother nature or environment). These six areas encourage comprehensive brainstorming to address all relevant issues. There is hardly any Six Sigma project completed without the use of a fish-bone diagram. An example of a template used to create a fish-bone diagram can be seen in Figure 7.14.

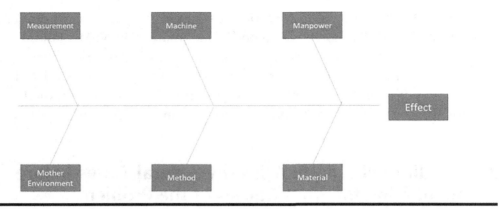

Figure 7.14 Template used for fish-bone diagram showing the 6 M's.

An example for the importance of root cause analysis is illustrated as follows: A device was attached to a machine, and one bolt often snapped. The first improvement solution was to make that bolt's size bigger, which only caused bolts in other locations to snap. The same solution was tried for the other bolts, but the problem still occurred. However, the root cause was found to be vibration, and it needed to be eliminated. On the other hand, this analysis can be taken even further, by ensuring the root cause for vibration is removed so that future designs do not encounter such a problem that testers failed to detect in the product design (Ishikawa, 1985).

When brainstorming using a fish-bone diagram, a skilled facilitator will ensure that all team members participate and share their views in a positive environment. A fish-bone diagram, which is also called cause-and-effect or Ishikawa diagram, cannot be proper if the root causes are not exhausted by the team. This cannot be achieved except by a skilled facilitator, who asks "why" several times until having reached the root causes. A smart facilitator would notice if the team members were reluctant or uncomfortable sharing their thoughts, due to the presence of a dominating manager, for example. The facilitator needs to address such an issue, by proper planning and effective communication with the manager to ensure that the session is successful.

In addition, FMEA is used to outline all possible failures at every single step of the process. These failures are prioritized using a risk priority number (RPN), which is the result of multiplying three quantified factors: severity for the failure effect on the system if it happens, the likelihood of occurrence, and the probability that the failure will pass without being detected.

7.9 Quality Pillar # 40: Tools Like Check Sheets Can Help Track or Compare the Performance of Different Teams and Then Elevate the Discussion from What May Seem like a Personal Argument to a Professional and Fact-Based Dialogue

A check sheet (or tally sheet) is a simple data collection tool, which is typically designed as a structured table. It can be created using Microsoft Excel in order to gather data from historical records or track it through future incidents as they happen. It also helps depict patterns and trends in data. Its goal is to ensure data is easily and accurately collected as required. Moreover, it triggers the user to ask the right questions based on the collected data and, hence, make informed decisions. The fields of the check sheet are designed to capture data based on the nature of the problem faced. These fields typically include information about the categorical inquiries or negative incidents and events, in terms of frequency, types, locations, time of occurrence, *etc*. In order to have an effective check sheet, a clear data collection plan is required, which guides the team to understand what to measure, how much data is required, how to measure it, how to collect it, and who will collect it. Table 7.4 shows an example of a filled template for a check sheet.

Table 7.4   An Example of a Check Sheet Filled Template

Project: Reduce customer complaints	*Department: Packaging section*	*Location: Plant A*	*Date: Jan 2–6*	*Shift: day*	*Data: Count of complaints by type by date*	*Process owner: A.B.*
Event (defect)/date	**Jan 2**	**Jan 3**	**Jan 4**	**Jan 5**	**Jan 6**	**Total**
Empty cardboard box	2	8	2	0	4	16
Color lighter than specification	7	8	11	6	8	40
Color darker than specification	1	0	1	2	0	4
Wrong color	0	0	14	0	3	17
Total	10	16	28	8	15	77

Source: Adapted from Six Sigma Training, personal communication (2008)

7.10 Quality Pillar # 41: Prioritize Your Improvement Efforts by Focusing on the Most Contributing Categories Using a Tool Like a Pareto Chart

Named after Vilfredo Pareto, an Italian economist, the Pareto chart is an effective tool that can be used to identify the relative importance of different categories and separate the vital few from the trivial many. It mainly helps in prioritizing improvement efforts to focus on the most frequent issues, which contribute to the majority of problems faced. The Pareto chart got generalized and publicized by Joseph Juran, who emphasized its importance and the 80/20 rule associated with it. This rule states that 80% of the problem, or its consequences, stem from 20% of the categories or causes. However, it is not always the case that a person will end up with data reflecting an 80/20 relationship, as it could be 60/40 or any other combination.

For example, a calling center can track data for all received calls, including various customer complaints. A Pareto chart can be used to present this data by showing all the categories of complaints, indicating which ones are more frequent than others and possibly amount to the majority (or 80%) of the total complaints count. These few complaints' categories will then be prioritized and selected for further analysis and rectification. For a company selling software products, the reasons why customers return the purchased software can also be tracked and depicted graphically, using a Pareto chart. These reasons might be software incompatibility, lower software quality than expected, software not deemed to be user friendly, *etc*. In addition, a drill-down Pareto can help analysts drill further into the top category's consecutive subcategories, such as customer geographical locations, customer segments, and types of product. In another example, maintenance failures at a factory can be tracked and depicted using a Pareto chart, to show which type of machinery failure occurs the most. In addition, business leaders explore division-wide data sets using Pareto diagrams to drill down and reveal which of the products and processes they must improve first.

LSS Black Belts and Green Belts frequently use Pareto charts to dive into the details of process-related issues, to find the biggest contributors to those issues, and to discover what types of categories relate to the problem under investigation. The example shown in Figure 7.15 is related to an LSS project, which was implemented at a retail store that sells kitchens. When measuring the output of the quotation process, the Green Belt collected the data from a sample of past sales' deals and created this Pareto chart. The KPI tracked was the duration of time in days from the moment an inquiry

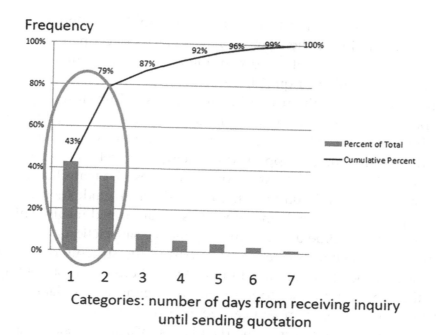

Figure 7.15   An example of a Pareto diagram for the frequency of won contracts, broken down by the time duration taken for processing inquiries.

is received from a customer until a quotation is sent back to the customer. Excluding the quotations that got rejected or ignored by customers, the Pareto chart shows the frequency of "closed deals" for the following categories: quotations sent within one day of receiving the inquiry, quotations sent within one to two days, quotations sent within two to three days, and quotations sent after three days. It revealed that most bids won (about 79% of them) were based on quotations delivered within two days from receiving the customer inquiry. It was concluded that if an inquiry is left unanswered by the sales team for more than two days, there is no need to waste any time responding to it, since the chance for winning that job is only 8% when sending the quotation on the third day. The sales team shall prioritize and focus more on the fresh inquiries. This practically meant that customers would be approaching competitors, and if they receive their quotations faster, they may proceed without waiting for other delayed quotations. Actually, a delay in a company quotation may be an indicator for lack of organization and eventual delay in execution. The team needed to focus on ensuring all inquiries are attended to within a maximum of two days. This eventually contributed to an overall higher winning rate, revenue, and net profit. Thus, the Pareto chart helped the sales team better understand customer behavior and how their own behavior needs to change if they want to improve their business results and winning rates (*i.e.*, the number of closed deals versus the number of quotations sent).

Another example for the use of Pareto is a case of unsatisfied patients at a hospital, where two major complaints' categories accounted for around 80% of the sum of complaints. Those two categories of complaints were as follows: delays in getting unapproved medicine, and delays in getting unapproved meals. To resolve the two prioritized issues, the team had to work closely with doctors and nutritionists to provide clear guidelines and to create lists of preapproved medicine as well as preapproved meals. This helped reduce the response time and enhanced patients' satisfaction.

Finally, a Pareto chart is often used as part of the structured approach of LSS DMAIC. Various tools are used in DMAIC, where one tool's output may become the input for another tool. In various organizations, data is logged into an ERP software system and can be exported into an Excel database for ease of analysis. However, if the data is not available to start with, then a simple check sheet can be used to collect data (see Section 7.5). This data can then be depicted using a Pareto chart to determine the prioritized area of concern. After that, a fish-bone (Ishikawa) diagram can be used to brainstorm potential causes for that prioritized area.

7.11 Quality Pillar # 42: Use Process Flowcharts and Maps as a Framework for Continuous Improvement (to Transform Processes from a Current State to a Future State)

Question every step in the process, eliminate unnecessary steps, balance the processing times of the steps by combining or dismantling them, and always streamline the flow of the steps. Optimize and simplify a process before automating it (see Section 9.1 for additional information on VSM).

Process maps are among the seven famous and basic quality tools, which are widely used. They provide a visual representation of the sequence of steps or activities taking place within the process under investigation. When mapping a process or reviewing an existing process map, the improvement team members need to consider the elimination of unnecessary steps. It is important to ensure that each process step adds value from the perspective of the customer of that step and ultimately from the perspective of the end customer of the whole process. If it does not add value, then the next logical question would be whether it can be eliminated or not. Some non-value-adding (NVA) steps may not be easily eliminated in the short term, due to regulatory or other requirements, such as the segregation of duties for better process governance. However, they need to be streamlined in the short term (cycle time and waiting time reduction) and then revisited in the long term for possible elimination. Another option for those NVA steps, if they cannot be eliminated, is to combine them with other steps. This will at least eliminate the waste of waiting associated with those steps.

Another important aspect to consider when improving a process would be to dream what an ideal process would look like from the customer perspective. An ideal process is a process that almost runs with the least exerted effort, the least amount of resources, and in the minimum time imaginable. This will eventually help the improvement team members to envision how a future-state process (or the "to be" process) will look like.

In process maps, different symbols are used to indicate different meanings. A rectangle is typically used to indicate a process step, which is best described using a verb and noun (to help visualize the process), such as "receive inquiry" or "send quotation". Diamonds mean decisions or approval steps, and thus, it is critical to examine if those diamonds are necessary and adding value or not (*i.e.*, available only as a formality). A feedback loop often indicates that a defect occurred, which is one of the types of waste in a process, as it requires rework. So the goal of the process team and the process owner shall be to ensure that the process step is done right the first time and every time. This can be achieved through revising the process design and learning from previous mistakes. Once that is achieved, the diamond is converted into a rectangle, indicating a regular process step. On the other hand, if an approval is eventually deemed not required anymore, then the whole diamond can be eliminated.

Table 7.5 shows a process maturity classification framework. It starts with a basic level of maturity, which is realized when a process is documented. The next step in maturity is when the process is actually implemented as per its documentation. Standard documentation usually includes a list of process metrics or performance measures. Thus, the next level of process maturity is realized when it is audited and found to be complying with applicable external and/or internal standards. Its performance needs to be measured regularly. This measurement is the basis for process improvement.

Table 7.5 A Process Maturity Classification Framework

Process maturity level	Process maturity level title	Process maturity level description
0	Not documented	Firefighting mode; reactive approach; process may exist, but there is no standardized way; verbal instructions; just get it done; *etc.*
1	Documented (in a SOP)	Standards are established, shared, and communicated; hard or soft documented SOP exists; current-state or as-is map exists
2	Implemented	Deployed and in use; SOP being followed; KPIs and SLAs are measured, even if not meeting targets, even if major nonconformities exist
3	Audited (as part of QMS or other standard MS)	Being regularly audited to check if complying to standards with zero or minor nonconformities, corrective plans exist to ensure closure of all nonconformities and achievement of all KPI targets
4	Improved	Improvement opportunities are implemented per the process future-state plan, performance is reviewed and improved regularly, waste is removed as per Lean rules, variation is minimized (process is under control, stable, and predictable), process is capable (meeting customer specifications), QCD (quality, cost, and delivery) metrics exist for evaluating process efficiency and effectiveness, clear evidence exists for continuous improvement trends meeting benchmarked targets
5	Optimized/ automated	Process is optimized, digitized, paperless, mistake-proof, proactive, sustainable in its performance, agile, and automated where appropriate or feasible, *etc.*

Hence, the next level of maturity would be achieved when the process is simplified and improved. Eventually, a higher level of maturity is realized when the process is stabilized and governed by random causes of variation. Also, it needs to be capable of meeting the specifications set by customers, experts, or government authorities. Finally, the highest level of maturity is achieved when the process is optimized, digitalized, and automated. Figure 7.16 shows these levels of process maturity in the form of a pyramid.

Another important consideration for any process to become more mature is to ensure that proper KPIs are selected and tracked. KPIs need to cover

Figure 7.16   Process maturity levels.

both efficiency and effectiveness aspects. Process efficiency has to do with maximizing the output of the process for the same input or less. Examples of efficiency-related metrics include production efficiency, labor utilization, delivery durations, rate of productivity, and cost proportions. On the other hand, process effectiveness is concerned with how close a process output is compared to what the customer requires. Examples of effectiveness metrics include customer satisfaction rates, complaints, percentage of SLA targets' satisfaction (could be related to delivery, quality, or cost).

Here are some important notes to take into account when reviewing any process:

a. It is advisable to use a standard template when documenting processes as part of a formal management system, such as ISO 9001. This can include the use of a standard flowchart template or swim-lane value stream map (see Figure 7.17, for an example). Typically, a VSM is a high-level process map (seeing the process from a 30,000-foot level). A SIPOC diagram is also a high-level process map often used in the define phase of Six Sigma (see Figure 7.18). It is used to provide a one-page summary of the process, listing all inputs, outputs, suppliers, and customers (internal and external), as well as the critical issues related to QCD. However, for process mapping, flowcharts can be used to describe the steps of the process in a detailed manner, including decisions and deviations. For transactional processes, it is often recommended to use a modified version of VSM, which is called a swim-lane VSM. This modified VSM can be drawn as a detailed map, not only as a high-level map. It is a cross-functional map, where each lane represents a stakeholder, a function, a department, a customer, an employee,

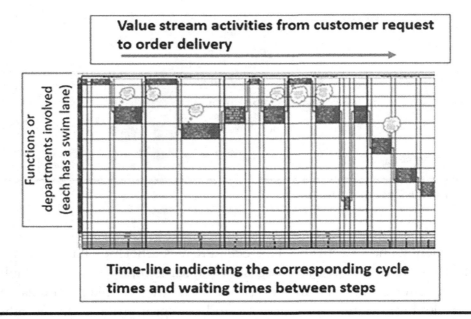

Figure 7.17   An illustration of a swim-lane VSM.

Figure 7.18   SIPOC diagram.

a manager, *etc.* Software like Microsoft Excel and Visio can help create
various types of maps and flowcharts. When mapping a process using a
swim-lane VSM, it is important to ensure that each swim lane (or function) is represented by a member of the mapping team.

b. The main difference between a VSM and a flowchart is that the VSM
includes time metrics, such as waiting time between the steps and the
cycle time for each step. This eventually makes up the total lead time of
a process from the starting point to the end point.

c. Recently, ISO management systems have drawn more attention to the
potential risks that may exist at different steps in any process. Thus,
it is advisable to capture those risks while constructing the VSM. The
presence of a cross-functional team that covers the whole scope of the
VSM does contribute to conducting a thorough risk analysis. Similar to
the approach of an FMEA, the team questions what failure mode might
be possible at each step of the process. This would eventually be dealt

with in the improve phase of Six Sigma as part of the improvement plan preparation.

d. Each process should have a clearly identified owner and a set of KPIs and their targets at the level of each process step, as well as the overall process.

e. Opportunities for automation can be also identified across the VSM, by examining each step, with an eye for feasible automation opportunities.

f. Approvals must be challenged and reduced whenever possible. For example, the use of a standard contract, which is preapproved by the company's legal team and commercial team, can replace the need to have every single contract reviewed for approval by those teams. The challenge is to design a standard contract that would take into account the reasons why some contracts in the past got rejected. This standardization approach needs to be biased for faster action while being balanced in terms of process governance. Another aspect of approvals simplification is to question whether a hard signature is still required or an electronic approval suffices.

g. Furthermore, it is recommended to get rid of unnecessary forms or at least to simplify their content (*i.e.*, eliminate some forms, combine some forms, reduce some sections, reduce some fields, or reduce the number of pages). For example, the improvement team can look at past filled records and eliminate the fields that are regularly not filled (if these fields are not necessary). They also need to question whether the stored records are necessary or not. If certain records are deemed necessary due to legal or other reasons, then it shall be clear for how long they shall be archived. Besides, the team can investigate if the archiving of scanned copies is sufficient or not.

h. For the swim-lane flow to be properly spread over the whole drawing page for ease of reading, it is recommended to start from the top-left corner of the page and end at the bottom-right corner.

i. The decision diamonds have to be analyzed, as they may indicate rework or defects.

j. The steps that do not have any delay between them may qualify to be combined.

k. The inputs and outputs have to be clearly identified.

l. It is also recommended to use workplace organization tools, like 5S and visual management.

m. It is also recommended to use flow enabling tools, like cell layout design and one-piece flow.

In summary, it is recommended to always challenge the process steps while reviewing the value stream, by considering the following points:

1. Are the process steps necessary and adding value? Is there any noticeable rework? Are there any duplicated steps performed by different employees or by different departments? Can these steps be eliminated?
2. Can some steps that include unnecessary meetings be eliminated?
3. Can the steps that include issuing unnecessary reports be eliminated?
4. Can they be combined and simplified to focus on the portion adding value?
5. Can multiple handoffs of documents and information (happening when crossing the swim lane) be reduced between departments to reduce potential errors? If not, then do service level agreements (SLAs) and checklists of specific requests (for standardized communication) exist to reduce delay and avoid receiving missing or incorrect information?
6. Can some steps be done earlier (as part of other steps) to eliminate the current step under study?
7. Can some steps be done in parallel (concurrently, not in series) to save time?
8. What challenges exist in relation to quality, cost, and delivery (QCD), which are based on tracked KPI data?
9. When reaching a decision diamond, always question the feedback loop of rejects, which indicates a clear waste, as the goal usually is to get a "yes" for all transactions passing through that step. Thus, by tracking those different rejects, a Pareto diagram can help identify the top frequently repeated issues, which can be then used as an input for a brainstorming session to find root causes, using tools like a fish-bone diagram. After that, another brainstorming session is required to identify the "high-gain" and "low-pain" solutions.
10. Also, approvals by department managers need to be questioned, especially if an approval becomes a formality without adding value.
11. Approvals by other departments are also important to investigate. If information is required by only on a "for your information" basis, then those other departments can be simply copied in emails (*i.e.*, cc'ed) or automatically notified by the system about any new contract for example.
12. In addition, for a legal department to review every contract is time consuming and may cause delays in some cases. Thus, a standard contract issued by the legal department itself can facilitate the process, and only

few exceptional cases need be sent for their approval. Thus, it is recommended to manage the flow by exception and not to make the exception the norm.

13. Concurrent engineering principles can be applied to ensure that the required parties are involved (as necessary) early in the process to avoid repeated work and waste of efforts.

In addition, regarding the forms or templates used in any process, here is a summary of additional points that need to be considered:

1. Are these forms necessary and adding value? Is there a duplicate form or a template somewhere else within the organization with repeated information of the same nature, filled by employees of the same function? Sometimes, the top section of a template can be repeated in various places, which can be frustrating to customers.
2. Is there a chance to reduce the number of pages?
3. Is there a chance to reduce the number of fields to the absolute minimum count of necessary fields?
4. Can drop lists and checkboxes be used to minimize incorrect information being filled? These are mistake-proof techniques that can be helpful.
5. Can guiding messages be added to avoid incorrect or missing information, which causes rejects and repeated work?
6. Can parts of the information be obtained by automating or digitalizing the forms to be filled online or uploaded online so that there is no need for other employees to key them into a system?
7. Can the same information be collected from other online systems by integrating the company's systems with other external systems? Of course, in this case, security issues need to be taken into account and resolved as well.

To properly map the process hierarchy, one can utilize a five-tier process for documentation, which is based on the process classification framework (PCF) published by the American Productivity and Quality Center (2018). This framework can help guide the documentation approach of these tiers for any organization. For the first tier, the core value processes and the enabling processes are identified. The second tier lists all departments under tier 1. The third tier includes the procedure documentation, which provides a description of each process, its KPIs, risks, and flowchart. The fourth tier provides a detailed work instruction guide for each activity with detailed screen snapshots taken for each low-level step. Finally, the fifth tier includes the relevant forms and templates (Salah and Rahim, 2019).

7.12 Quality Pillar # 43: Effectively Manage the Stakeholders of Your Improvement Project, and Understand the Basics of LSS Project Management

An important step in any LSS project is to ensure that the different stakeholders are identified, including process owners, employees, customers, subject matter experts, suppliers, investors, community members, and others. All these stakeholders might be affected by the project. Thus, it is necessary to recognize how each of the stakeholders can influence the project. Stakeholders' level of interest in the process and its products and outputs may vary depending on various influencing factors, such as economic or contractual factors. Assessing the stakeholders helps in creating action plans to ensure the success of LSS projects. Customers can be identified by brainstorming, SIPOC, analysis of marketing data, and the tracking of products or services. SIPOC helps capture the customers' needs and translate them into CTQ characteristics to be taken into account in designing a product that is manufacturable and a service that can be consistently deliverable to clients. Structured design methods may include the use of the process capability analysis, the Pugh concept selection matrix, and FMEA (Farmer and Duffy, 2017).

The basics of project management include the use of project charters (including problem statement, objective statement, scope, baseline data, and team members), communication plans, project planning and monitoring (using work breakdown structure (WBS) and Gantt charts), project management or management and planning tools (tree diagrams, matrix charts, relations charts, activity network diagrams, prioritization matrices, process design program charts (PDPC), and affinity diagrams), and project tollgate reviews throughout the DMAIC cycle (Breyfogle, 2003; Farmer and Duffy, 2017). A Gantt chart is a project management tool used to show a list of project activities, their planned dates, actual start dates, and completion dates. It helps in monitoring the progress of project tasks against the plan. Typically, any delay in any critical task can delay the whole project. These tasks form a critical path in any project. However, to further understand the dependencies of tasks and details of activities as well as critical paths' tasks, one can use program evaluation and review technique (PERT) and critical path method (CPM) (Breyfogle, 2003).

Project management is generally about balancing three aspects: project goals, resources, and time. Managing project resources includes the allocation of committed and skilled staff. Their skills can be evaluated and easily managed by using a cross-skill matrix. A project manager needs to understand the flexibility a project has in terms of these three aspects, using tools like a 2D matrix, which can help prioritize them, and achieve a trade-off between them. Errors in estimating time and cost can lead to failure. In addition, critical tasks that may get forgotten without target dates or clearly assigned owners can lead to failure. This can be avoided when one ensures that project tasks follow a work breakdown structure (WBS). WBS is about breaking down the project into digestible and manageable parts, by mapping them in a detailed manner. It helps in simplifying complex projects, understanding the logical links of tasks, and evaluating how realistic they are (Breyfogle, 2003). Thus, WBS is a project management planning tool used by a team to brainstorm and break the project down into high-level tasks from start to end. These tasks are broken down further to include subtasks and units of work to be performed. These units of work are typically displayed using a tree-type diagram. When managing any project, addressing logistics is essential for success. Logistics management involves planning, applying, and monitoring the flow of information and material from suppliers to customers, to ensure that the overall process is efficient and effective. Various issues arising in the logistics cycle can negatively affect teams' work, such as team members' connectivity, locations, communication means, meeting arrangements for brainstorming or Kaizen events, workload distribution, coordination, meeting agendas, and action items (Farmer and Duffy, 2017).

When considering the enhancement of a supply chain, a VSM can be used along with other tools like process design program chart (PDPC), which helps organize and evaluate processes within the SC. It also helps in the evaluation of process implementation from a high-level perspective and in creating contingency plans in the case of variations or deviations, by assigning probabilities and priorities (Breyfogle, 2003).

Communication methods used in LSS projects include meeting agendas, minutes (meeting record capturing key decisions and SMART actions), and progress reports. Agendas typically cover the meeting objective, defined topics, responsible presenters, and the allocated time. Communication plans help establish a communication protocol, indicating the "what", "where", "who", "when", "how", and the frequency of communication, which depends on project complexity. A simple project may need physical or virtual meetings, on a daily basis, to discuss the status or progress of tasks and their relevant risks. A formal communication plan is often needed for complex projects, which includes an escalation protocol, escalation threshold, and verification of communication effectiveness. Other factors affecting communication include geographical locations (infrastructure, distance, and time zones) and cultural diversity. Finally, project planning is about setting up a comprehensive tracking system to ensure synergy across all project elements, processes, tools, communications, *etc.* It requires skills in communication, information processing, negotiation of resources and securing commitments, assuring measurable milestones, and incremental and modular planning and management involvement (Farmer and Duffy, 2017).

7.13 Quality Pillar # 44: Learn about the Usage of the Seven Basic Management and Planning Tools in LSS Project Management

The basic project management tools, which are also called the management and planning tools, include the following: tree diagrams, matrix charts, relations charts, activity network diagrams (ANDs), prioritization matrices, process design program charts (PDPC), and affinity diagrams. They are often referred to as the seven basic management tools. They help teams to work with their ideas as opposed to the seven basic quality tools that mostly focus on working with numbers (Breyfogle, 2003).

Also known as a CTQ tree, a tree diagram is a project management planning tool that helps in displaying and analyzing a main topic as well as its subtopics' branches. It looks like an organization chart, and it is used by teams to capture inputs and map out the subtopics or possible root causes (Farmer and Duffy, 2017). In addition, a tree diagram helps uncover a hierarchical relationship of different goals or events, which might be desirable or undesirable as in a fault tree diagram. Logical "AND" or "OR" gates can be used to connect different components of ideas for easier analysis (Breyfogle, 2003).

Another project management planning tool is the affinity diagram,, which was introduced by Jiro Kawakita in the 1960s. Affinity diagrams depend on teams' creativity and intuition. They are used to naturally group a huge number of brainstormed ideas or identified issues (typically between 100 and 200), into themed categories for better understanding and problem solving. An affinity diagram can be initiated with each member of the team writing his/her brainstormed idea on a sticky note and posting it on a wall. Then each member is asked to go through all ideas and move them closer to other ideas where they best fit. Each group of sorted ideas is then given a header name that describes the overall common theme of these grouped ideas. Also, subgroups can then be formed if needed (Breyfogle, 2003; Farmer and Duffy, 2017). The use of an affinity diagram is typically followed by the use of another project management planning tool, which is the relations diagram (or interrelationship diagram), to draw arrows of relationship between the ideas or their themes, indicating drivers and driven categories.

Interrelationship diagrams help classify ideas into causes or drivers versus driven outcomes. To implement this diagram, the brainstormed ideas or statements are organized in a circular pattern. Then, starting with each of these ideas, draw a line connecting them with each other if a relationship is present. The arrows shall be pointing from drivers or causes to driven ideas or outcomes. After finishing the assignment of arrows pointing out of all ideas, as applicable, the team will count the number of arrows in and out of every idea. The idea with the highest number of outgoing arrows is prioritized as the main root cause or driver affecting others, which shall be addressed for improvement (Breyfogle, 2003). Overall, interrelationship diagrams can be used to analyze a causal relationship, find solutions, create QA policies and TQC plans, resolve customer complaints, eliminate defects, facilitate small group activities, and reform departments (Farmer and Duffy, 2017).

In addition, matrix diagrams are prioritization tools used to explore and illustrate relationships between two groups of items, such as the sections of a training program listed on top of a matrix and its objectives listed on the side. Using numbers or symbols, each intersecting square in the matrix is then evaluated by the team for the strength of the relationship, the prioritized root cause connections, and for possible conclusions or corrective actions (Farmer and Duffy, 2017). A matrix diagram typically utilizes a 2D matrix to assign weights and ranks for prioritizing different ideas, tasks, or goals. A prioritization matrix is often used along with matrix diagrams to help prioritize the items listed within them. These items can be goals, activities, or characteristics resulting from a tree diagram, a cause-and-effect diagram, or other diagrams. Examples of matrix diagrams are prioritization matrices, cause-and-effect matrices, and relationship matrices. QFD is a good example of the use of prioritization matrices. To set up proper criteria for prioritization, tools like analytical hierarchy process (AHP) can be used. AHP helps decision-makers integrate their priorities into matrices using paired comparisons (Breyfogle, 2003).

Similar to the program evaluation review technique (PERT) chart and critical path method (CPM), the activity network diagram (AND) is used to show interdependencies between different project tasks at different levels, the type of sequential flow path of tasks (serial or parallel order), and the tasks' durations. It illustrates the efficiency of the overall planned project schedule and reveals potential issues in scheduling as well as in the allocation of adequate resources. This is particularly important in the case of calculating a critical path of a project, where a delay in any of its steps affects the duration of the whole project (Farmer and Duffy, 2017). Sometimes, AND diagrams are called arrow diagrams. They use nodes to represent the start and finish times of activities (Breyfogle, 2003).

Process decision program charts (PDPC) are used in the initial planning stages of a project, to evaluate a list of processes for their possible deviations or failures affecting the project and to come up with contingency plans to mitigate their impact. The priority of these deviations is decided by their assigned probabilities. Some PDPC forms resemble tree diagrams. The first step to create a PDPC is to identify the purpose of the process and its basic events. Then the second step is to identify the potential deviations and their corresponding contingency activities (Breyfogle, 2003).

Chapter 8

Fundamental Pillars Related to Additional Six Sigma Tools

8.1 Quality Pillar # 45: Uncover Defects Using Concentration Diagrams

Concentration diagrams are used to investigate the location of incidents over a geographical map or a drawing of a product. These incidents might be accidents or defects. The diagram will present the layout of a facility, product, or even an application document form, highlighting the fields having the most errors or missing information. Data is typically collected, and a dot is inserted at the exact location where the wrong or missing important information occurred (in the case of a form) or the component location where the defect or incident happened (in the case of a facility or product). By following this process, and after allowing some reasonable time to collect a representative sample (the general rule of thumb is to use about 20–30 samples as a start), a concentrated pattern may start to emerge indicating where a problem keeps appearing. Thus, a prioritized approach is possible, which involves investigating the reason a problem is frequently happening at that location and not as frequently at other locations, until the team can identify potential causes and verify them through testing data and perhaps experimenting with feasible solutions.

Following are some examples for the use of concentration diagrams, which are sometimes used as part of Lean Six Sigma training. The first example is the case of World War II (WWII) fighter planes. A team of American engineers examined the bodies of the air force planes as they

DOI: 10.4324/9781032688374-11

returned from battle to decide what locations they needed to fortify with additional metal armor. To expedite this process, they used concentration diagrams to collect data and locate where the planes were hit to determine which areas required reinforcement. The diagram looked similar to what is depicted in Figure 8.1. Based on that, which part did they decide to armor?

Well, the part of the plane they decided to armor was the tail. Although it did not show any damage on the diagram, they concluded that planes hit in the tail did not return. The tails were the weakest part of the plane.

Another example is the cholera epidemic in London during the 19th century. A doctor decided to examine which neighborhoods had the highest number of cases per capita. He used a concentration diagram where dots represented each infected person's house location on a map of London (which was used as the background of the graph). A pattern emerged eventually, which helped him determine that the water in one neighborhood crossroad was contaminated. The corrective action he took was to remove the water pump handle at that location to prevent further spread of the disease.

A third example from the automotive industry concerns the leather interior used in car doors. The location of wrinkles (a type of visual defect) was examined, helping to identify and, thereby, resolve the root causes of the problem. Finally, even in transactional processes, defects within forms or templates, such as invoices, can be tracked to determine which fields more often suffer from wrong or missing information so that they can be fixed.

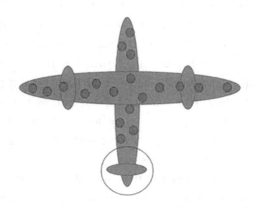

Figure 8.1   A concentration diagram for the body of a fighter plane. Dark dots represent areas where various planes were hit.

8.2 Quality Pillar # 46: Use a Box Plot to Show the Data Distribution, Compare Teams, and Compare Performance before and after Implementing Improvements

A box plot or box-and-whisker diagram is a graphical tool used to enable a clear understanding of the data distribution and variation. It summarizes the data by the minimum value, the second quartile, the median (50th percentile), the third quartile, and the maximum value (Juran and Godfrey, 1999). It can be useful even for small sample sizes (Breyfogle, 2003). Figure 8.2 shows an example of a box plot, with its detailed annotation.

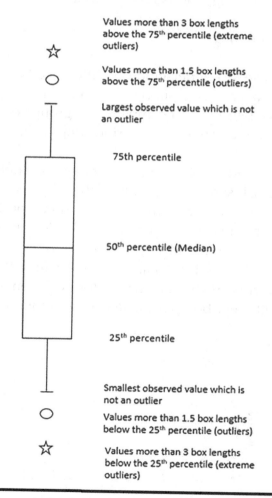

Figure 8.2 A generic example showing a box plot and its detailed annotation as adapted from Pyzdek and Keller (2019).

A box plot is considered a graphical display of data, showing various features such as the following (Montgomery, 2001):

1. A box marked by three lines (first quartile or 25th percentile or Q1, second quartile or Q2, and third quartile or Q3) as well as two whiskers extending to the extreme values. Some references indicate extreme values as outliers if they fall outside the calculated ranges and extend away from the bulk of data (more than 1.5 times Q3 minus Q1). They are designated with asterisks and may be typically investigated to find underlying causes.
2. Location or central tendency, which shows the median position, at the second quartile marking, and is referred to as the 50th percentile or Q2.
3. Dispersion.
4. Departure from symmetry.

Box plots can be used to understand the difference between two or more groups of data, such as groups of suppliers or branches. Figure 8.3 shows an example of the use of box plots to compare two groups of efficiency data before and after the implementation of various improvements in a Lean Six Sigma project.

For the same data used in Figure 8.3, the individual control chart, which is depicted in Figure 8.4, shows the trends of the efficiency data in three stages: before improvement, during the Lean Six Sigma project, and after improvement. The data indicates a change in behavior of the process in terms of variation and central tendency.

Also, box plots can be used to compare revenue in dollars. Figure 8.5 shows the data for various retail branches in four different cities. Finally, Figure 8.6 displays different box plots matched with their corresponding distribution.

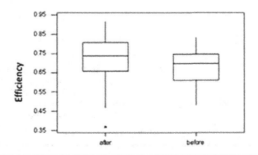

Figure 8.3   An example of two box plots for efficiency data collected before and after improvement generated by Minitab.

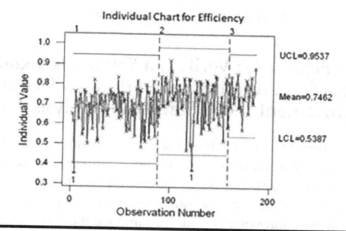

Figure 8.4 Individual control chart for production efficiency showing three stages generated by Minitab.

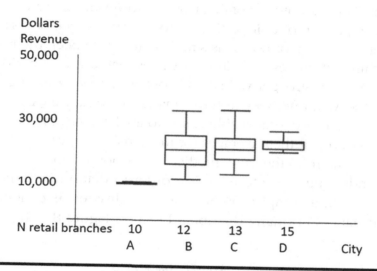

Figure 8.5 Comparison of revenue in dollars for various retail branches in four different cities as adapted from Pyzdek and Keller (2019).

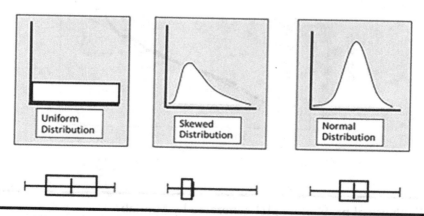

Figure 8.6 Different generic box plots matched with their corresponding distribution as adapted from Six Sigma Training, personal communication (2008).

8.3 Quality Pillar # 47: Verify if a Sample Is Significantly Different from Another Taken Prior to Treatment or Improvement Using Statistical Analysis Tools

To illustrate this idea, the following example of a certain metric, measured as a percentage, when two samples are taken and compared before and after implementing improvement, can be considered. A point estimate comparison can easily be conducted by focusing on the average or the median of the first sample taken before improvement and the same for the sample taken after improvement. In this example, the median for the data taken prior to improvement was 70%, which is less than the median value of 74% for data taken after improvement. This indicates favorable results. However, one cannot merely rely on the comparison of point estimates to conclude whether a significant improvement took place or not. This simply could have been the result of variation within that process, resulting in values that range from 65% to 80%, for example. A much stronger validation is obtained when running statistical tests such as the Mann-Whitney test, the analysis of variance (ANOVA), and two-sample *t*-test. These tests enable teams to analyze the variation of any two samples to judge if their averages (or medians, in the case of the Mann-Whitney test) come from the same mother population or not.

Before conducting those tests and in order to determine which tests are suited for such a comparison, a data normality test is conducted to determine if data is normally distributed or not. Figure 8.7 shows an

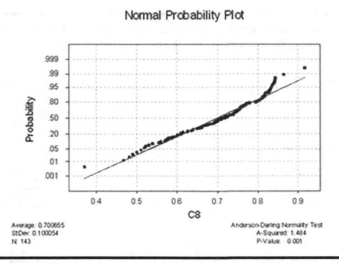

Figure 8.7   Normal probability plot generated by Minitab.

example of normality test for a sample of data. Here are the normality test hypotheses:

Ho (null hypothesis): Data is normal.
Ha (alternative hypothesis): Data is not normal.

The hypotheses test, carried out using Minitab statistical software resulted in a *p*-value of 0.001, which is less than the threshold of 0.05, indicating that the null hypothesis must be rejected, which means the data is concluded to be not normal. This matches with the normal probability plot, which shows various points not falling on the line.

Since data is not normally distributed, comparing the medians will provide a better indicator for central tendency or a shift in the process than means or other averages. Thus, a Mann-Whitney test is used as a way to judge if the medians of the two samples taken before and after implementing improvement come from the same mother population or not. This test analyzes variation in each sample to judge the medians of nonnormal distributions. What is hoped to be proven is that they are indeed different, indicating that whichever improvement actions have been implemented, have actually resulted in a significant change, hopefully in the targeted direction (whether the higher, the better, or the lower, the better). Here are the Mann-Whitney test hypotheses:

Ho: Medians are equal.
Ha: Medians are not equal.

The Mann-Whitney hypotheses test, performed using Minitab statistical software, resulted in a *p*-value of 0.0027, which is less than 0.05, indicating that the null hypothesis must be rejected. This indicates the medians are concluded to be statistically and significantly different. Therefore, the medians are not equal (median *before repair* = 70% and median *after repair* = 74%). This indicates that the improvement actions implemented did indeed result in a favorable impact and verified improvement.

Here is another example, which assumes that the observations are random samples from normally distributed populations with equal variances. Thus, analysis of variance (ANOVA) can be used. ANOVA is a method used to dissect the variability within a data set into the sources and causes of that variability and determine the strength of those sources. ANOVA is often used along with main effects and interaction plots. ANOVA is used to do the following (Six Sigma Training, personal communication, 2008):

- Identify sources of variability in the process output.
- Verify whether the presumed causes are real or not.
- Determine the significance of a regression equation.
- Decide which factors affect the output in a DOE.

ANOVA has two types of analyses to determine if input variables significantly affect the average output:

- One-way ANOVA, which is performed by analyzing the output response or result by varying one category or factor.
- Two-way ANOVA, which is performed by analyzing the output response or result by varying two categories or factors.

In one-way ANOVA, one compares the observed difference or variability "between" treatments' means (or averages) to the variability due to repetitions "within" each treatment. If the "between treatment" source of variability is significantly greater than the "within treatment" source, then it can be concluded that there is a difference between treatments, which is not simply a result of chance (see Figure 8.8).

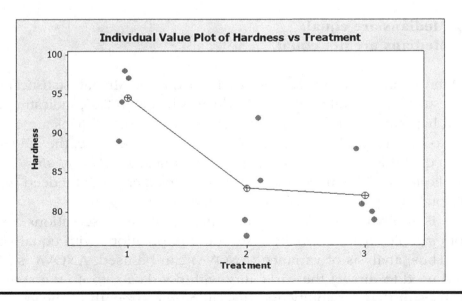

Figure 8.8 A generic example of a main effects plot as generated by Minitab and adapted from Six Sigma Training, personal communication (2008).

Thus, an ANOVA test is used as a way to judge if the means of the two samples taken before and after improvement come from the same mother population or not. It is also used to judge if at least one of the means of the three or more samples taken from different populations (branches, departments, *etc.*) differs from others. It analyzes variation in each sample to judge whether the means come from the same distribution or not. Once again, what is hoped to be proved is that they are indeed different, which means that whichever improvement actions one has implemented, have actually resulted in a significant change, hopefully in a favorable direction (whether the higher, the better, or the lower, the better). Here are the ANOVA test hypotheses:

Ho: Means are equal.

Ha: Means are not equal (or at least one mean is different from the others).

The ANOVA hypotheses test, carried out using Minitab, resulted in a *p*-value of 0.01, which is less than 0.05, indicating that the null hypothesis must be rejected. This indicates the means are concluded to be statistically and significantly different. Therefore, the means are not equal (mean *before improvement* = 10 hours, and mean *after improvement* = 6 hours). This indicates that the improvement actions implemented did indeed result in a favorable impact and verified improvement.

8.4 Quality Pillar # 48: Slow Down to Do More— Use Evolutionary Optimization (EVOP), which is a Slow-Motion DOE, as a Great Way to Test Potential Factors Affecting a Response

It sounds counterintuitive, but it is nonetheless highly effective. Several years ago, an LSS project led by a Black Belt, was to improve the production line efficiency at a lumber factory. During this project, one key potential factor or root cause for the factory's downtime, which negatively affected production line efficiency, was production line speed. While brainstorming to reflect on the process, some team members raised the issue that perhaps because the line was running faster than its designed capacity, it was frequently stopping and failing at various locations.

Testing the speed requires shutting down the production line as part of a designed experiment to conduct a number of runs at different speeds for different products, which is very costly. Design of experiments (DOE) is an important tool often used in firms and factories that focus on designing new products or reviewing an existing product by examining the relationship between various potential factors (independent inputs) and a dependent output as well as the interaction between these factors (Gitlow *et al.*, 2015). Originally developed by the British statistician Ronald Fisher, who introduced two important books about statistical methods (Box *et al.*, 1978), DOE is a very effective approach that can be applied to various industries, although many sectors are unaware of its potential benefits. The Japanese statistician Taguchi developed the robust design approach, which is a modification of the traditional DOE approach (Breyfogle, 2003). DOE is often used in manufacturing, but various researchers have explored its use in the service industry as well.

In order to conduct a DOE, the team needs to brainstorm a list of possible factors (inputs or variables) that they suspect to affect the output response (the key indicator being studied). These factors can be tested at different levels, and their interactions can be checked to reveal whether they are mutually dependent through different experimental combinations of settings. Main effects plots can be used to test the main effect of each factor, and interaction plots can be used to test for dependencies between factors (see Section 8.7). Figure 8.9 shows how a factor may affect the output in terms of its variation and/or average. The goal is first to find the factors

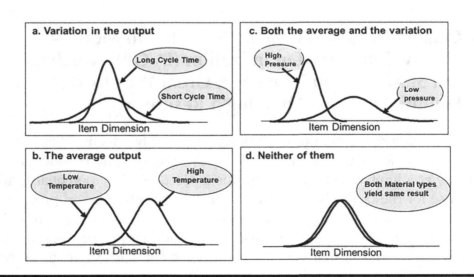

Figure 8.9 Types of effects of factors on a process output as adapted from Gee *et al.* (2015).

that affect variation and to set them at the level that minimizes variation. The next goal is to find the factors that affect the central tendency of the output (without affecting variation) and set them at the levels that shift the distribution of the output into a favorable direction toward the target. If all combinations are tested, then the experiment is called a full factorial experiment, which is the type typically used when one investigates four or fewer factors. For more than four factors, one can use fractional factorial experiments. Also, screening experiments (for seven or more factors) can be used to economically identify the most vital factors. Some of these factors might be control factors, which can be adjusted (to achieve less variation and then to bring the average output closer to the specified target), and some might be noise factors, which are typically not easy to adjust, as they relate to the environment or natural variability in raw materials, for example. Noise factors are difficult to control and, therefore, may be expensive to manipulate. The goal is to find strong control factors that can minimize the effect of noise factors and to find ways to reduce their impact directly or indirectly by compensation. By following the stages of the process flow, it can be confirmed that all potential factors are included. The DOE enables simultaneous investigation of multiple factors. It helps to discover the most critical factors affecting the output and the best setting for these factors. This can be seen through the graphical analysis of main effects plots and interaction plots.

In order to conduct a successful experiment, a relevant output measure is needed, in addition to a rigorous experiment design, solid plan, reliable measurement system, and proper tracking of experimental units. The following are the recommended steps for designing and conducting a DOE (Gee *et al.*, 2015):

1. Analyze the available historical data, or collect new data to evaluate the current process capability.
2. Define the purpose of the experiment.
3. Decide what to measure as the output of the experiment.
4. Determine the control and noise factors that could affect the output of the experiment.
5. For each factor, decide on the number of levels as well as their corresponding actual values.
6. Choose an experimental layout that will accommodate the selected factors and their levels.
7. Select the number of repetitions or replications.
8. Validate the measurement systems.

9. Plan for the experiment, and organize the resources, including staff and materials.
10. Decide whether to randomize the runs or not, and create a test plan.
11. Conduct the experiment. Ensure that all units are labeled with proper information indicating the experimental condition in which it was delivered. Randomize the runs to minimize the influence of any noise factor.
12. Measure all the experimental units.
13. Perform analysis of data to identify the strong factors.
14. Find out which combination of factor levels is the best to achieve the aim of the process.
15. Conduct a confirmation experiment using those optimal settings.
16. Use visual controls, and create standard operating procedures to ensure these optimal settings are sustained over time.
17. Recalculate the process capability indices.

However, there is another choice for a modified approach of DOE, where the testing is performed at a relatively slower pace without interrupting the actual or regular manufacturing process as in the traditional DOE approach. This approach is called evolutionary optimization (EVOP), or evolutionary operation, which would take longer, but its advantage is that it will not interrupt the production operation, so the cost is way lower (Juran and Godfrey, 1999). EVOP is typically used in the analyze and improve phases of a Six Sigma project.

In the same project, it took great effort to convince the management team to consider slowing down the production speed as an experiment to validate such a hypothesis. Finally, a plan was approved to run various production shifts using various speeds over several weeks. Experimenting with the speed of the production line resulted in a better understanding of which speeds are more suited for maximizing efficiency. To the surprise of both the factory management team and the project team themselves, the project team managed to put more products out of the factory doors when the speed was slower. This was indeed a breakthrough improvement enabled through the structured approach of LSS DMAIC.

This also exemplifies one of the principles of the Lean methodology: namely, "one-piece flow" (Imai, 2012). Typically, operators tend to batch work between stations due to various reasons. One important reason is the poor layout of the workplace, which may not be organized according to the sequence of the process steps. The waste of motion or movement is high in such layouts, which leads to operators holding finished work and delaying its release to the next step until they have enough batched subassemblies or transaction documents to justify the trip from their location to the next station, typically far away. Another example is batching various emails to process all of them at once using an online platform that has numerous access steps.

To illustrate this idea of "one-piece flow", here are two scenarios that involve two stations, each with one operator taking 1 minute to process each product. A customer ordered 10 products. In the first scenario, the first operator takes 10 minutes to process 10 products as a batch and then hands them over to the next operator, who also takes another 10 minutes before the products finally reach the customer after 20 minutes. Note an additional negative aspect of this scenario—namely, that the second operator was idle for the first 10 minutes because of batching. Also, had the customer ordered only one product, it would still have taken the same 20 minutes for it to reach him/her, again due to batching.

However, if one considers a second scenario (the ideal Lean approach of one-piece flow), in which the first operator takes 1 minute to process one product and directly hand it over to the next operator at the second station, who takes another minute to process it, the first product would reach the customer in 2 minutes only (compared to 20 minutes in the first scenario). That is a 90% reduction in lead time, despite the seeming inefficiency of working product by product. It should also be noted that it would take only 11 minutes for the full order of 10 pieces to reach the customer (instead of 20 minutes as in the first scenario). That is equivalent to a reduction in lead time by 45%, or almost half. Moreover, the idle time (waste due to waiting) incurred by the second operator is only 1 minute (compared to 10 minutes in the first scenario). See Figure 8.10.

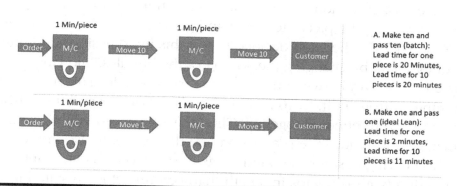

Figure 8.10 Lead time for batching versus one piece flow.

Had these minutes been hours or days, the scale would definitely indicate a huge difference, which further emphasizes the enormous percentage of time reduction between the two scenarios.

An organization's Gemba readiness for high standards of quality is measured by 5S (see Section 10.2.). Similarly, lead time is a measure of management capability and strength. Lead time essentially represents the turnover of money. It starts when the company pays for raw materials and supplies and ends when the company receives payment from its customers for products sold. Shortening the lead time is a key indicator for the health of the organization.

Obviously, automating processes can eliminate such waste by, for example, electronic transfer of documents in the case of transactional processes. Similarly, enhancing the design of a layout brings stations closer together following the sequence of steps. Some employees might advocate for a handling medium such as conveyor belts as the solution. However, it is always recommended to think about how to minimize conveyor belts and the distances between stations, unless there is a strong justification or need. The longer the distance and the conveyor belts, the more time it will take the products to travel, the more operators will be required to maintain and manage the line, the greater the likelihood of defects occurring along the way, and the more overall cost required.

In the Black Belt project mentioned earlier, another major issue was related to the production line suffering failures and increased downtime due to lumber pieces getting jammed at a specific perpendicular transition point within the line. This 90° shift in direction allows for the longitudinally fed pieces coming out of the planer mill to travel in parallel. After brainstorming, the project team determined that the wide range of 4 ft. for lumber board length within each bundle was a potential root cause. The same bundle contained boards with a length range of 12–16 ft. When the shorter pieces were pushed by longer pieces at that 90° transition point, they acted as a pivots, causing the pieces to rotate and get jammed, causing production line downtime. The team decided to test this hypothesis and minimize the pivoting effect by changing the sorting of the bundles, allowing a range of only 2 ft. in length between the pieces of each bundle. This means that boards ranging from 14 ft. to 16 ft. were bundled together and those from 10 ft. to 12 ft. were bundled together. This strategy proved effective, and the team managed to reduce the production line downtime. It also indirectly affected the drying cost for the bundles, as more wood was fitted into each of the bundles (with less gaps in length than before), which resulted in a very significant cost-saving as well.

8.5 Quality Pillar # 49: Learn to Use Offline Simulation to Improve Your Process

One of the most helpful tools used in the analyze and improve phases of DMAIC is simulation. It involves the creation of a model to test various offline "what-if" scenarios (Gitlow *et al.*, 2015). Simulation software products such as Arena are used by practitioners to simulate real-life process behaviors to help identify areas of improvement, test various options, and check potential solutions. Also, machines may come with a built-in simulation software to help in testing and checking for areas of improvement. The advantage of using a simulation software is that it is ready and easy to use and provides a safe environment to experiment in without interrupting or negatively affecting the regular production operation.

Sometimes the challenge to improve a process recovery may not lie in the raw material or the employees who run the process but, rather, in the machine setup itself. This sounds simple, but it can be complicated by a large number of machine parameters. Sometimes machines are set up by specialized suppliers based on given relevant conditions applicable at the time when the machine is first set up. However, those conditions and circumstances change over time, depending on market metrics, as an example. If manufacturers are not aware of this, some excellent opportunities can be missed.

My first Six Sigma Green Belt project concerned enhancing the process recovery by understanding why recovery for low-grade lumber was only averaging 27%. The process involved taking low-grade sorted lumber boards, scanning them for defects (such as stains, knots, and dimensional defects), cutting them into blocks ranging only from 6 to 12 inches, sorting them into different bins classified by different types or levels of product grade, and finally feeding them to a finger-jointing machine to make new boards of higher grades, which were then sold for higher prices. The material was classified under softwood lumber used for aesthetic, rather than structural, considerations. Although the focus was on a low-grade raw material to start with, the 27% recovery was still considered low. The project team investigated various hypotheses related to potential causes, including raw material quality, operator skill level, scanner software accuracy and decision logic, cutting saw accuracy, and sorting system accuracy.

The project team found that the main issue, which was eventually tested and confirmed as significantly critical, was the software setup for the cutting decision rules. The team needed to understand how the scanner made its decisions. The prices of the different grades were critical, and an updated price list was therefore obtained from the sales team to help in the setup. Selecting a sample of around 500 boards and then obtaining the software program from the supplier enabled the team to run various recipes of tests for the grades' relative price ratios, which helped the software decide the grade to aim for and the length to cut the board pieces, while maximizing the potential revenue and recovery. After several offline-simulation trials, the team managed to come up with the improved values. Once these were inputted, profit increased, and the recovery reached 41%, indicating a great success. It can therefore be seen that the offline tests using the scanner's simulation software led to a breakthrough improvement without any interruption in the production process.

Another potential cause of low recovery was related to the scanner's accuracy as a measurement system (see Section 3.1). Measurement system analysis (MSA) is a key tool often used within the measure phase of a Six Sigma project (Breyfogle, 2003). The team designed a number of MSA tests of gauge repeatability and reproducibility for both the scanner machine and the cutting saw machine. A sample of 20 boards was carefully selected to represent an unbiased variety of boards. These boards were numbered and fed into the scanner three times each, in order to test the repeatability of the scanner's resulting decision. The result was 96%, which was acceptable relative to the supplier's promised target of 95% accuracy. For the reproducibility test, the same 20 boards were examined by the chief grading specialist at the factory whose assessment was very close to the machine's in terms of the resulting blocks and their grades. Similar tests were then done for the cutting saw machine, but since the tests were destructive, the pressure of the saws was lowered to allow for the team to collect a somewhat intact board with partial saw marks, indicating where the cutting was executed. To repeat the test, the same scanner results were used repeatedly but with an equivalent board (of the same size) fed into the cutting saw machine. This test worked, and the team was able to confirm that the cutting saw machine was consistent in its execution of the scanner's cutting orders, which were also confirmed to be consistent. Thus, there was not enough evidence to qualify this potential root cause as a critical one. In short, the supplier fulfilled his/her promise in terms of machine accuracy.

8.6 Quality Pillar # 50: Stratify Data by Various Categories to See if a Pattern Emerges

Ishikawa listed data stratification as one of the seven basic quality tools (Antony *et al.*, 2021). This tool has sometimes been referred to as a graphing tool, which in some cases has been replaced by flowcharts, as noted in various Six Sigma training and educational resources, such as ASQ (2021) and SPCFOREXCEL (2017). However, stratification is a fundamental and important quality tool that helps separate data by different sources or groups so that patterns may appear.

One case study used in Six Sigma training to illustrate the power of data stratification as a quality tool is the case of an American manufacturer of fiber optic cables. This manufacturer struggled to find the root causes for an unexpectedly high defective rate in finished products. The case was not solved until the project team decided to look at the data arranged in strata by each day of the week. Strata are subpopulations or segments of the population, which are likely to be differentiated by the characteristic under investigation (Juran and Godfrey, 1999). As the data was investigated, Sundays presented suspiciously unique values for failure rates that were not perceived within the other days. This enabled the team to narrow down their scope and manage to isolate the precise difference. This is also known as part of Kepner-Tregoe's (KT) approach to revealing what is unique about a problem in terms of the "what versus what not", "where versus where not", "when versus when not", *etc.* (Kepner and Tregoe, 2006). Apparently, the high failure rate occurring on Sundays was due to external vibration affecting the highly sensitive manufacturing process. When the team analyzed the root causes, they found that every Sunday afternoon, there is a high traffic flow on the adjacent highway due to commuters returning back to the city after spending their weekend out of town.

Obviously, the same conclusion could have been reached by examining a control chart showing a cyclic effect, where failures would peak on Sundays. However, data stratification can quickly depict such behavior by comparing each day with the other days of the week. Other examples of data stratification are data grouping and classification by age, gender, location, source, *etc.*

8.7 Quality Pillar # 51: Use Main Effects Plots and Multi-vari Charts to Investigate the Effects of Suspected Factors

One effective approach used to investigate the effects of multiple factors in an experiment is the use of a factorial design or a DOE. The advantage of this approach is that the main factors are varied simultaneously and viewed in terms of mutual variances as opposed to a weaker approach considering only varying one factor at a time. Typically, these factors are varied within two levels: low and high. The effect of each primary factor alone is called a main effect and is defined as the change in response by the change in the factor's level (Montgomery, 2001). Thus, the main effects plot can help quantify the differences of the averages between different settings of one factor, independently of other factors (Breyfogle, 2003).

Multi-vari charts are simple yet very powerful in data analysis and graph assessment. They also provide similar results to those obtained through design of experiments (DOE). They help study variations such as positional variation (within piece or within batch), cyclical variation (piece-to-piece changes or patterns in batches) and temporal variation or time-to-time variation (Pries, 2009). Leonard Seder is credited for introducing the multi-vari chart in 1950, which allows for visual decomposition to identify the components that affect variability the most (Breyfogle, 2003). Variation components examples are time periods, part-to-part or within-part variation, production tool or machine differences, shifts, *etc.*

Here is a hypothetical example of a process that involves three types of transactions required by customers. Three operators are allocated to handle this process and are trained to perform all types of these transactions. Customers require that the process shall not exceed three days in duration. The manager of the department received some complaints by customers who had experienced some delays. The manager decides to use a main effects plot to examine the gathered data about the process duration by the operators. The main effects plot shown in Figure 8.11 clearly indicates that operators A and B comply with the customer-specified requirement or service level agreement, whereas operator C does not. The manager decides to investigate further before taking any corrective action.

Using a multi-vari chart similar to the one depicted in Figure 8.12, the manager concluded that all operators had incidents that exceeded the customers' acceptable limits, particularly when dealing with transaction type 1. Operator C happened to have handled more transactions of type 1 than the others. Thus, the manager decided to focus on the reasons why transaction type 1 took longer to process than other transactions and to determine whether the agreed target was reasonable or not.

Sometimes, the response differs between the factor's levels depending on the chosen levels of another factor. This happens due to an interaction between the two factors. Testing one factor at a time fails to detect the interaction between factors when one factor masks the influence of another (Montgomery, 2001). This means that the effect of one factor will depend on

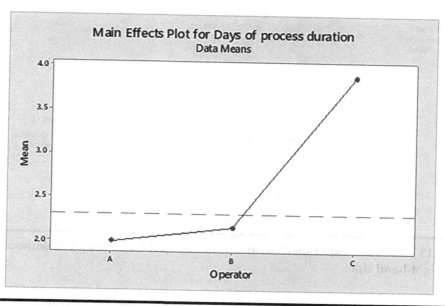

Figure 8.11   Main effects plot example.

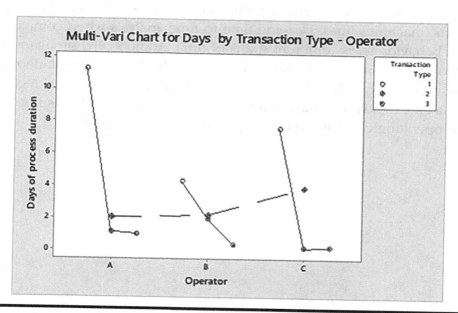

Figure 8.12   Multi-vari chart example.

another factor. To investigate whether such a case exists or not, interaction plots can be used, which are often used as part of factorial experiments. Figure 8.13 shows two examples: one with interaction and another without interaction.

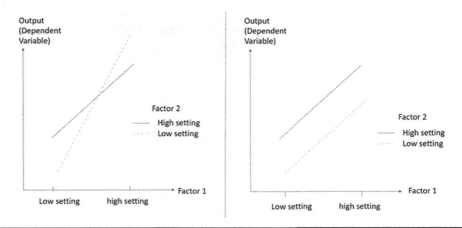

Figure 8.13   Factorial experiment with interaction (left-hand side) and without interaction (right-hand side).

A standard method in testing theories related to problem solving is process dissection, which includes testing intermediate stages to locate defect origin; stream-to-stream analysis when dealing with multiple suppliers, shifts, machines lines, *etc.*; and time-to-time analysis when comparing process behavior across different spans of time. Additionally, simultaneous dissection utilizes multi-vari charts to test multiple theories simultaneously (Juran and Godfrey, 1999). DOE can complement these two visual techniques, as it extends the analysis into other factors and sets levels beyond normal operating conditions (Breyfogle, 2003).

LEAN MANAGEMENT IV

Chapter 9

Fundamental Pillars Related to Lean Management

9.1 Quality Pillar # 52: Use Value Stream Mapping (VSM) as a Framework for the Improvement of the Supply Chain (SC) or Any Process

For someone who is about to begin their quality improvement journey, one of the most effective tools or methods they can utilize is value stream mapping (VSM). It is a set of all sequential activities happening in a process, whether adding value or not (explicit and hidden waste), from the moment a customer makes an order to the delivery of products (including design and manufacturing). It is typically of a high-level and cross-functional perspective, including various parties involved in the delivery of value across the stream. It includes three types of flow:

- manufacturing (raw material and subassemblies);
- information (schedules, forecasts, and documents); and
- time (each process time and the waiting time between process steps).

Figure 9.1 shows an example of one form of a VSM often used in transactional process improvement, which is called a swim-lane VSM.

Value stream management connects and aligns the needs of management teams and operations teams (Tapping *et al.*, 2002). VSM allows team members to step out of their typical processes and see firsthand how their work affects others and vice versa. In addition to these types of flow, VSM

DOI: 10.4324/9781032688374-13

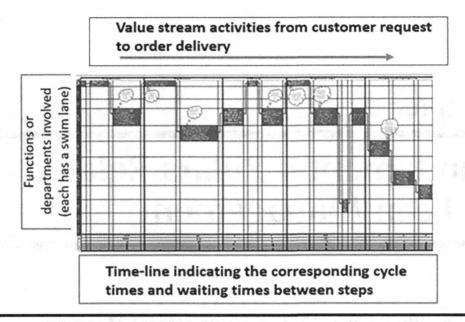

Figure 9.1   An example of what a swim-lane VSM looks like.

identifies areas of improvement such as bottlenecks, wasteful activities, delays, and integration or automation opportunities.

Lean uses VSM the way Six Sigma uses the DMAIC framework for improvement. A VSM can be created using a Kaizen event. The term "Kaizen" is derived from two Japanese words, "kai" and "zen", and means to change for the better, or "improvement". Kaizen implies continuous improvement and is mainly concerned with self-discipline (Imai, 2012). In a Kaizen workshop, which might last a few days, a team's scope might be to improve, transform, and enhance a current process design. The term "stream" implies that value is flowing toward the customer as a river flows down a valley. The earlier one discovers the rocks, or errors, the cheaper it is to fix them. The focus is to ensure quality and build it early into the process, even starting at the design stage. Typically, a high-level process map is created in which the focus is on overall lead-time reduction. However, some companies use a more detailed swim-lane (cross-functional) VSM,, especially in transactional processes, to highlight the following information (Six Sigma Training, personal communication, 2008):

1. Process steps.
2. Details of each step, including inputs and outputs.

3. Inventory of products or documents.
4. Error rate.
5. Cycle time and processing time.
6. Waiting times between steps (including queuing time) and the overall lead time.
7. Process availability and changeover time.
8. Number of operators.
9. Information flow, reports, schedules, *etc.*
10. Opportunities for improvement (types of waste, obstacles, queries, *etc.*).

Any obstacle or query on missing or incorrect data is highlighted using a cloud (or another symbol) to be included later in the migration action plan that will transform the process from the current state to the more sustainable future state. This brings the process one step closer to an ideal state or vision. The clouds can be tackled using the Kaizen approach. Kaizen is the vehicle that enables teams to implement Lean tools such as 5S, quick changeover, material Kanban, labor scheduling, a training cross-functional matrix, and visual yard inventory. It can even be used for strategic planning retreats.

Typically, the list of improvement actions is focused on operational issues or automation issues (*i.e.*, a wish list) with the support of a company's information technology team. The VSM may be revealing for the management team and employees. It enables them to see the proportion of non-value-added activity within any process. For example, instead of focusing on eliminating a second, or even a minute, in processing time at one particular step, the VSM shifts the focus to the wastefulness of waiting times between steps, which can add up to days or weeks, if not months.

Only around 5% of typical employee activity counts as value-added work, as depicted in Figure 9.2 (Tapping *et al.*, 2002). VSM shifts the focus from micromanaging employees to increase that small percentage of value-added work (usually by reducing the steps' cycle times), into a macro-level of management to reduce the 95% of non-value-added work (usually by reducing the process's lead time, where waste typically occurs, and thus, where a huge opportunity for improvement lies).

Some may think this is exaggerated, but it is not. Imai (2012) illustrated this in a story about being at an airport terminal and trying to get a ticket stamped. He waited in line until the service agent told him to walk to another terminal, where he waited in line again until he finally received the stamp. The sound of the stamp being "banged" onto his ticket represented

Work Activites

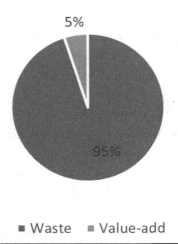

5%

95%

■ Waste ■ Value-add

Figure 9.2 Work activities classification and proportions as adapted from Tapping *et al.* **(2002).**

the very moment when "value" was added. This "bang" took much less than the typical 5% mentioned earlier.

Usually, a team of five to eight representing all the functions involved in VSM is invited to participate in a three-day basic Lean training session and begin the mapping exercise. They engage in discussions to describe the current process from their perspective. They step out of their daily work so that they can map and reflect on the process. They empathize with one another and with their external customers as they become more aware of how their work affects others. This includes going to the Gemba to observe and collect data to complete the mapping exercise. The result is a finished, current-state VSM.

The same team is invited to design an ideal state, which is almost impossible to achieve but helps to design a future state with a list of improvement initiatives that form an improvement plan to migrate from the current to the future state.

The benefits of VSM include the following (Six Sigma Training, personal communication, 2008):

1. It serves as a platform and a framework for process improvement.
2. It transforms the current-state process into a more sustainable future-state process.

3. It enables cross-functional teams to see the process from one another's perspective and the customer's perspective.
4. It exposes waste and enables a better understanding of the process and its metrics.
5. It enables the team to identify opportunities related to the physical operation, integration of activities, and automation of tasks.
6. It helps transform the business culture.

In an integrated Lean Six Sigma methodology following DMAIC, VSM fits well within the DMAIC framework, as it is used in the measure phase to map the current state and in the improve phase to map the future state. If one starts their journey with process improvement (PI), they should start by looking at their current VSM, diagnose their activities, determine whether they can recognize different types of waste, quantify the impacts of waste, and then discuss with their team how to design a future-state VSM that focuses on adding value. They are then ready to start their PI journey.

The approach would begin with the following steps (Tapping *et al.*, 2002):

1. Establish a commitment to waste elimination.
2. Choose the value stream process to start with.
3. Learn about Lean and VSM.
4. Map the current-state VSM, and go to the floor (the Gemba).
5. Add the VSM metrics.
6. Map the future-state VSM.
7. Plan for Kaizen events.
8. Implement the Kaizen plan to transform the process from current to future state.

When examining a process through a Gemba walk, it is important to look for defects, rework, queries (the need to ask for information), bottlenecks, backlogs or queues (piles of work), different ways of doing the same type of work, work being done in series when it could be done in parallel, several approvals, multiple handoffs, "feast or famine", batches, and interruptions. In addition, the team should look for indicators of instability such as inconsistent approaches, exceptions, chaos, repeated quality problems, missing information (required to do a process step), interruptions, variations in cycle times, and work backlogs. The following steps should be followed to start constructing a current-state VSM (Six Sigma Training, personal communication, 2008):

1. Start with the customer icon on the top-right corner.
2. Add customer-triggering demand and requirements.
3. Add the production control box in the center and the shipping forecast information, including schedules and plans.
4. Add the supplier icon on the top-left corner to start indicating the flow of steps from raw material to finished products.
5. Draw the manufacturing or transactional steps.
6. Add process data at every step, including metrics.
7. Add the information flow.
8. Draw the inventory icons, and add inventory data.
9. Draw the flow arrows indicating push, pull, and first-in-first-out (FIFO) locations.

For transactional processes, indicate the required information and providers. The process steps may start from the top-left corner with the customer triggering the process as a request received by the organization; this continues until it is fulfilled and the service is delivered to the customer at the end of the flow.

For the future state, one needs to consider designing a new process where unnecessary steps and waste are eliminated. Additional considerations include customer and supplier information; demand rate (pitch and takt time) (Section 9.8); a safety inventory requirement and finished goods supermarket requirement (Section 10.6); Kaizen events required for process transformation (Section 11.2), such as a redesign of the cell layout (Section 11.7); line balancing (Section 9.7); changeover (Section 11.6); Kanban systems (Section 9.5); 5S (see Sections 10.2, 10.3, and 10.4); total productive maintenance (TPM) (Section 11.5); error-proofing (Section 11.3); autonomous operation and maintenance (Jidoka) (Section 11.4); standardized work (Section 11.1); and the paced withdrawal or Heijunka system for visual control (Sections 10.1 and 10.5). To illustrate the benefits of VSM, see the case study in Appendix A.

9.2 Quality Pillar # 53: Become Lean. Recognize Value and Eliminate Waste. Make Sure You Can "See" Waste; Then Proceed to Eliminate It

The use of bananas as a means of illustrating the concept of waste or as a tool for understanding process improvement can be introduced in the following story. A man once picked a few bananas in a store and had a cashier weigh them. When asked to pay, the man said, "I refuse to pay for the total weight because it includes the peels, which I will throw away. I will only eat the fruit. So, I shall pay only for the fruit." This example might be an exaggeration, but it perfectly explains and illustrates Lean philosophy.

Lean is a simple process improvement strategy that focuses on eliminating waste and maximizing value. Value is the opposite of waste; waste is anything that does not add value. Value is what the customer, if given the choice, is willing to pay for.

Value is also anything above the absolute minimum necessary to make a product (Breyfogle, 2003). It includes any activity that takes material or information and converts or transforms it to meet the customer's expectations. It is a physical feature that is added to a product to enhance it and make it more appealing to the customer, who would then appreciate it and be willing to pay more for it. Value is that portion of the performed work that is directly useful to the customers and benefits them, exactly like the fruit (but not the peel) in the banana story.

When adding attributes or features that are above the absolute minimum required by clients, the Kano model is utilized to attract customers and position the offered services or products competitively against other providers. However, this comes at a cost that must be recognized. A feasibility assessment can be used to help decide whether it is recommended or not. Examples might include when auto-dealers provide free maintenance options or free insurance for a year or more. Some of these features might become essential in the future as customers get used to them and therefore begin expecting them as basic features, and not attributes.

Thus, waste is anything that the customer, if given the choice, is not willing to pay for (Six Sigma Training, personal communication, 2008). It is the banana peel, which costs money but does not generate any value for the customer. The first challenge in becoming Lean is to be able to see waste. Lean thinking is really about wearing a new set of glasses that enables viewers to recognize that the peel of the banana is in fact waste that they pay for. It is similar to the activities people do habitually without questioning whether they add value to their customers or not. Once they can "see" waste, the challenge is to eliminate it. This is typically done by using a wide variety of simple tools from the Lean tool kit such as value stream mapping (VSM), 5S, visual workplace, quick changeover (single-minute exchange of dies, or SMED), mistake-proofing (Poka-Yoke), total productive maintenance (TPM), Kaizen, Kanban, cell layout, and work standardization, among others.

In addition, similar to how a river flows downstream toward a village, a process value stream (often referred to as a map) is the set of activities that carries the value toward the customer. Waste is any activity that hinders the flow of the value to the customer, exactly like how rocks impede the flow of water in the river. The earlier the problems related to the flow of the stream are fixed, the cheaper it will be. This is similar to water being cleaner upstream than downstream.

Some researchers have indicated that there are 7 "deadly" types of waste (Breyfogle, 2003; Tapping and Shuker, 2003), and others such as Imai (2012) indicated there are 8 types of waste, or Muda, including waste of time. However, based on the author's literature review and own experience, 13 types of waste can be identified. Table 9.1 describes these 13 types of wastes that can be found in any organization along with their causes and effects. These types of waste are strongly related to one another and, in many cases, cause one another and share overlapping and common characteristics.

The key challenge of waste or Muda is to see it and then use the proper tools to eliminate it.

Lean began at Toyota in the 1950s with the engineer Taiichi Ohno (Juran and Godfrey, 1999). It was influenced by the production line approach of Henry Ford, who brought work to the people, not people to work. The approach was initially called Toyota Production System (TPS). In the late 1980s, an American team from the International Motor Vehicle Association in Boston visited Toyota in Japan and introduced a similar approach called the "Just-in-Time (JIT)" system upon their return to the United States. In the 2000s, it famously became known as Lean systems. Just as "fat" is removed from meat to make it lean (*i.e.*, red meat), waste is removed from any system to make it a Lean system. Lean evolved from Lean manufacturing to Lean enterprise or Lean management. Nowadays, many companies implement an integrated Lean Six Sigma approach. One of the key reasons why Toyota came up with TPS or JIT was to cut down on wasted inventory and its associated costs. While inventory is a financial asset, it is considered a waste from the Lean perspective. In the past, Toyota carried huge inventories of supplied assembly parts and finished cars, which tied up tremendous amounts of cash. Cash is critical for any organization to survive. It is not enough to manufacture and push products out of the production line to be considered successful in business. If these products are not produced based on secured demand, they will end up unsold, costing the company substantial amounts of money to store, manage, handle, count, and preserve

Table 9.1   The 13 Types of Waste or Muda in Lean Management

Type of waste	Definition	Causes	Effects
Overproduction	Producing more items or documents or information than the customer requires	Producing quicker than the following step Batching work or batching movements for economic reasons Unbalanced resources	Queues Intermediate stocks Accumulated emails and reports Finished inventory
Waiting	Unnecessary time delay between the tasks where value is added	Responding or producing slower than required and poor design Unavailable resources Waiting for answers	People wait Machines and material wait Documents and transactions wait
Transportation	Unnecessary movement of an item, a product, a document or a piece of information	Distant suppliers and customers Long distances between work areas and poor layout Work areas set up by similarities instead of product flow	Lots of movement back and forth Cost of transportation from suppliers or to customers Batching, inventories, and high cost
Overprocessing	Any task or action done upon the item or document that is not required by the customer	Lack of knowledge or failure to know what the customer needs No standardized work Multiple inspections and approvals	Added time Added costs Variability
Inventory	Permitting more than one item to be in line or in a queue for the same process step, which appears as a backlog or a safety buffer or could be accumulating at a bottleneck	Takes too long to make or get a product or part Economic order quantity (buying larger amounts equivalent to years' worth of consumption) Batching	Cash tied up More space to store Obsolescence and time expiries Handling cost (receiving, storing, counting, and issuing)

(Continued)

Table 9.1 (Continued)

Type of waste	Definition	Causes	Effects
Motion	Excess movement done by the person to execute a process task	Poor organization Lack of visual controls Lack of standard methods	Cannot find things readily Running in circles and fatigue Back-and-forth movement
Defects (bottlenecks and inquiries)	Any damaged product or any rejected item by customers; any task not done right the first time or redone more than one time; asking for required information, which might be missing or provided incorrectly	Process variations Process complexity Lack of skills or knowledge Poor design Damaged while waiting Rushing	Extra resources for inspection and rework Delays Warranty claims Unsatisfied customers
Poor people utilization	Not using the abilities of people; inefficient utilization of people's time	Using hands while ignoring minds Not valuing ideas Fighting internally, turf protection Mistrust, not working as a team No mechanism Belief that people do not know enough or do not have the big-picture knowledge	Inefficiency Low morale Slow decision-making Change resistance Slow rate of improvement Lost opportunities Building barriers
Other resources	Not using the capabilities of equipment; inefficient utilization of material or energy	Underutilization of equipment or facilities Failure to maintain equipment Overconsumption of energy Failure to economically use, reuse, and recycle material	Low return on invested capital Equipment failure Extra cost for energy Environment damage

Inferior process	Not using standard approaches, best practices, or proper tools that are suitable to do the work efficiently, effectively, and safely	Inefficiencies Defect, extra motion Injuries Frustration
Information	Not tapping into useful insights based on data and reports, not providing correct data or not sharing it and delaying it	Missing or untimely information Incorrect information Withholding information Unusable information Using opinions and emotions, ignoring facts Mixed messages Bad decisions Ignorance Frustrations Lack of motivation
Reprioritization	Facing too many interruptions, multitasking and shifting back and forth between tasks without any plan and before finishing any task properly	A lot of work-in-progress Too many interruptions by colleagues, customers, or management demanding different tasks Poor planning Overproduction Lost time Customer/employee frustrations Higher cost
Time	Stagnation of material, products, and information or sitting in one place	Waiting for decision Waiting for signature or approval No delegation of authority No bias for action

them. They may even become obsolete or get damaged or expire (Six Sigma Training, personal communication, 2008).

If inventory is represented by water level, then lowering that inventory level can reveal other types of problems and waste in the same way that lowering the water level in a river can reveal rocks. These rocks can be a lack of proper scheduling, machine failure, quality issues, long transportation times, vendor issues, production line imbalances, long changeover times, poor housekeeping, miscommunication, and absenteeism (Suzaki, 1987; Juran and Godfrey, 1999).

Lean benefits include the reduction of lead time, costs, labor required, space, inventory, and defects. They also include an increase in customer responsiveness, capacity, employee satisfaction, and flexibility against demand fluctuation. Lean enables improvement teams to see from different perspectives: the customer perspective, the part or service perspective (as the part or information moves or stops) and the "start to end" perspective (from order to delivery).

One great example of waste is illustrated in house building. A typical house might take anywhere from 6 to 12 months to build. However, some companies build a house in a few weeks, or even days, using precast and assembled modules, fast-curing concrete, or 3D printing. This confirms that a huge portion of the 6- to 12-month period is a waste. If all the waiting time is eliminated and all the people involved are brought in to work simultaneously using an effective plan, the majority of waste can be eliminated. In one training session, the trainer showed a video (from 1992) of a competition organized by the Building Industry Association (BIA) in San Diego. A house building record of 2 hours and 45 minutes was announced by inspectors from the city's Building Inspection Department. This demonstrates the difference between processing time (value-added time) and the waiting time or wasted time between the value-added steps (Six Sigma Training, personal communication, 2008).

Lean is based on the following simple principles (Tapping and Shuker, 2003):

1. Understand the meaning of value versus waste.
2. Map the flow of the value using VSM.
3. Make the value flow, and remove waste.
4. Pull instead of push.
5. Seek perfection and continuous improvement.

For the operational cost to be reduced and for the waste to be eliminated, Imai (2012) suggested focusing on the following:

1. Enhance quality and productivity.
2. Lower the inventory levels.
3. Reduce the length of the production line, which leads to fewer people needed to manage it, fewer mistakes, less work-in-progress, and less lead time.
4. Minimize the machine downtime.
5. Minimize the space, and lower the lead time.

9.3 Quality Pillar # 54: Do Not Perform an Inspection or an Audit Unless It Adds Value. Signatures Often Become Formalities (Waste of Overprocessing and Waiting)

If a product or document is inspected without finding any mistake or gap, then there is no need for that inspection, as it did not add any value. Inspectors should never lose sight of their goal in inspection, which is to identify defects and areas of improvement. Like inspectors, managers review their subordinates' work for approval. Their goal should be to train their subordinates, provide them with the right tools, and convey their experience so that they find no issues with their employees' work. Once that goal is gradually achieved, that step of inspection can be eliminated, and the responsibility can be confidently delegated. Performing the same audit repeatedly and identifying the same type of gaps is not logical, as it indicates the previous audits did not rectify the gaps.

Similarly, approvals and applying signatures to documents are considered a waste of time unless they add value. Often, multiple signatures become routinely bureaucratic, as a top manager will sign once, confirming a certain member of their team has signed without even reading the document. It becomes a redundant formality, adding an unnecessary step to the process, in addition to the waiting associated with every signature. Repetitive types of contracts that are typically sent to a legal department for approval can be standardized into one contract with standardized terms, which can be preapproved by an organization's legal team. That way, only a small percentage of contracts with negotiated special terms are sent to the legal team for review. This speeds up the process and allows the legal team to focus on adding value somewhere else. Think of what managers can do with the time gained from similar initiatives, where they can spend more time with customers and generate more business and revenue.

Approvals and audits play key roles in governance. However, they need to be challenged and improved. Removing approvals and inspections should not be done all at once. It is recommended to do this gradually, while ensuring the customers' interests are protected.

When investigating why some processes have multiple approvals, the following scenario often takes place. When a problem occurs and two teams start blaming each other, one of the common—though incorrect—solutions is to add more layers of approval, assuming that this will prevent or rectify mistakes. In fact, it only introduces more delays into the process because it does not address the root causes.

Audits are important to ensure processes are conducted per standard criteria and documented best practices. However, auditors need to ensure that audits add value every time one is conducted. Audits cost time, effort, and money. If an audit keeps revealing the same gaps, someone needs to question whether the audit is useful. An audit can be an effective tool to challenge the current procedures and to identify the gaps in a process's performance against the documented processes. These gaps can be analyzed and eliminated to enhance the process performance, and audits can add value following Deming's famous plan-do-check-act (PDCA) cycle.

9.4 Quality Pillar # 55: Do Not Waste Money and Effort on Automation and Technology to Optimize Your Process before You Streamline It

Automation can be a catalyst to get teams to streamline and improve their processes. When automating a process, it first has to be prepared for automation. Automating redundant, unnecessary, or complex steps would be a waste of time and resources. Customers and employees alike would suffer from using automated platforms that contain inferior processes.

Similarly, if a process includes multiple templates or forms with many fields to be filled by the customer, these should be reviewed and simplified before they are automated.

For repetitive tasks, the robotic process automation (RPA) solution is becoming a trend. This tool is used to assist staff in adding value by performing repetitive manual tasks, thereby freeing up their time. Once again, simplification is a prerequisite for such task automation.

Imai (2012) stated that automation should not be perceived as a threat to human jobs because the Japanese introduced robots and automated solutions in their industries decades ago, and the market maintained its growth, while providing more jobs for people.

9.5 Quality Pillar # 56: Pull Instead of Push

The majority of companies use a push system in their manufacturing approach and end up with large amounts of costly inventory (Imai, 2012). During the industrial revolution, factories focused on producing more quantities to become profitable. This was evident in the United States after World War II, when mass production in factories "pushed" products to global markets. Decades later, competitors enhanced the quality of their products and grew their market shares gradually. This caused American manufacturers to face sales reductions and increased the amounts of product inventory. Mass production and pushing products to the markets were not proven to be economically feasible.

A few decades ago, Toyota's top management realized they had a large number of cars and subassemblies within their inventory. This tied up much cash and led to higher operational costs due to the need to build more warehouses to store the extra inventory and hire employees to manage it. When this happens, companies have to borrow money from banks to finance their operations. Even companies with good sales records may have to cease operations due to a lack of cash and poorly managed working capital (inventory, accounts payable, and accounts receivable). The Toyota team decided to embrace a Lean approach, where production was more synchronized with customer demand. Customers pull products instead of factories pushing them out. When customers are ready to receive products, they get made and delivered just in time. Toyota managed to improve its supply chain in a way that enabled them to partner with their best suppliers and bring them closer to their locations. They also partnered with their customers to create a continuous flow of deliveries instead of pushing out huge batches of products. This has been achieved to the extent that subassemblies and parts arrive every morning at a Toyota factory, and trucks depart with finished cars at the end of the day for dealers' facilities (Six Sigma Training, personal communication, 2008).

Pulling has great advantages in terms of economic profitability and customer responsiveness. It became easier for Toyota to adapt to customers' changing requirements, as they were not stuck with large amounts of finished products waiting to be forced onto the customer.

In an office environment, manually processing documents in a process stream involving various departments can be challenging, especially if their physical locations are not close to one another. This encourages employees to batch their work and wait to send their finished files to the next department in the stream for processing. These batched files arrive in a large bundle at the desk of an employee who can become demotivated due to the large amount of work suddenly appearing on their desk, which negatively affects their productivity and the quality of their work. Obviously, the solution to this situation lies in changing the flow into a pull system where batches are gradually reduced until they reach a single-piece flow. This often requires hiring a delivery person or changing the physical location of offices. Automated workflow solutions introduced by information technology teams within an organization can effectively ensure smooth flow, visibility of transaction queues, fewer delays, and less paperwork.

The use of Japanese Kanban also enables pulling instead of pushing. Kanbans are signals for pulling work or material from the supplying units or work centers. They can consist of a visual signal, such as a light, a computer message, or cards that instruct or authorize the replenishment of specific types and quantities of parts. Sometimes, they are simply an empty paper tray or floor space, indicating that the production unit is ready to receive another order or subassembly for processing. Kanbans help control the flow without the need to schedule it at every location within the value stream. Figure 9.3 shows an illustration of Kanban card movement as well as product movement. Thus, the customer station gets what the customer needs and the supplier station produces what is needed to replenish consumed orders.

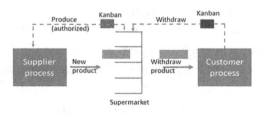

Figure 9.3   A lean system with visual means (supermarket and Kanban) to control production between processes without scheduling as adapted from Six Sigma Training, personal communication (2008).

A good example is the vending machine, where only what is consumed (pulled) by the customers is replaced. In a factory, "supermarket" shelves or floor locations can be established to organize flow in a "pulling" manner to gradually move closer to the one-piece flow, or an ideal lean flow. This sounds slower than pushing in a production environment, but it is much faster in reality. A Lego exercise can be used to simulate various scenarios and enable teams to visualize and feel how an ideal Lean flow system works.

The objectives of a pull system include providing a method of controlling and balancing the flow of resources, eliminating waste (transporting, storing, *etc.*), supplying the product at the rate of consumption, and achieving a visual workplace where abnormal conditions can be quickly spotted.

9.6 Quality Pillar # 57: A Single Point of Chaos

Several years ago, while passing through an airport, a long wait was experienced in a customs queue. It was noticed that some travelers were processed slower by the officer because their fingerprints and eye scans had to be captured. Obviously, there was a language barrier. However, in such delays and bottlenecks in any process, one can see how important it is to isolate such process steps so the majority of transactions (which are defect-free or do not form a special case requiring complex processing) can flow smoothly through the system stream. In another airport, all these first-time entry cases are processes in a separate flow, making it easier and faster for regular travelers to pass through customs.

Another example comes from an accounting department. In a retail company, the accounts payable department was composed of 12 accountants, who handled all suppliers' invoices in a three-way matching process. The invoices sent by the suppliers had to match the original purchase order issued by the procurement department and the delivery note issued by the receiving employee at the distribution center. First, all incoming invoices were sorted into 12 piles, one for each accountant, containing their handled suppliers' accounts. Then each accountant would process the payment after confirming that the details of the three documents mentioned previously matched, including supplier details, goods description, quantities, and prices. In the case of a mismatch, the accountant would try to contact the supplier, receiver, or buyer to rectify the situation. However, this troubleshooting step was tedious and not easily resolved. This resulted in a backlog of unresolved invoices, which filled about 30 boxes and caused suppliers to complain of payment delays; they also threatened to stop any future shipments. In addition, if an accountant was on vacation, all their suppliers would experience additional delays. Using a Lean Six Sigma Kaizen approach, the team mapped the process and came up with a new process design where sorting was minimized and the 12 accountants were divided into three groups of 4 accountants each. Each group had a rotating troubleshooter position so that any mismatch is passed directly to them, isolating the point of chaos and focusing the efforts of the other three accountants within the group. Within a couple of months, the team was able to catch up on and clean up all the delayed invoices. This also allowed for cross-training of accountants and enabled the effective resolution of various mismatching problems. Eventually, the team planned to move into a first-come-first-serve process or first-in-first-out (FIFO), where no sorting took place at all, as all accountants work in one group with only one troubleshooter. Other benefits included more flexibility for taking vacations and offering suppliers an earlier payment, provided they granted a reasonable discount on the payment due.

In a similar process, Mazda moved from using hundreds of accountants to a handful, by eliminating the need for creating invoices. Payment can be initiated automatically through the enterprise resource planning (ERP) system once the receiver approves it based on matching the goods received with the purchase order information in the system itself or once the cars are shipped out of the factory because no car can leave without the supplied parts installed (Six Sigma Training, personal communication, 2021).

In addition, more companies now use robotic process automation (RPA) to enhance similar cases that involve substantial manual work. The software solution mimics the repetitive steps an accountant takes to automatically execute the processes efficiently and effectively while learning from special cases as they arise and which are resolved by the software engineer or the reviewing accountant.

Receptionists also act as single points of chaos to sort and ease the pressure on other employees who are handling various types of transactions. However, the ultimate goal is to determine how to automate processes after simplification and provide user-friendly processes, so clients can expend the least amount of effort and time on them. For example, clients can request a service online instead of coming to an office, and the provider can either visit them or provide the service remotely.

9.7 Quality Pillar # 58: Ensure the Production Line or Streamline Is Balanced

When tracing value offered through a stream of steps from the moment a customer order is received to the moment it is delivered, it is important to consider the work balance in that value stream. Imbalance, or Mura, as the Japanese call it, happens when one step takes more time than the other steps, causing a bottleneck that results in more pressure on the employees working on that particular step, as they appear to be working more slowly. This will also result in much idle time in steps that have shorter cycle times, creating significant waste (*i.e.*, Muda of waiting) and costing the manufacturer.

Fixing such a challenge lies in understanding the customer demand rate and aligning all steps' cycle times to the demand rate. The customer is like a maestro, and the demand rate dictates the beat or rhythm at every step in the value stream. This can be achieved by adding more workers to that bottleneck step or by breaking down its components and reassigning some parts to other steps. Figure 9.4 shows an example of a value stream consisting of three steps, where the second step was the bottleneck and how it was balanced.

Work imbalance is also related to variations in the process, as it requires stability and consistency. Balancing the process enhances it and makes it more economical, predictable, and manageable.

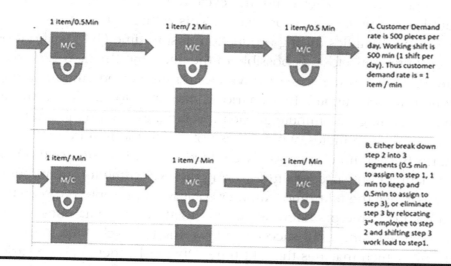

Figure 9.4   A work balance chart showing a portion of a value stream before and after balancing.

9.8 Quality Pillar # 59: Aim to Match the Cycle Time with the "Takt" Time

If production is a symphony, then the customer is the maestro. Per the lean pulling system, the customer dictates the rhythm of the operation. If an operation runs at a slower rate than the customer demand, the customer will be unsatisfied and will seek an alternative competitor. On the other hand, if an operation is running faster than the customer demands, it will result in a high waste of inventory, which is costly to the manufacturer.

To design a production line with many work centers, one needs to study the customer demand rate and conduct a workload analysis. This will help decide the number of employees and the breakdown of tasks or work elements to achieve time balancing.

When studying the customer demand rate, an important term often used is the "takt" time, which refers to the pulse of the market. "Takt" is a term borrowed from the German language, referring to the baton used by an orchestra conductor (Imai, 2012). The demand rate or pace is calculated by dividing the total daily demand of the customer by the number of working minutes per shift. For example, if the demand is 500 units per day and the factory operates for 500 minutes per day shift, then the demand rate is 1 unit per minute. This means that for every takt time of 1 minute, a unit has to flow from one workstation to the next, causing a domino effect across all VSM workstations so that a unit would reach the customer every 1 minute (*i.e.*, takt time). On the other hand, the cycle time represents the actual time taken until one unit leaves a workstation. This actual time can be affected by various abnormalities during production. Just-in time (JIT) is about bringing the cycle time as close as possible to the takt time (Imai, 2012).

Figure 9.5 shows three scenarios with a takt time of one minute (demand rate is one unit per minute). In scenario A, one operator works on three machines, spending one minute at each machine, amounting to a total cycle time of three minutes, which does not match the required takt time. In scenario B, two more operators are added, which is costly (one operator per machine) but succeeds in lowering the cycle time to one minute per unit and matches the takt time. Another solution is presented in scenario C, where a total of three operators work on a total of nine machines (an additional cost in machines) but succeed in lowering the cycle time to one minute per unit, which matches the takt time. Obviously, there can be various solutions. However, the more feasible solution will be selected. In this case, scenario B appears to be more feasible.

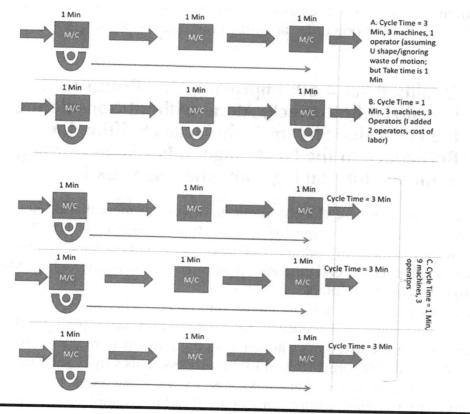

Figure 9.5   A work balance chart showing three scenarios of cycle times compared to a fixed demand of one unit per minute.

Typically, the number of operators needed is equal to the total cycle time divided by the takt time. For example, if a cycle time is 3 minutes and the takt time is 1 minute, then three operators are required. If the result is a fraction, such as 3.25, then the process needs to be changed to reduce the cycle time, and only 3.0 operators are required. A standardized work approach is used to ensure all operators follow the best work practices so that they always satisfy the required takt time (Tapping and Shuker, 2003).

Another tool used to orchestrate the flow between process steps is called a "pitch". A "pitch" is a measure of paced withdrawal that serves as a basic unit of the work scheduled to flow from one step to the next. It represents the frequency at which finished items are withdrawn from a step in the process and the amount of work scheduled to be released to that process step. Pitch is a multiple of takt time (by the selected number of work units), and it establishes a consistent workflow for a work unit to move from the beginning to the end of the value stream. It is used when it is not realistic to monitor the flow of one order at a time (Tapping and Shuker, 2003).

9.9 Quality Pillar # 60: Improving One Process Stage (Localized Bottleneck) Alone without Considering the Full Value Stream Only Means Shifting the Bottleneck to the Next Stage. It Is Like Rewarding Someone for Making Someone Else Look Bad

This is the problem with localized efforts of improvement that do not pay attention to the wider perspective of the whole value stream map (VSM). Narrowing the focus to optimize one step is not the best approach because it may not impact the end customer positively. This is exactly why a VSM approach is always favorable.

The right approach, and the first step in process improvement, will always be to map the cross-functional process from start to end per the perspective of the external customer with the participation of representatives of all the functions involved in the process. This way, a solid plan and a structured approach are followed across the value stream steps, where various opportunities of improvement are listed in an implementation action plan. One of these improvement actions can be focused on improving one process step. However, it is more likely that the selected step would be prioritized for potentially being the bottleneck and would be looked at from the perspective of the whole VSM. This approach from a holistic VSM perspective has many advantages, such as the following (Six Sigma Training, personal communication, 2008):

1. It enables managers and employees from various functions to see the value stream from other functions' perspective.
2. It enables them to see the value stream from the external customers' perspective.
3. It enables them to see the value stream from the product or service perspective.
4. It enables them to see the value stream from the full end-to-end perspective.
5. It enables them to collectively identify areas for improvement and concurrently work on redesigning the whole value stream to enhance it.

Chapter 10

Fundamental Pillars Related to Visual Management

10.1 Quality Pillar # 61: Visual Management: Abnormalities Should Be Made Visible at a Glance

When driving a car, knowing the speed, fuel level, and engine temperature at various times is important to avoiding problems (*e.g.*, exceeding the speed limits, running out of fuel, and facing mechanical failures). The vehicle's dashboard design enables the driver to monitor these indicators and receive any other message that is important to know while navigating. Similarly, in any process, employees and managers alike must have dashboards or visual means that enable them to monitor process performance over time.

If a picture is better than a thousand words, then a visual workplace is better, as it provides just-in-time information (Tapping *et al.*, 2002).

The visual workplace is one of the great tools in the Japanese Lean approach, focusing on transparency of performance and waste identification. Truly, waste that is easy to see will become easy to eliminate. Consequently, more effort can support value-adding activities.

Hiding problems, bottlenecks, work imbalance (Mura), and various types of waste (Muda) will hinder process improvement efforts. This is an essential part of the quality culture, as well as the employees' responsibility and discipline, in any organization, which directly impacts the level of quality the customers receive.

In addition to Mura and Muda, a third term that Lean management often uses is "Muri", identifying strain and fatigue that operators endure during

DOI: 10.4324/9781032688374-14

their work, especially when they must perform repetitive tasks in a workplace that is not ergonomically designed according to proper human-factors' engineering rules. Muri leads to Muda because it impacts quality and leads to product defects.

Visual management practices include a clear display of products and performance records that remind all employees of Gemba status, in terms of quality, cost, and delivery (Imai, 2012).

The goal of a visual factory (or visual management, in general) is to give the management and employees control of the workplace. Mistake-proofing techniques can help achieve high levels of control, eliminating causes of errors or at least flagging (using alarms) and mitigating them (Tapping *et al.*, 2002). This control is a result of information availability in real time for everyone to see. At a "glance", anyone should be able to tell whether the team is operating in a normal or abnormal state.

The first step in improvement that a manager must take is acknowledging that the process he or she is managing is not perfect. If they do not admit it, they will never improve, as they continue to work busily in a firefighting and reactive mode. As a matter of fact, the process will never be perfect. Process improvement is a continuous journey toward a virtual and ideal state that can be almost impossible to achieve but is at least possible to approach, one step at a time. As Joseph Juran described it, the journey of continuous improvement happens one breakthrough project at a time. Each project delivers a breakthrough improvement that significantly enhances the process KPI of focusing in the desired direction and reducing variation, to achieve better process consistency and stability. One project at a time means that the project team maps the current (as-is) state of the process and follows an improvement plan to migrate to the future (to-be) state, which eventually becomes the new current state, and the journey continues.

Visual management is a great way to motivate employees. For example, the employees were greatly motivated in a facility that displayed a live score of bonuses tied to production, almost the same as displaying a sports game score live in any match. If a machine fails, the bonus score decreases until employees can fix it (money is not the only motivator, but it does encourage focus). Live scores of productivity, defects, or any KPI generally will lead to advanced employees and management team involvement in daily operations. Implementing that positively and progressively and achieving it through visual dashboards—monitors, or simple boards, to indicate the status of current KPIs relative to corresponding targets—can make the lives of employees much easier. Alphanumeric labeling, color-coded characters, magnetic shapes, manual boards, and electronic screens can display visual information to all employees at a glance. This will enhance communication, so managers can see where and at what time they must intervene to offer support and add value. Examples of visual boards include the following:

a. A board showing the layout of a yard with all the storage locations, with magnetic cards or tokens with written information readily indicating the shipments staged at each location. Thus, shipments become easy for both a yard employee and a delivery-truck driver to locate.
b. A board showing where each employee is working during the shift for better communication and planning of work. Each employee's name printed on a medal gets hung on a location pin.
c. A board showing targets versus actual trends of KPIs (*e.g.*, cost, productivity, quality, delivery, safety, daily operational tasks).
d. A board showing maintenance teams or contracting teams and locations at projects by day of week or by the hour of the day.
e. A board to show the status of projects (*e.g.*, installation status, stages with progress levels, assigned teams, challenges, performed inspections, work certification, and payment status).

Also, the visual management of files is essential. Frequently used files (associated with live projects) require proper labeling and organization at specific shelf locations, also properly labeled and visible from a distance, to avoid waste of time spent walking or opening cabinet doors to see if files are available. Removing cabinet doors to eliminate the waste of motion or at least using glass doors one can see through is more convenient. For example, to enable the visual management of files, use colored tabs arranged as per an index page; fold drawings, like the German DN-40 standard for large engineering drawings, into A4-sized sheets that leaves an edge sufficient for punching and box-filing. Another example is a meeting room that has a clear electronic screen, indicating if it is available (green) or already booked (red) for a certain meeting.

Another form of visual management is the andon system. A display device of visual control, usually positioned above the production cell or line, provides information about the present condition of the operation and warns the operators of any developing problem. Sometimes, an audible signal might accompany or replace a visual one. Thus, visual management includes using signs, measurements, pacing devices, and real-time visual or audible feedback, easily allowing recognition of the difference between normal and abnormal conditions. Errors register quickly, increasing efficiency and maintaining it over time (Six Sigma Training, personal communication, 2008).

According to Imai (2012), managers must ensure having a visual display of the 5Ms (*i.e.*, manpower or operators, machines, material, methods, and measurements). Some examples are operators who must view morale, tracking it in terms of counting suggestions and absenteeism, skill levels using cross-training matrices, and the quality of operator output. Applying it for machines, managers must see the quality of output and whether it stops automatically, along with lubricant levels and internal malfunctions, visible through the transparent housing of machines. For material, they must see if the flow is smooth, the storage location is clear, and inventory levels are appropriate. For methods, they must see standardized methods showing sequence and quality information. For measurements, they must see the status of the operation and actuals versus targets.

Visual management helps workers gain control over their workplace, the focus of the 5S tool (Tapping *et al.*, 2002) that the next section discusses.

10.2 Quality Pillar # 62: Use 5S as a Measure or a Thermometer for Indicating the Health of the Company in Terms of Its Internal Culture, Focused on Employee Discipline and How Organized the Workplace Is

Have you ever misplaced some notes or wasted time searching for a document location? Have you helped somebody find a file, the latest form, or a tool? Have you wondered how others perform a certain process or filled in for someone on vacation? Have you wondered how your team is doing right now, how they are progressing toward their goals, or what their priorities are?

All these questions can be answered with the help of "5S". 5S is a tool for enhancing workplace organization, the work environment, and cleanliness. It supports a zero tolerance for waste, enabling workers to visually manage their work area and see all types of waste there so that they can eliminate them. It includes cleanliness, but that is only one part of it.

Prior to implementing 5S, operators typically do the pre-5Ss: scrounge (borrow), snip (take), stash, scramble, and search. These are all symptoms for the lack of 5S implementation, reflecting the health of a company. As a matter of fact, 5S comprises five steps described by five words starting with the letter *S* in the Japanese language. Each *S* designates a progression in implementation that can be translated into the following (Six Sigma Training, personal communication, 2008):

- Sort: Separate everything (Gembutsu) in the work area into two groups—things needed to perform tasks and things that can be removed because they are not needed. Using red tags to indicate the status of the unrequired items (*e.g.*, functioning, obsolete, broken, misplaced) is recommended.
- Set in order: Organize the needed items in order of priority and usage. Label them properly, and use visual identification tools, such as color-coding, categorizing shapes, and alphanumeric labeling for ease of tracking. A famous saying often used in this step of 5S is: "A place for everything and everything is in its place" (*i.e.*, everything is returned back to its place). Thus, it mainly concerns self-discipline in ensuring that waste is not tolerated and defects are not accepted. Also recommended here is finding adjacencies that work well together, to minimize the waste of movement. The "milk run" concept can be used as applicable, where a runner (similar to a postman) or a device can move information and documents, enabling flow to happen without delay. Simplify the flow, so it requires minimum movement and space. Unnecessary items are typically unsafe, defective, obsolete (outdated), unused, or more than required (extra or duplicate). Necessary items are typically used by someone on the team for daily or periodic work. Red-tagged items are the unnecessary items taken to the holding (quarantine) area for auctioning and disposal. For required items or documents, the rule of six can be used to organize them (see explanation in the following).
- Sweep: Clean, shine and ensure that the workplace is "customer inviting". How a customer would feel and form an impression when walking into an organized office or another office that is not organized is clearly different. Also, inspect for damages and abnormal conditions while cleaning. Clean, inspect, detect, correct, and finally prevent a recurrence. Some factories paint their machines white to make spotting any leaks or failures easier, which helps in rectifying problems at early stages. Also, when firefighters wash their trucks themselves, it enables them to inspect their equipment, rectify any issues, ensure reliability while cleaning, and avoid surprising failures.

■ Standardize: Use a standard process, communicate the guiding instructions visually, train the team, audit progress, and adjust as required. Set a standard best practice to which the team must adhere, to stabilize the process and minimize defects or problems. Obviously, this leads to expending more efforts on improvement rather than on firefighting and corrective actions. Follow Deming's famous PDCA cycle.

■ Sustain: Ensure the standardized process is followed and maintained regularly, using audits, and follow up until it becomes a habit ingrained in all employees' behavior. Continuously improve these practices to become the best in one's domain.

Some of the advantages of 5S (Six Sigma Training, personal communication, 2008) include the following:

■ Safety: Better organizations reduce unnecessary motion, decreasing the "opportunities" for accidents, such as slipping, tripping, and falling. Aisles become clear, and problems are identified easily. "Safety" can also be added to the five parts of 5S to indicate the importance of safety in all aspects of organizing any workplace, making 5S "5S+1" (not 6S, which could be confused with Six Sigma).

■ Quality, customer responsiveness, and visual control (easy control of stock levels).

■ Time management (faster communication of transaction status).

Imai (2012) presented a story about workplace organization. An auto-manufacturer visited a plant in another country to evaluate whether it was suitable to become their automotive parts supplier. Upon their arrival at the facility, the visiting team directly asked for a tour of the shop floor (the Gemba), where the actual work happens, before sitting in any meeting room. Once the tour ended, the visiting team regretted the plant was not ready for designation as their parts supplier and left the hosts, in shock, asking how the visiting team decided even before hearing the service offering. The visiting team explained they did not find the required level of self-discipline in the Gemba. Workers did not care how organized or clean the work area was, and they put out their cigarettes on the floor next to the production machines. They simply could not trust those workers with the required attitude to produce high-quality parts, as they lacked the discipline to keep their manufacturing cells clean. Therefore, 5S helps to gauge how committed a team is to quality.

5S is about providing employees with control over their workplace (Tapping *et al.*, 2002). It is about employee discipline to always maintain the Gemba state of mind. As Imai (2012) put the Gemba state of mind: "Don't accept defects, don't make defects, and don't pass on defects".

5S is applicable in any industry or facility. For example, Romanians implemented 5S Kaizen in some of their cities' municipalities (Imai, 2012).

The level of workplace organization is the same as a thermometer reading. They both are a true reflection of health. The same as a thermometer can measure the temperature to indicate if the body is healthy, 5S is a tool to gauge how disciplined and healthy an organization is. 5S templates can provide a strong auditing tool that can not only indicate current health but also provide a plan for improvement, showing how a team can score higher.

In another case, a factory team had not conducted proper cleaning and workplace organization for quite some time. Ironically, after removing all the dust, one frame appeared to praise keeping the place as clean as "home". The team engaged in a Kaizen event that included a full revision of the layout design and machine locations; tools organization; new paint for all walls; shiny paint for all isles, indicating safe walkways; full cleaning of windows to allow light to shine in, and even buying some flower pots to decorate the entrances. All this had a great impact on the morale of the operators, making them feel like it was a new factory, instilling pride in the place, enhancing their discipline to ensure keeping it organized, and motivating them to be more productive with fewer defects.

In a case encountered in another factory, the team conducted a Kaizen event and managed to sort and organize various items of raw material used in product assembly. All were properly set in order, using various fixtures to allow for ease of identification and access. Also, inventory levels were studied, and Kanban cards were used to easily place orders when a reorder point was reached after consuming a portion of the inventory, often indicated by the color "red". Sometimes, yellow was used to mean coming close to red, while a green color meant "safe", in terms of inventory level. Red meant that there was enough material to last long enough until an order was placed and goods were received from a supplier. A buffer is a good idea when gradually starting to implement Kanbans. Once the system is stabilized, these buffer amounts can be challenged and further reduced.

A general rule of thumb is to remove any item not for use during the next 30 days (Imai, 2012). Another rule often mentioned in Lean training relevant to 5S is called the "rule of six". Items or documents needed every six hours or in less than a day are kept handy, accessible, and typically placed on the desktop. Items needed within six days or a week are kept in a drawer or cabinet close by. If required once every six weeks, the item is kept in a shared cabinet away from a busy work area and regularly needed files and tools. If needed every six months, then whether it is really needed or not probably should be questioned. If still required, it can be stored away in an archiving area or a warehouse. If not needed, it can be auctioned or disposed of. Archived documents must have a clear process of deciding what to keep, for how long, and how to properly dispose of them. This is usually prepared in consultation with the firm's legal department, to ensure proper file management. Of course, archiving physical documents is recommended only if online archiving is not sufficient. Archiving is typically required for legal reasons or regulatory compliance. However, it is important to specify the required period for keeping the file before disposal, bearing in mind the cost of archiving.

Generally anticipated as a result of proper 5S exercise is the ability to locate any item in 30 seconds or less. Taking a long time to locate a file is an indicator of low-level efficiency and does not reflect professionalism during audits (audits on their own are not the goal). One can easily tell when running low on something and reorder before running out. Items that might typically be missing are quickly identified without searching.

5S is considered the first step in the Kaizen journey, making abnormalities quickly visible (Imai, 2012).

10.3 Quality Pillar # 63: There Shall Be a Place for Everything, and Everything Shall Be in Its Place (Related to 5S, Detailed in Section 10.2)

When technicians or employees who work as a team in a maintenance garage, inside an office, or even at mobile locations share tools or files, establishing a clear system for ease of location and retrieval of the shared tools and items is essential. In various cases, buying additional tools to eliminate sharing can be feasible, as each team member will be better off with no chance of missing the required tools to perform the assigned jobs. If no system exists, employees will often get frustrated as they try to urgently locate a tool or a catalog to use in a task they are trying to finish. This frustration will lead to low morale, negative attitudes among the team members, and thus, low productivity. Notably, employees who pick these items to use in their daily tasks are not to blame for the loss of the items because they do not know where to put them back when they finish using them. There is no "home" specified for these items as part of a standard system that can drive proper behavior and discipline. Having such a system will resolve this matter once and for all. 5S can help achieve this workplace organization and is easily implemented in offices and factories using a Kaizen approach. The second *S* in 5S refers to setting things in order, focusing on ensuring a specified location for everything, and each thing is always staged in its location.

Another example of a tool for organizing items' places is the shadow board, where tools can be placed in a specified place indicated by a visual picture or a shaded drawing of the tool on a desk or a board, hung on a wall. This is also sometimes associated with an alphanumeric label as well. This board enables the team to always find the needed tool, provided that everyone follows the process for putting the tool back in its specified place, once done using it. A daily audit at the end of each shift is required at the beginning of this process implementation to ensure it becomes the new habit (typically in a few weeks).

Similarly, for electronic files, the discipline to properly name and file all documents ensures ease of access at any time. For example, properly storing large drawings can be challenging. Obviously, if soft copies are not sufficient, among the best practices for filing physical drawings is using the German DN-40 standard for folding large drawings into an A4 size, leaving an extended edge suitable for punching and box-filing.

10.4 Quality Pillar # 64: Tools Shall Be Stored at the Point of Use (Related to 5S, Detailed in Section 10.2)

In addition to the previous principle of assigning each tool a specific location, ensuring that the assigned location or "home" is as close as possible to the place where the tool is often used is important. This will minimize the waste of motion, transportation, and waiting.

This applies to materials as well. The frequency of usage shall determine the priority of which material location will be closer to the work area (usage or processing area). In an office, all required stationary items, paper forms, or the required electronic tablets, and scanning tools are placed handily for immediate service provision, to waste less time on non-value-adding activity. Various examples illustrate this idea, based on actual improvement projects that were encountered by the author (Six Sigma Training, personal communication, 2008):

■ Placing a laminated sheet of the most frequently used tags or barcodes next to the radio frequency identification (RFID) reader, to scan them easily when issuing material from inventory.

■ Using a mobile RFID reader to scan and receive goods instead of carrying the goods to the RFID location.

■ Properly placing tags or barcodes on the shelves in a warehouse for ease of processing material.

■ Feeding a sawmill with two types of logs (raw material) while ensuring that the most frequently consumed material is stored closer to the mill infeed than the other material. This directly relates to properly analyzing the time and motion of the loaders handling the raw material in the yard.

■ An engineer who must walk from his office on the ground floor to his manager's office on the second floor to have a drawing stamped because the only stamp is kept there is easily noticeable as part of a Lean Six Sigma (LSS) value stream mapping (VSM) exercise, following a Gemba walk through the process. The distant location encourages waiting until a batch of drawings is ready to be stamped all at once in one trip, increasing the waste of waiting.

■ In an airplane parts manufacturing facility (as part of a benchmarking visit), the following case was encountered. As a result of various improvement projects, production cells required fewer operators, and thus, the best of them were selected and reassigned to work in a newly created innovation center. This assembled team focused on creating jigs, fixtures, and tools or equipment that could enhance quality and productivity across the facility. One of their projects was the introduction of small ovens built specifically for curing the airplane parts produced in a specific cell. Previously, operators had to carry the parts all the way to a shared large oven and often had to wait their turn—the curing cycles for various items are not equal, and a curing cycle cannot be interrupted to feed other parts. Putting this small oven right at the point of use avoided much waste, and operators could better utilize their time, focusing on adding value to other activities.

10.5 Quality Pillar # 65: Use Paced Withdrawal or a Heijunka System for Visual Control

Heijunka or "level loading" is about the leveling and distribution of workload proportions over a day or a shift, balancing them while ensuring the capacity can cater to customer demand, in terms of volumes and variety of products. Production is leveled using concepts or tools such as paced withdrawal, a Heijunka box and the runner (water spider or Mizusumashi). Paced withdrawal is used when there is no product variety as all pitch increments are identical. Production slots are divided using standard pack-out quantities batched according to customer requirements. In Heijunka, the paced withdrawal is broken into units based on the volumes and variety of ordered products. It helps to establish a Lean pull system when dealing with a variety of products. The Heijunka box is used by dividing it into slots representing pitch increments. Pitch refers to the amount of time, based on takt time, at which a work-in-process (WIP) quantity or a standard required pack size is released to a downstream operation. Each slot typically has a Kanban authorizing the making of customer orders. The arrangement is based on volumes and variety (Tapping *et al.*, 2002). The runner role (water spider or Mizusumashi) is created to enable frequent pickup and delivery of material in a plant (Imai, 2012), by a material handler who plays a critical role in ensuring flow occurs across the value stream. The runner must also assess the ability of the flow to meet the targets, flag abnormalities, and challenge the team to solve problems. The position of a runner can result from freeing up employees through Kaizen events that improve the efficiency of work cells. The runner uses a Heijunka box similar to how a postman uses mailboxes (Tapping *et al.*, 2002).

Here is a simple example for the purpose of illustration. If a shift spans 500 minutes daily and a customer requires 500 pieces of product A and 250 pieces of product B daily, in batches of 25, then the total daily requirement is 750 pieces and the takt time is 500 minutes/750 pieces, equal to 0.67 minutes or 40 seconds per piece. This means the pitch is equal to 25 pieces per standard pack times 40 seconds, or 1,000 seconds per pitch or pack. Every Kanban corresponds to a pack of 25 pieces, and thus, product A requires 20 Kanbans, and product B requires 10 Kanbans. Leveled production can be realized based on the ratio of (A:B = 2:1), reflected in the way the Heijunka box is loaded with Kanbans. These Kanban cards are physically placed in the slots of the Heijunka box corresponding to the pitch increments, in which production lots will be released to shipping and eventually replenished. This cycle takes place every 1,000 seconds (Table 10.1 illustrates the

Table 10.1 Heijunka Box and Kanbans Example

Start time of each Kanban	7:00:00 AM	7:16:40 AM	7:33:20 AM	7:50:00 AM	8:06:40 AM	8:23:20 AM	8:40:00 AM	8:56:40 AM	9:13:20 AM	9:30:00 AM	9:40:00 AM
End time for each Kanban	7:16:40 AM	7:33:20 AM	7:50:00 AM	8:06:40 AM	8:23:20 AM	8:40:00 AM	8:56:40 AM	9:13:20 AM	9:30:00 AM	9:40:00 AM	9:56:40 AM
Kanban number	1	2	3	4	5	6	7	8	9	BREAK	10
Product A	1	1		1	1		1	1			1
Product B			1			1			1		

Start time of each Kanban	9:56:40 AM	10:13:20 AM	10:30:00 AM	10:46:40 AM	11:03:20 AM	11:20:00 AM	11:36:40 AM	11:53:20 AM	12:10:00 PM	12:30:00 PM	12:46:40 PM
End time for each Kanban	10:13:20 AM	10:30:00 AM	10:46:40 AM	11:03:20 AM	11:20:00 AM	11:36:40 AM	11:53:20 AM	12:10:00 PM	12:30:00 PM	12:46:40 PM	1:03:20 PM
Kanban number	11	12	13	14	15	16	17	18	BREAK	19	20
Product A	1		1	1		1	1			1	1
Product B		1			1			1			

Start time of each Kanban	1:03:20 PM	1:20:00 PM	1:36:40 PM	1:53:20 PM	2:10:00 PM	2:20:00 PM	2:36:40 PM	2:53:20 PM	3:10:00 PM	3:26:40 PM	3:43:20 PM
End time for each Kanban	1:20:00 PM	1:36:40 PM	1:53:20 PM	2:10:00 PM	2:20:00 PM	2:36:40 PM	2:53:20 PM	3:10:00 PM	3:26:40 PM	3:43:20 PM	5:00:00 PM
Kanban number	21	22	23	24	BREAK	25	26	27	28	29	30
Product A	1	1	1			1	1	1	1	1	
Product B				1							1

same example). Obviously, this approach works more effectively when used to simplify complex combinations of numerous products that customers demand daily.

10.6 Quality Pillar # 66: Use a Supermarket of Inventory to Enable a Continuous Flow of Goods (See Section 9.5 on "Lean Pulling Principle"), Buffer Inventory to Meet Changing Patterns of Customer Orders, and Safety Inventory to Meet Demand in the Case of Disruptions

A supermarket is a system for storing a specific amount of WIP or finished inventory and replenishing what internal or external customers pull. It sustains a continuous flow when it is difficult to maintain. In addition, the buffer inventory will meet variations in demand due to fluctuations in ordering patterns and takt time. Safety inventory meets customer demand in the case of disruptions. Typically, supermarket inventory can equal one day's worth of inventory, whereas buffer and safety inventory might not exceed two days' worth of needed inventory. However, all staged inventory is still considered waste that ultimately must be challenged and reduced (Tapping *et al.*, 2002).

For example, one may consider how a vending machine works. The runner will only replenish the exact type and quantity of what was emptied or customers purchased. This setup enables pulling. In another example, a supermarket can stand between steps of the operation, in the form of shelves, trays, or simply empty spaces on the shop floor. Several rectangles painted on the floor right before a production cell indicate the places where subassemblies waiting to be processed by the next production cell can occupy pallets or trollies. This mechanism will control the amount of inventory allowed to accumulate before a production cell. An empty rectangle can be considered a Kanban, signaling the authorization for a preceding production cell (or warehouse) to send another subassembly or material, specified using a visual board and Kanban cards containing the required information. Figure 10.1 shows an illustration of Kanban card movement as well as product movement.

In a Kaizen event at a truss plant that specialized in the design and assembly of wooden house roofs, the goal was to create a value stream map to identify opportunities for improvement. Initially, it was evident that two separate teams were blaming each other for process deficiencies. The first team was the office team, including sales, engineering, and production planning, who complained that it took almost one full week for an order to go through the required production steps on the shop floor. The second team included the shop floor crew, who complained of frequent production interruptions forcing them to stop what they were doing, remove the subassemblies, and change the machine setup to start working on a VIP urgent order. It can be imagined how frustrating this might be for operators who take pride in their work and dislike wasting their time and effort.

The team members were trained on the basics of Lean management, types of waste, and value stream mapping. They were asked to leave their differences outside the Kaizen event as they engaged to cooperate in mapping the current state while highlighting areas of opportunity. They were encouraged during the event to see the flow of value from the customer's perspective and to reflect on how each person's work affects others. Once the value stream was done, the team was assigned to collect data and conduct an analysis of the gaps in preparation for another Kaizen conducted three weeks later to map the future state of the process value stream.

A key result of the current-state Kaizen was that the process took one week on average both at the office as well as on the shop floor. So, no more complaints about delays on the shop floor were heard, since they found that it took one week from the moment a customer inquiry arrived until a production order was released to the shop floor. The reason is the several steps of initial and final design modifications and approvals required before a customer would agree to proceed with production.

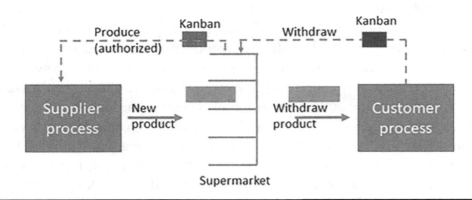

Figure 10.1   A Lean system with visual means (supermarket and Kanban) to control production between processes without scheduling, as adapted from Six Sigma Training, personal communication (2008).

In terms of the shop floor operation, an early step was noticed to be taking a shorter cycle time than the other steps. This step simply included the cutting of various lumber pieces into various lengths and arranging them on trollies to await assembly in a later step. However, the shop floor was literally flooded with many trollies already staged for many future production orders. This was a clear example of waste of inventory. In addition, there was no clear tagging of trollies indicating the jobs to which they belonged. This added more waste of waiting and searching, frustrating the assembly team as their step functioned as a bottleneck, and they could not easily locate the trollies that the next job order needed.

The team decided to use a supermarket of three painted rectangles on the shop floor, in three different colors, to indicate which colored trollies would line up in each rectangle. Typically, each job order included an average of five trollies. Also, if a VIP order were to be rushed, the production manager would not need to interrupt the assembly team at all. The manager must wait for the next empty rectangle and arrange to stage the rushed-order trollies in it. A red tag can indicate that the order is urgent. Thus, once the assembly team finishes the current order, they move ahead to start arranging the jigs and fixtures to assemble the urgent order. Finishing one order took about four hours, just about the maximum time the urgent order needed to wait. The assembly team was very excited and happy about the new arrangement. The use of a simple supermarket setup enabled all teams to communicate visually and effectively, creating a positive atmosphere at the plant.

Chapter 11

Fundamental Pillars Related to Additional Lean Tools

11.1 Quality Pillar # 67: Standardize after Every Improvement to Maintain the Gains (See Section 6.4)

A standard work method entails an agreed-upon set of work-related procedures that help establish the best-known methods and sequence for each process in the value stream. It is the basis for consistently achieving high levels of quality, efficiency, and safety (Tapping *et al.*, 2002).

Supervisors and managers must spend time in the Gemba listening to operators and seeing the challenges in a typical day. They can help look for root causes and then standardize processes to prevent recurrence and eliminate waste from the process (Imai, 2012).

One of the golden rules of Gemba management is standardization. The plan-do-check-act (PDCA) cycle serves in achieving improvement over time. However, using a standardize-do-check-act (SDCA) cycle between improvements is essential to stabilize the process and maintain improvements (Imai, 2012). Thus, standardization stabilizes processes after every improvement. Eventually, another improvement cycle begins by creating the flow to connect different stages of the process, again requiring standardization. Finally, the scheduled workload gets leveled, requiring another SDCA cycle. Thus, the Lean Six Sigma journey includes applying standardization throughout, with the establishment of work methods and preventing the recurrence of defects. One way to develop a standard work

DOI: 10.4324/9781032688374-15

Figure 11.1 Standardization approach, as adapted from Imai (2012).

method is using the Kaizen approach. Figure 11.1 illustrates how standardization works.

According to Imai (2012), standards have the following characteristics:

1. They describe the best, easiest, and safest way to perform a task.
2. They offer the best way to preserve knowledge.
3. They provide ways to measure performance.
4. They show the cause-and-effect relationship.
5. They provide a basis for improvement and maintenance, including training.

Standardized work is the best possible way to perform work with the least amount of waste, producing the best-quality service at the lowest cost. Standardized work defines who, what, where, when, and how work performance will occur. This includes all work elements, their detailed description, and their cycle time. People who do the work themselves create standardized work. Ensuring that employees can see and follow standardized work is important. The characteristics of "good" standardized work (Six Sigma Training, personal communication, 2008) include the following:

- Visual display.
- Stable and repeatable process.
- Work interruptions more than 10% of the time, due to quality issues, require fixing the quality issues first.
- Process steps represent the best work method.
- Abnormalities are immediately visible.
- Clear reaction plan to respond to occurrences of abnormality.

Strategies to assure adherence to the standard work method include (Snee and Hoerl, 2018) the following:

- Assuring that the people who do the work create the standard.
- Removing options from the work area.
- Creating signals that immediately flag abnormalities.
- Creating clear rules about what to do when abnormality occurs.

In Lean Six Sigma, the main objective of the control phase is to develop and implement a control plan to institutionalize the new process or design and to maintain the gains. Typically, handing the plan over to the process owner enables follow-up and validation of transitioning toward the newly designed process. The new process may include a new policy, standard operating procedure, learned best practices, methods and metrics for future audits, budget, and training documents. In addition, the new process or design is statistically validated to ensure that it meets the objectives and benefits sought through the project. Using statistical process control (SPC) can accomplish this. Standardized improvement changes become a baseline for further improvement and candidates for implementation elsewhere, as applicable.

11.2 Quality Pillar # 68: Kaizen Is a Very Powerful Approach to Mobilizing People Toward Change. It Puts People at the Center of Change to Ensure Success

Kaizen is a Japanese tool equivalent to an improvement team event. Often referred to as a blitz or a quick event, an improvement team focuses in a short time on a specific objective. Tapping *et al.* (2002) notes that "kai" means "take apart", while "zen" means "make good". Thus, Kaizen means "change for the better" or, simply, "continuous improvement". Essentially, it encompasses "self-discipline". Employees strive for high levels of quality, not allowing defects to pass from their stations to others in the production value stream (Imai, 2012). Thus, a Kaizen event is a quick change that a group of employees executes in a short time to achieve a certain scope of improvement. The bias is mainly toward action, as the team is not too worried about perfection in such a short event (typically lasting between one and five days).

Farmer and Duffy (2017) state that Kaizen indicates implementing gradual and incremental improvement over a long period, as Masaki Imai put it. Kaizen blitz or Kaizen event is a team approach that lasts three to five days and focuses on the implementation of an improvement technique, such as cell layout design, quick changeover, or increased throughput. Intense and short, it may even last for less than a day in the form of a mini-kaizen. The people who do the work in the process execute it by challenging themselves to improve their process in small, cheap, and steady steps. It empowers employees to submit ideas for review, piloting, approval, implementation, and recognition.

Obviously, preparing a plan prior to the event and arranging the required resources will ensure success. Kaizen is all about empowerment. Top management simply assigns a specific challenge to a team. As the team gets mobilized, they become unstoppable, feeling that they own their work area, the gap is theirs to realize, and the solution is theirs to create. They truly feel proud and energized to embark on the challenge. Often, these employees or subject matter experts come up with surprising solutions that managers themselves do not expect. This approach overcomes resistance to change, as the employees feel responsible for their work area. However, it is important that the top management team is engaging and on board with the changes proposed. The members must ensure that they provide proper supervision for the Kaizen plan implementation. For example, in a Kaizen event that lasts three days, top management would typically be present at the event kick-off to provide a brief and listen to the plan and, at the end of every day, to get feedback on the progress and challenge team members for potential opportunities they may have missed. This will help with the SDCA validation cycle that typically follows the PDCA improvement cycle.

Kaizen can function as a vehicle for implementing many other improvement tools. For example, a Kaizen event can achieve drawing a current-state value stream map (VSM) and filling it with data and information. Then, in turn, the map itself can help identify several opportunities, in the form of scheduled Kaizen events that comprise an improvement action plan for migrating toward the future state.

Besides a VSM, other examples of establishing scope for Kaizen events or blitzes may include focusing on (Six Sigma Training, personal communication, 2008) the following:

1. Reduction of waiting for unavailable information, people, or responses and emails.

2. Reduction of storage space.
3. Enhancement of the cell layout to include evaluating the workflow (*e.g.*, using spaghetti diagrams), the location of workstations, and the sequence of operation.
4. Utilization of staff, including evaluation of the number of people involved, their skills, job rotations, cross-training, staff scheduling, and balancing workload.
5. Setup of schedules, including the use of Heijunka boards for workload leveling, takt time frame, and status of performance, whether ahead of or behind the plan.
6. Setup of a visual workspace that can include visual flow, Kanbans, andon signals, and key performance indicator (KPI) results—*e.g.*, the number of transactions completed.
7. Reduction of batch sizes to create flow.
8. Freeing up capital cost.
9. Reduction of warehouse and work-in-process inventories.
10. Reduction of transportation and motion.
11. Standardization of work, including best practices.
12. Workplace organization and self-discipline, using the 5S approach.
13. Reduction of reprioritization, by creating specific work intervals, rechanneling calls and emails, setting up a single point of chaos, and working on one task at a time instead of multitasking.

More details of many of these improvement approaches are included in other sections.

Kaizen events must be aligned with the strategic goals of any organization. If a strategic priority relates to cost efficiency, then Kaizen events on the shop floor must address relevant activities, such as productivity and quality defects. According to Imai (2012), Kaizen principles include the following:

1. Challenge the status quo.
2. Get rid of past assumptions.
3. Keep improving without costing too much (reach for the mind before the wallet).
4. Seek good ideas coming from a problem that is tough to solve.
5. Involve all team members, and do not rely on one person's opinion (no ranks, no criticism).
6. Ignore excuses, and look for solutions.
7. Do not seek perfection.

8. Implement quick-fixes on the spot (be biased toward action).
9. Find the root causes.
10. Make Kaizen a habit.

From time to time, Kaizen events result in reducing the number of workers a production cell needs. Fewer workers means lower costs and fewer hands present to make mistakes. However, Kaizen and productivity improvement must not result in employee firings. Rather, utilize the freed-up staff for other value-adding activities and innovation efforts. Firing people as a result of improvement initiatives will discourage any other employee from participating in any improvement activity or future Kaizen event. Thus, the approach should seek a win-win goal for both the employer and employees.

Taiichi Ohno once said that his team starts their Kaizen efforts by observing the way their operators work because it costs them nothing. Thus, a starting point to identify waste is through a motion study. Frederick W. Taylor laid the foundation for industrial engineering time-and-motion studies as part of his work-standards design. Kaizen functions as a manifestation of motivation, resulting from realizing achievements, and matches the highest level of Abraham Maslow's hierarchy of human needs, self-actualization (Breyfogle, 2003).

11.3 Quality Pillar # 69: Design a Product or a Process for Zero Defects Using Mistake-Proofing Techniques or Devices

Also known as error-proof, fail-safe, fool-proof, or Poka-Yoke (*i.e.*, to avoid inadvertent errors), this quality tool is attributed to Shigeo Shingo, a leading engineer and manufacturing expert for Toyota (Breyfogle, 2003). The idea behind this tool is to ensure that the design of processes, products, services, and templates would prevent certain errors from occurring. Such errors demonstrate the difference between desired and actual behavior or performance. They can result from, for instance, forgetfulness, misunderstanding, improper identification, slowness, nonsupervision, surprise, lack of training, absent knowledge or concentration, distractions, working too fast, and lack of practice. Sometimes an error might even be intentional—typically rare but hardest to prevent. However, if preventing or eliminating errors generally cannot occur, then at least easily flagging them should, so if they happen, workers would know and can correct them. Moreover, if achieving that

Table 11.1   Error-proofing Principles

Principle	Objective	Example	Level
Elimination	Eliminate the possibility of error.	Redesign the process or product so that the task or item is not necessary anymore.	Most favored
Replacement	Substitute with a more reliable process.	Automate tasks.	Medium high
Facilitation	Make the work easier to do.	Use color-coding.	Medium
Detection	Detect the error before further processing.	Use computer software to warn workers in the case of a typing error.	Medium low
Mitigation	Minimize the effect of the error.	Use fuses for overloaded circuits.	Least favored

Source: Adapted form Juran and Godfrey (1999)

cannot occur, then the least to expect should be to design the process so it would enable people to mitigate the impact of an error when it goes undetected, containing and minimizing the negative impact as much as possible (Six Sigma Training, personal communication, 2008).

Mistake-proofing can help to establish better controls and improvement actions that lead toward a zero-defect status. This requires the discipline to continually check for error sources and root causes. It also does not necessarily require heavily investing in technology or costly solutions. Ideally, error-proofing implementation takes account of three components: physical (using such fixtures as mirrors to help eliminate conditions leading to errors), philosophical (using empowerment to eliminate situations leading to defects), and operational (using devices that reinforce correct procedure sequence). Table 11.1 shows the logical principles or steps to follow when designing a mistake-proofing device (Juran and Godfrey, 1999).

Here are some additional examples of error-proofing (Six Sigma Training, personal communication, 2008):

- Color-coding of components or files to distinguish them easily.
- Products equipped with sensors for easy tracking and finding.
- Trucks electronically connected to a security gate through a code scanner, so only equipped trucks can pass.

■ Barcode scanning in a grocery-checkout process to help minimize mistakes and time.
■ Machine lock-out safety procedure that ensures electricity is not reconnected unless all electricians are done fixing the machine and out of the danger zone.
■ Guiding laser beams to guarantee proper alignment.
■ Simple mechanical counters.
■ Use of statistical process control.
■ Devices to prevent incorrect feeding of parts into a machine.
■ Physical devices, audible signals, visual displays, and warning lights.
■ Electronic forms with drop-down options and auto-filling features.

Here is an example of various levels of control in a process, ranging from basic soft controls—such as verbal instructions that are easy to misunderstand, miscommunicate, or forget—to a hard control level, where process design aims for perfection, as in error-proofing and design for Six Sigma (DFSS), shown in Table 11.2 (Six Sigma Training, personal communication, 2008).

Error-proofing design includes considering zero defects in such contexts as manufacturing, shipping, use by customers, maintenance, or environmental recycling. Manufacturing often associates it with Jidoka (autonomation).

No matter how observant or skilled workers are, errors will likely occur without implementing preventive measures (Dale *et al.*, 2016). The source of an error requires inspecting, analyzing, and rectification, using mistake-proofing. This leads to preventing defects from occurring (Poka-Yoke) or at least detecting defects when they do occur and stopping the process (Jidoka).

Table 11.2   Levels of Control in a Process

Type of control	Level of control
DFSS	Extremely hard (high strength)
Error-proofing	Hard
SPC and visual controls	Medium high
Operational method sheets	Medium low
Written instructions	Soft
Verbal instructions	Extremely soft (low strength)

Source: Adapted from Six Sigma Training, personal communication (2008)

Mistake-proofing new products from the design stage is much easier than doing so with old ones. A multidisciplinary team approach that utilizes the knowledge and skills of workers who first identified the cause of mistakes and participated in corrective measures, as well as quality control specialists, can achieve mistake-proofing.

Error-proofing has the advantages of reducing both defects and the cost of poor quality, enhancing workers' knowledge of processes and error prevention, and increasing consistency. Sources of errors relate to people's skills and knowledge, material in use, lack of information, miscommunication, inferior methods, and machine problems. To prevent defects, Shingo (1986) identified different types of inspection systems for discovering defects: reducing defects by self-checking and successive checking and eliminating defects at their source. Common transactional errors include missing or incorrect information. Common manufacturing errors include processing errors, missing or wrong parts, and adjustment errors. Operators should be careful not to make mistakes when making adjustments, changing tools, taking measurements, using mixed types of parts, following multiple steps, using symmetrical and asymmetrical parts, and engaging in rapid repetition.

Typical action verbs that indicate waste include adjust, approve, change, copy, inspect, move, reconcile, repair, review, return, update, wait, reschedule, and rework. Other "warning signs of waste in processes" include unclear responsibility, multiple handoffs or signatures, stress, complexity, and exceptions. Detecting problems may relate to any function (*e.g.*, temperature, electricity, or time), and sometimes preventing them can involve using such various instruments as gauges, sensors, or sensitive switches (see Table 11.3).

Table 11.3   Common Detection Functions and Devices

Detection Function	Devices
Pressure	Gauges, pressure-sensitive switches
Temperature	Thermometers, thermostats, thermistors, thermocouples
Electric current	Meter relays, current meter
Vibration	Sensors
Cycles	Counters, stepping relays, fiber sensors
Time	Timers, delay relays, timing units, time switches
Information	Buzzers, flashing lamps

Source: Adapted from Six Sigma Training, personal communication (2008)

Table 11.4 Common Types of Visual Management Tools and Their Uses

Type of visual management	Use
Signs/labels	Show where tools, inventory, *etc.* should go.
White demarcators	Tape or paint points off pathways, inventory locations, *etc.*
Red lines/floor marks	Outline inventory levels. Sometimes written on storage area.
Andons	Alarm lamps that warn supervisors when abnormalities occur.
Production boards	Display the actual versus the target for an output of a production cell.
Standardized work chart	Easy-to-read, graphical representations of process layout, work procedure, *etc.*
Displays of faulty items	Display the types and count of defective units using tools like Pareto charts or check sheets

Source: Adapted from Six Sigma Training, personal communication (2008)

Table 11.4 shows common types of visual management tools and their uses (Six Sigma Training, personal communication, 2008).

11.4 Quality Pillar # 70: Seek to Achieve Autonomous Operation and Maintenance Using Jidoka

Jidoka (autonomation) is a method that uses automation with a human touch to mistake-proof a process and prevent defects, enabling a smooth flow with workers focusing on value-adding tasks. The goal of Jidoka is to achieve zero defects and eliminate the risk of passing on an undetected defect to customers. Jidoka is about separating human work from machine work and developing devices for defect prevention. Jidoka enables people to rethink the design of processes, in terms of defect prevention, holistic process linking parts together, and inexpensive automation that supports smooth flow. It utilizes Poka-Yoke principles and Six Sigma methodology (Tapping *et al.*, 2002).

Practically, Jidoka is implemented at three spots in production: in the case of a defective product, by stopping the process before it starts; or a defective unit leaving a production cell; or passing to the following production cell (Six Sigma Training, personal communication, 2008).

Imai (2012) used a simple example to illustrate mistake-proofing with a simple human touch. A factory was using a high-speed machine that fed input material along with some unwanted scraps on top of it. This scrap caused jams, and thus, the machine underwent costly downtime. The first solution workers implemented was to hire and assign an attendant to watch the input material and stop the machine in the case of scraps. However, the team then introduced a simple solution by fixing a broom brush at the machine input, right above the infeed, to sweep off any unwanted scraps. This inexpensive solution prevented the machine from jamming.

A common example of Jidoka is a printer that stops printing in the case of a paper jam or low toner ink. Another famous example is the Toyoda automatic loom type G machine that Sakichi Toyoda invented, in which a falling pin automatically stopped a run whenever a thread broke, to prevent the production of defective products. This resembles the case of workers pulling down a wire to stop production, signaling an error, and requesting team and management help (Roser, 2021).

11.5 Quality Pillar # 71: Ensure Machines Are Ready and Available All the Time by Implementing Total Productive Maintenance (TPM) and Eliminating Machine Idle Time

At one factory, calculating efficiency involved multiplying two percentages: namely, the production or machine availability, the percentage of time the machine is available to work when required (machine availability or production line uptime, the opposite of downtime), and the percentage of performance, the occupancy ratio or product fill ratio related to not missing any opportunity or production slot available to fill and occupy. Typically, multiplying these two percentages by a third quality percentage (*i.e.*, 100% minus the defectives percentage) results in a commonly used metric, overall equipment effectiveness (OEE). OEE is the highest-level TPM metric (Nakajima, 1988) (for more on OEE, see Section 3.2).

Total productive maintenance (TPM) seeks to ensure that machines are available and ready for production when needed. This entails all activities required to maintain machines and the plans to do so, considering their usage, lubrication, condition, spare parts, consumables, diagnostic tools, and corrective or preventive measures. The totality of maintenance concerns the skills of not just the maintenance teams but also the users trained to properly use the machines, flag any issues, and perform all required basic and regular checks or maintenance activities. Moreover, it concerns the awareness and skills of the cleaning team, to ensure they do not use improper or incompatible cleaning materials that may damage or negatively affect the machine. Finally, it concerns the awareness of all other employees working around the machines of what is best for the machine, in terms of keeping the surrounding work area organized and clean. TPM is not only about maintenance but also productivity enhancement, mainly focusing on proper planning and employee training, to overcome obstacles that relate to the following:

- equipment downtime (during operation and setup),
- equipment reduced speed (related to design speed versus actual idle or stoppage time), and
- equipment reduced yield (related to reworks, defects, scrap, and stabilizing after changeover) (Breyfogle, 2003).

An industrial workshop team finished an engineering exercise for producing a new assembly machine, and when they tested it, it did not start at all. They struggled to find the reason. After several attempts to investigate and get it started, they found that the power lines feeding it were somehow internally disconnected. Apparently, the frequent handling of the metal scrap by the cleaning staff using a heavy metal trolley that crossed over the electrical wires cut off the invisible inner conductor, leading to power disconnection. The problem got fixed, and training enhanced awareness of how cleaning-staff work could affect production and machine availability.

In a lumber-manufacturing facility, the oil for lubricating sprockets and chains for lumber board handling was leaving dark marks on the boards. A scanner misread the marks as physical defects, causing it to reject the boards as lower grade. In this case, the maintenance team's awareness was crucial to ensuring that the machines functioned properly and the unexpected issues of using some inappropriate consumables did not negatively affect production yield.

Tapping *et al.* (2002) indicated that autonomous maintenance is a basic component of TPM. It includes cleaning, inspecting for abnormalities (such as inadequate lubrication and excessive wear), eliminating sources of contamination, lubricating components, establishing standard procedures, training operators to inspect all components, and continuously improving the whole system.

TPM involves every employee at the facility in focusing on improving equipment efficiency and quality through a comprehensive method of preventive maintenance that extends over the machine's life span, helping to enhance the productivity and life cycle of the machine. It utilizes 5S as a foundation for TPM (Imai, 2012). A machine down interrupts production, affecting operating cost and causing more batching, inventory between stations, finished inventory, and scrap and rework.

Ultimately, TPM strategy that aims for zero downtime is associated with accident-free Gemba (Imai, 2012). TPM combines both preventive and predictive maintenance. It drives total quality control (TQC) and depends on total employee involvement. Each company must develop its own customized TPM action plan through an integrated team approach involving both the maintenance and production departments.

TPM training programs can help develop the right procedures and empower operators to feel like owners (Imai, 2012). Using a 5S approach, cleaning includes checking to cite abnormalities needing rectification, leading to a continuous work environment and equipment improvement.

Thus, within the systematic approach of TPM, "total" means equipment effectiveness, maintenance programs, and the involvement of all staff, to form an atmosphere that encourages focusing on innovation, productivity, lead time, elimination of defects, and workers' safety.

11.6 Quality Pillar # 72: Execute Changeover Quickly to Reduce Idle Time by Externalizing All Possible Internal Elements

When employees finish the processing of one transaction and shift the focus to starting a new one, the process they go through is called a "changeover". This process consumes time, the non-value-adding time between two different manufactured products or transactions or customers served. Hence, the goal is to minimize this time as much as possible.

The changeover cycle is the time that converting a specific process or equipment from doing one type of work to the next type requires. Figure 11.2 shows the total changeover time, from the moment the last good part of product type 1 is produced until the moment the first good part of product type 2 (in the next batch) is produced. This includes the process

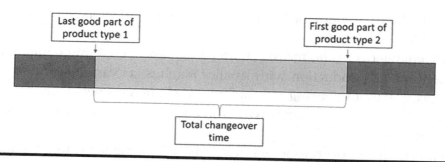

Figure 11.2 Total changeover time.

stabilization time, during which the first few produced items may need to be reworked until the production machine is optimized and fine-tuned.

Quick changeover originated with a methodology called single-minute exchange of dies (SMED) that Shigeo Shingo developed at Toyota (Tapping *et al.*, 2002). This type of thinking started in production. For example, in a plastic injection molding process catering to a variety of product demands, the challenge was to change the tools and dies with minimal interruption of the production flow. As Imai (2012) stated, the goal of SMED is to reduce the changeover time and the production rejects. Quick changeover applies to both manufacturing and transactional processes. Its recommended approach is as follows:

1. Go to the Gemba where the changeover process is taking place.
2. Video-record the process from start to finish.
3. Meet with own team to discuss opportunities to minimize the change-over time while watching the video (step by step).
4. Eliminate unnecessary waste—*e.g.*, motion, waiting, transportation.
5. Combine steps wherever practical.
6. Run some steps in parallel instead of series, to minimize the overall changeover time.
7. Ensure all required tools, materials, and info are at the point of use.

A good example of a quick changeover is the pit stop in Formula One car racing. The pit stop is the process used when race cars stop for refueling, replacing tires, and mechanical tuning. Decades ago, it was customary for this process to take around 60 seconds. However, it is now as little as 2 seconds. The main difference lies in externalizing many elements of the changeover and the allocation of a devoted and well-trained team ready to perform the internal elements in a very short time. All tools and resources are available on the spot.

Quick changeover time means shorter lead times, enabling companies to implement mixed production with smaller batches, as various products can be produced without wasting too much time changing over. Thus, minimal downtime means more inexpensive setups, leading to quicker response to client demands.

The quick changeover approach takes the following steps (Six Sigma Training, personal communication, 2008):

■ Document the current changeover process.
■ Separate the internal steps (done during changeover, operations performed while the machine or process is stopped) from external steps (done prior to changeover, operations performed while the machine or process is running).
■ Convert as many of the internal steps to external steps as possible (ensure all parts and tools are staged and ready prior to changeover).
■ For the remaining internal steps, create parallel internal steps.
■ Reduce complexity, and eliminate waste (divide the work among people, use interlocking devices instead of bolts, use fixtures, eliminate adjustments, and mechanize wherever necessary) (Tapping *et al.*, 2002).
■ Create a new changeover procedure (ensure smooth flow of such elements as staged items, tools).
■ Test the new changeover procedure.
■ Document the new procedure.
■ Chart changeover time to compare and monitor.

11.7 Quality Pillar # 73: Ensure You Have a Proper Cell Layout Design to Enable the Most Efficient Flow (Small Lots or One-Piece Flow)

Work cellular design enables efficient arrangement of work elements to maximize value-added content and minimize waste. It ensures that the production machines' arrangement follows the required sequence of manufacturing steps, not grouping by machine categories. Thus, the workflow organizes the processes.

A work cell is a self-contained entity that consists of various value-adding operations. Here are some principles to follow when designing a cell layout (Tapping *et al.*, 2002):

- Arrange processes by their sequence.
- Set the work cell up for counterclockwise flow. This will encourage the use of the right hand for tasks while the worker moves from one activity to the next within the cell.
- Locate equipment close together, and consider safety for material and hand movement within a smaller area.
- Place the last process step close to the first.
- Select a suitable shape for the cell, depending on equipment and resource constraints.

For example, in a U-shaped circuit cell, workers complete all elements of work as they naturally pace the work. Such a cell is easy to implement and promotes fully skilled operators. Creating a work cell considers dividing work into elements. A work element is the smallest increment of work that can be shifted to a different worker. Work elements are typically stacked on a chart in which each grid represents a unit of time. Then, using a paper Kaizen, the unnecessary walking, waiting, unloading (where auto-ejection makes sense), out-of-cycle, and any other wasteful activities are removed. Other types of designs include C-, L-, S-, and V-shaped cell layouts, depending on equipment constraints and resource availability. Product demand and mix are important to keep in mind when designing a work cell, to adapt to customers' changing demands (Tapping *et al.*, 2002). Figure 11.3 illustrates the U-shaped work cell design.

Figure 11.3 U-shaped work cell layout design (a top-view showing one operator moving between three workstations).

11.8 Quality Pillar # 74: Use Quality Function Deployment (QFD) to Identify and Convert Customer Needs into Design Features Embedded in Your Products and Services

Quality function deployment (QFD) is a proactive design approach introduced by Akao in Japan in the 1960s as a quality improvement and communication tool (Tan and Shen, 2000). It is used by cross-functional teams to convert customer needs or requirements into product and process technical design features or engineering characteristics (Imai, 2012). Examples of North American companies using QFD include Ford, IBM, Xerox, Hewlett-Packard, and Procter & Gamble (Chen, 2007). After the first phase of QFD of product planning and identification of engineering technical characteristics using HOQ, the second phase is the product design, including the product performance during its life cycle, and the feasibility analysis. Then the third phase is process design, and the fourth phase is process quality control (Salah *et al.*, 2009b).[1] Foster (2007) explained the following steps of QFD: list the customers' requirements; list the technical design characteristics; assess the relationship between customers' requirements and design characteristics; assess the correlation between technical design characteristics themselves (in the roof section of the HOQ); evaluate the importance of customers' requirements, and compare own organization to competition; prioritize the needs of the customers and the technical characteristics; and conduct final assessment of absolute and relative weights to determine engineering decisions. Finally, QFD enables companies to increase their efficiency, reduce prelaunch lead time, and reduce costs (see Figure 11.4). It helps employees make trade-offs between what customers need and what their companies can afford to manufacture (Matzler and Hinterhuber, 1998).

11.9 Quality Pillar # 75: Use the Kano Model to Gain a Deep Understanding of the Customer's Voice

Created by Kano *et al.* (1984), the Kano model is an effective method used to obtain a profound and creative understanding of customers' needs and the ones more critical to satisfaction than others. It classifies product characteristics into three types: attributes that are expected by customers to exist in a product without asking, attributes that are proportional (the better they are, the higher the satisfaction), and attributes that are attractive, which attract customers, but do not cause dissatisfaction if absent. In other situations, three

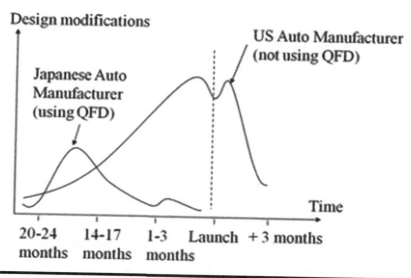

Figure 11.4   A Japanese auto manufacturer using QFD versus a US auto manufac-turer who is not, as adapted from Sullivan (1986).

other attributes may result such as indifferent, reverse, and skeptical attributes. It is generally recommended to fulfill all *must-be attributes*, be competitive on the *proportional attributes*, and then include some of the *attractive attributes* (CQM, 1993; Robertshaw, 1995). It is important to note that customer needs are dynamic in nature, and what is currently attractive may become a *must-be* in the near future. A Kano questionnaire can be used to help researchers in the classification of customers' needs according to Kano's categories (Salah *et al.*, 2009b). The improvement in one customer requirement may not grant the same satisfaction as in another one. This is why it is necessary to weigh them. The Kano model can be used to distinguish the influences of the needs on customer satisfaction (Chen and Chuang, 2008). It is important to understand customer requirements and the company's own capabilities. Salah *et al.* (2009b) explained, through a case study, how the Kano model can be utilized along with Six Sigma structure and QFD to contribute to new product innovation and the enhancement of existing products or services.

Note

1. Sections 11.8 and 11.9 are mainly prepared based on our published work: Salah, S., Rahim, A. and Carretero, J. A. (2009). Kano-based Six Sigma utilising quality function deployment. *International Journal of Quality Engineering and Technology, 1*(2), 206–230.

CURRENT AND FUTURE QUALITY IMPROVEMENT TRENDS, RECOMMENDATIONS, AND CONCLUSIONS

Chapter 12

Current and Future Quality Improvement Trends, Recommendations, and Conclusions

12.1 Quality Pillar # 76: Use an Integrated Management System (IMS) for Quality, Health, Safety, Environment, and Other ISO Standards Relevant to Your Business

The most popular set of standards for a Quality Management System (QMS) is the International Organization for Standardization (ISO) family of standards. Its basis is such various principles as customer focus, leadership, people involvement, process focus, and a management approach focused on systems of processes (Pfeifer *et al.*, 2004). In addition to the ISO9001 quality management system, ISO45001 for health and safety management and ISO14001 for environmental management are widely used systems. Several years ago, ISO introduced various new versions of these systems and other ISO systems that all follow a standardized structure, to enable and encourage organizations to integrate these systems. Its sections include an introduction, context of the organization, leadership, planning, support, operation, performance evaluation, and improvement. In addition, due to its strong relation to business continuity, risk management has become a main part of the ISO approach, gaining further attention during the COVID-19 pandemic.

DOI: 10.4324/9781032688374-17

Many organizations started realizing that the three common ISO systems mentioned earlier could start saving them much effort, time, and money by avoiding duplication and managing their processes and systems more efficiently. In addition to quality, health, safety, and environment (QHSE), an IMS can be the umbrella that easily includes many other ISO standards, such as ISO55001 for assets management, ISO22301 for business continuity management, and ISO27001 for information security management. Among the standardized sections in many ISO standards are common ones that can be satisfied using a set of documented procedures but are usually duplicated when not using an IMS approach.

The use of an IMS of various ISO standards greatly benefits many organizations through improved performance, fewer interruptions to business, risk management and enhanced business resilience, combined audits, reduced but consistent documentation (*i.e.*, less administrative overhead), fewer necessary approvals, improved communication and teamwork, standardized information, effective utilization of resources, enhanced synergies, less redundancy, reduced costs, enhanced process maturity, and greater efficiency.

Also, the savings realized by implementing an IMS include the following:

1. Fewer fees paid to certifying bodies and auditors due to fewer days required to audit an integrated system than stand-alone systems.
2. Fewer days required for the audit, saving employee hours. These employees include quality assurance personnel, employees in audited departments, and managers.
3. Fewer opening and closing meetings and fewer auditor visits for combined systems.
4. Fewer management review meetings.
5. Less documentation and effort to create and manage.

As a best practice, one organization managed to combine 12 standards under one IMS and, as a result, achieved annualized savings of millions of dollars. IMS is an essential part of process management, a major component of the integrated company-wide management system (ICWMS) discussed earlier in this book.

12.2 Current and Recent Quality Improvement Trends and Challenges

QM evolved greatly over the past century, and that continues to be noticed as various trends start to emerge, including recent QM developments, such as (Dale *et al.*, 2016) the following:

- Increased use of basic tools of statistical quality and process control.
- Recognizing internal improvement constraints and the need to involve external partners, such as the suppliers, in the improvement approach.
- TQM becoming the umbrella for various initiatives for enhancing quality.
- Acknowledgment of the necessary consideration of people issues in quality management.
- Increased use of advanced techniques as part of a modern quality planning process. These include tools like failure mode and effects analysis (FMEA), the Kano model, design of experiments (DOE), and quality function deployment (QFD).
- Increased use of such quality techniques as total productive maintenance, Lean, and Six Sigma.
- Increased importance of benchmarking, business process reengineering (BPR), and self-assessment excellence award models.
- Recognition that many quality tools and improvement techniques have the same goals.
- The effect of globalization, especially the emergence of new economies.

The transition from "old" to "new" QM includes the following trends (Dale *et al.*, 2016):

- Companies offer a wide range of product customization and have switched to modular assembly.
- Suppliers take more responsibility for the development of the end product.
- Driven by profit, companies experiment with materials, suppliers, and technologies that can result in cheaper and more effective outcomes.
- In many industries, all simple technological advances are complete.
- There is more focus on innovation, especially when related to a technological breakthrough.
- Changes in patterns of distribution with fewer powerful supplier points.

"New" QM focuses on subjects relating to (Dale *et al.*, 2016):

- Durability expectation of product lifetime.
- Aesthetic considerations related to the brand image, as well as the non-technical and soft aspects, such as feel, smell, look, and taste.
- Compatibility of components, software packages, and updates.

■ Cooperation between internal functions and with external supply chain partners to speed up innovation, prevent poor quality, and respond quickly to fix defects.

Future QM issues and challenges include (Dale *et al.*, 2016) the following:

1. Adapting quality and improvement tools and techniques to the e-commerce environment.
2. Developing a quality system beyond ISO 9001 serving only as a paperwork system audit to provide preventive approaches and a process-integrated system.
3. The impact of corporate culture on quality and process improvement, in terms of commitment, change tolerance, and communication across multiple cultures.
4. Moving from traditional function-oriented organizational structures into process streams aligned to satisfy customer groups and exploit specific market opportunities.
5. Seeking the best ways and structures for managing across different locations and countries with different challenges and needs.
6. Revitalizing quality and improvement initiatives continuously and after any period of stagnation.
7. Developing effective relationships with suppliers and pursuing joint improvement opportunities.
8. Using the e-commerce environment as a basis for QM research, especially as it impacts the value chain to become flat.
9. Market improvement initiatives add real value to the organization and are not just for regulatory purposes or for compliance's sake.
10. Preventing suffering from change fatigue as a result of repackaged improvement initiatives.
11. Ensuring product costs remain competitive, as quality alone does not guarantee an organization's success.

In summary, QM success depends on its introduction to the organization, focusing on proper communication, training, infrastructure, teams and projects, people involvement, measurement, and basics of quality (Dale *et al.*, 2016).

Some important concerns relating to the use of quality tools and techniques include their need to be appropriate, understood, data based, action aimed, and validated for successful usage (Snee and Hoerl, 2018).

12.3 Future Quality Improvement Trends and Challenges

Similar to how innovating new products determines the success of an organization, the adoption of new Quality 4.0 (Q4.0) technologies, such as internet of things (IoT), Big Data, blockchain, robotic process automation (RPA), artificial intelligence (AI), and virtual reality (VR), will determine whether an organization will survive competition or not. Learning about and adopting modern Industry 4.0 (I4.0) technological tools to enhance, optimize, and digitalize processes is essential for business sustainability. The following section will explore this important topic of future trends of quality improvement.

12.4 Quality Pillar # 77: Understand What Quality 4.0 (Q4.0) and Industry 4.0 (I4.0) Are about, How They Relate to Your Business, and How You Can Utilize What They Can Offer

Learn about and adopt modern I4.0 technological tools to enhance, optimize, and digitalize your processes such as internet of things (IoT), blockchain, Big Data, data analytics, drones, robotics, 3D printing, robotic process automation (RPA), mobile applications, mobile tablets, automated workflow system, digitized forms, artificial intelligence (AI), sensors for data collection, digital twins, and virtual reality (VR).

So many changes in the world today affect every individual in various ways. These changes are fast and not easily predictable, making reaching the right decision at the right time more challenging. However, the good news is the various new technologies and advanced approaches in the market that can help us navigate better and enhance our chances of success.

The mechanization of manufacturing and the invention of the steam engine represented the first industrial revolution. Mass production lines shaped the second industrial revolution. The introduction of automation, computers, and the internet formed the third industrial revolution. As part of the fourth industrial revolution (I4.0), technological enhancement shifted the focus to connecting humans to machines and integrated processes (Jamkhaneh *et al.*, 2022).

Moreover, to overcome the pressure that global competition poses, digital technologies can help enhance processes through automation and real-time monitoring, leading to higher efficiency, lower cost, and fewer defects. The technology acceleration trends provide various opportunities for innovation and disruptive ideas of business operation. Accordingly, many organizations started formulating a digital transformation strategy for deploying cyber-physical systems (CPS) to digitize and automate their processes (Soldatos *et al.*, 2019). This marks the start of the fourth industrial revolution (Industry 4.0 or I4.0), introduced in 2011 and aimed at timely communication between physical and digital units. In addition to the internet of things (IoT), I4.0 includes such various technologies as the use of sensors, Big Data, artificial intelligence (AI), visual examination, virtual reality (VR), augmented reality (AR), integrated systems, cybersecurity, advanced material, neural networks, machine learning, and cloud computing. These technologies relate to such quality management (QM) practices as management commitment, strategic management, suppliers management, process management, resources management, customer focus, and data management.

In addition to the digital effects, I4.0 exerts social, economic, and physical effects on industrial systems. Strategic intelligence, part of the World Economic Forum (WEF), listed the following implications of I4.0 (in alphabetical order), quoted from Babatunde (2021):

(1) 3D printing, (2) advanced manufacturing and production, (3) advanced materials, (4) agile governance, (5) artificial intelligence and robotics, (6) arts and culture, (7) behavioral sciences, (8) biotechnology, (9) block-chain, (10) circular economy, (11) cybersecurity, (12) digital communications, (13) digital economy and society, (14) drones, (15) entrepreneurship, (16) future of economic progress, (17) future of health and healthcare, (18) gender parity, (19) geopolitics, (20) global governance, (21) global risks, (22) human enhancement, (23) information technology, (24) innovation, (25) international security, (26) internet of things, (27) justice and legal infrastructure, (28) mental health, (29) neuroscience, (30) public finance and social protection, (31) space, (32) sustainable development, (33) values, (34) virtual and augmented reality and (35) workforce and employment.

Thus, the application of these I4.0 technologies to digitalize QM represents the fourth quality revolution (Quality 4.0 or Q4.0), which integrates technology into daily operations to affect people and processes (Carvalho *et al.*, 2021). Q4.0 presents a new opportunity for any organization to utilize technological advancements to reach higher levels of operational excellence, performance, and innovation (Sony *et al.*, 2020). These advancements include automation and information and communication technology (ICT). Q4.0 is a joint optimization of human and technical systems (Sony *et al.*, 2021). It is not the goal of Quality 4.0 to replace the basic quality approaches. On the contrary, it aims to boost them, increase technology users, and enhance processes (Jamkhaneh *et al.*, 2022).

Sony *et al.* (2020) listed the following eight ingredients for the implementation of Q4.0 in any organization:

> (1) handling big data, (2) improving prescriptive analytics, (3) using Quality 4.0 for effective vertical, horizontal, and end-to-end integration, (4) using Quality 4.0 for strategic advantage, (5) leadership in Quality 4.0, (6) training in Quality 4.0, (7) organizational culture for Quality 4.0 and, lastly, (8) top management support for Quality 4.0.

Furthermore, I4.0 is about the adoption of CPS systems in factories to digitally interconnect machines and operational technology (OT) with information technology (IT) systems, such as enterprise resource planning (ERP), manufacturing execution systems (MES), computerized maintenance management (CMM), supply chain management (SCM), and customer relationship management (CRM) systems. It utilizes advancements in the internet of things (IoT) and connectivity technologies to gather and utilize data to make industrial systems intelligent (Soldatos *et al.*, 2019). The integration of all elements of a product life cycle, including ERP as well as physical control systems, the use of algorithms, IoT and cloud computing, smart glasses, smart gloves, barcodes, quick response (QR) scan codes, autonomous vehicles, simulation, virtual reality, and collaborative robots, are all features of I4.0 (Sony *et al.*, 2020). Additional relevant technologies being researched include adaptive software, interface technology, speech recognition, modeling of complex systems, collaborative problem solving, reasoning under uncertainty, and neurophysiological models of cognition (National Research Council, 1997). Table 12.1 lists examples of these recently emerging technologies or terms, their brief explanation, challenges or opportunities, and benefits. Table 12.2 lists some technologies considered part of I4.0 and Q4.0 and their relationship with several QM practices. In addition, Table 12.3 shows a description of the use of some Lean quality tools before and after I4.0.

Table 12.1 A List of Various Terms or Types of Technologies Considered Part of I4.0 and Q4.0, Their Brief Explanation, Challenges or Opportunities, and Benefits

Technology or term	Explanation	Challenges or opportunities	Benefits
Industry 4.0 and Quality 4.0	I4.0 is about the launch of new technological enhancements that shifted the focus of industries to connecting humans to machines and integrated processes (Jamkhaneh et al., 2022). Q4.0 is about the application of I4.0 technologies to digitalize QM (Carvalho et al., 2021). It is about strategically aligning QM with I4.0 in a company-wide approach (Sony et al., 2021).	The acquisition of human technological skills to adopt I4.0. The learning and development of effective relational and collaborative skills to manage the sociotechnical changes (not just technological capabilities) and the understanding of how I4.0 influences digital servitization (Chiarini, 2020).	Higher efficiency, lower cost, and fewer defects (Soldatos et al., 2019).
Big Data analytics	The automation of data collection, data analysis, and data sharing (Chiarini, 2020). The large amounts of structured data in a system and unstructured data, such as social media feeds, associated with data analytics (Agnellutti, 2014).	The automation of data collection, data analysis, and data sharing. The use of prescriptive business analytics (Chiarini, 2020).	The use of an evidence-based decision-making process. The ability to predict machine failures (automatic detection during manual and machine works fostering a new kind of digital Poka-Yoke), reduce downtime, improve maintenance (predictive maintenance), and acquire self-learning machines that are connected and able to make independent decisions (Chiarini, 2020). Exploiting text analysis to analyze customer satisfaction and solving problems through modeling, prediction, and relation analysis (Rifqi et al., 2021).

Artificial intelligence	Solving problems using predictive software to make complex decisions related to quality (Rifqi et al., 2021).	The use of predictive software for problem solving and decision-making, combining Big Data methods to identify rational subgroups, potential causes, and correlated patterns in data sets (Chiarini, 2020).	The enhancement of optimization, operational performance, and quality (Chiarini, 2020). Neural networks and deep learning can help in categorizing defects for better detection and recognizing complex patterns for better prediction (Rifqi et al., 2021).
Internet of things	The ability of devices to communicate using sensors linked through networks using the internet to transmit, gather, and analyze data (Agnellutti, 2014).	IoT (including intelligent sensors) enables humans to have a better visibility and to take timely data-driven actions (Carvalho et al., 2021).	Monitoring and auditing for quality and safety using automation sequence control and drones (Rifqi et al., 2021).
Blockchain	A blockchain is composed of various connected (chained) blocks that contain uniquely identified transaction data, a communication network, and a shared ledger for data storage (Vimalajeewa et al., 2010). It also consists of validity rules (logic), consensus mechanisms (protocols and algorithms), and cryptography (like usernames and passwords). Thus, a blockchain can be thought of as a database located on various computers simultaneously (Banafa, 2020).	Using blockchain to authorize trusted transactions that meet quality objectives (Rifqi et al., 2021).	A blockchain facilitates transactions without a central trusted entity, secures data via cryptography, makes data truthful or transparent and indisputable, automates auditing, and reduces the risk of disputes to enable real-time settlements. If corrupted, a database can be restored simply by rerunning all the transactions in a blockchain (Prusty, 2018). It can help improve the security of transactions in banks and verification and validation of information in a supply chain and other networks. It can provide an actively distributed ledger to save time when recording transactions among various entities, eliminate intermediaries, and minimize the risk of tampering (Banafa, 2020).

(Continued)

Table 12.1 (Continued)

Technology or term	Explanation	Challenges or opportunities	Benefits
Cyber-physical system (CPS)	The integration of networking, computation, and physical processes within an organization (Sony et al., 2020).	Customer value cocreation and customer experience through CPS including: the automation of service or servitization, capturing continuous timely input of customer, customer relationship management (CRM) system, AI, fragments of software, and social media and business analytics (Chiarini, 2020).	QC and QA through CPS and ERP, including: the monitoring of products' progress (smart product QC to satisfy specifications, where value of product in use is determined by the customer), the use of process automation, the setup of a smart factory utilizing IoT to interconnect CPSs, new and traditional technologies embedded in cyber entities (including additive manufacturing, smart sensors, robots and collaborative robots (COBOT), augmented reality (AR), virtual reality (VR), smart human interface (SHI), Big Data and analytics, artificial intelligence (AI), and autonomous vehicles and simulation). The data obtained from the supply chain flow is managed through product life management (PLM) and manufacturing execution system (MES) software connected with the automated document control process of the QMS (Chiarini, 2020).
Smart sensors and RFID	The identification, tracking, and registration of data connected with raw input material, work-in-progress, and finished items (Chiarini, 2020), as well as maintenance issues. Smart factory is about being equipped with real-time sensors, actors, and autonomous systems (Sony et al., 2020).	The automation of data collection and data analysis related to QC and QA, including inspection, audit results, defective products, and calibration results (Chiarini, 2020).	Using RFID and auto-identification for better communication, real-time data sharing, product traceability, and error-proofing of transactions like ordering correct items when inventory level is low. Using smart sensors, VR simulation, smart watches, and smart glasses to manage noncompliance and better quality control (Rifqi et al., 2021).

Table 12.2 A List of Various Terms or Types of Technologies Considered Part of the I4.0 and Q4.0 and Their Relationship with a Number of QM Practices

I4.0 technologies vs. QM practices	Management commitment	Customer involvement	Supplier involvement	Employee involvement	Benchmarking techniques	Process management	Information analysis	Strategic planning
Data science	X					X	X	X
IoT, VR, AR, cloud computing	X	X	X	X	X	X	X	X
Big Data	X	X	X			X	X	
Blockchain and AI	X			X			X	
Machine learning	X						X	X
Neural networks and deep learning	X					X	X	

Source: Adapted from Carvalho *et al.* (2021)

Table 12.3 A Description of the Use of a Number of Lean Quality Tools Before and After I4.0

Lean tool	Before I4.0	After I4.0
Kanban	Using pull production based on a signal by cards, boards, *etc.*	Using pull production electronically based on sensors, RFID tags, wireless LAN network, *etc.*
Poka-Yoke	Using basic devices to eliminate errors	Eliminating errors using automatic tools like barcode scanners, RFID tags, and electric fastening tools
Standardized work	Using best practices and lessons learned	Using 3D information, AR, and digital mockup model
Heijunjka (production leveling)	Converting orders to smaller ones and into batches	Using graphic user interface (GUI) linked to regular manufacturing execution system (MES)
TPM	Planning maintenance to ensure machine availability	Using AR to detect abnormalities prior to failure

Source: Adapted from Rifqi *et al.* (2021)

Companies that intend to cope with and benefit from I4.0 opportunities must assess their future strategic plan from a digitalization perspective and invest in hiring empowered technology-related professionals, such as software developers, data scientists, electronic commerce (e-commerce) specialists, and social media experts (Jamkhaneh *et al.*, 2022). Quality practitioners must have the ability to exploit the information as the processes they are managing require (Carvalho *et al.*, 2021). Technical training to use these technologies is critical to successfully implementing them. In addition, employees must have transformational and adaptability skills (Sony *et al.*, 2020).

In terms of I4.0 competencies, the Occupational Information Network listed the following (in alphabetical order) (Babatunde, 2021):

(1) active learning and learning strategies, (2) analytical thinking and innovation, (3) attention to detail and trustworthiness, (4) complex problem-solving, (5) coordination and time management, (6) creativity, originality and initiative, (7) critical thinking and analysis, (8) emotional intelligence, (9) instruction, mentoring and teaching, (10) leadership and social influence, (11) management of financial, material resources, (12) manual dexterity, endurance and precision, (13) memory, verbal, auditory and spatial abilities, (14) persuasion and negotiation, (15) quality control and safety awareness, (16) reading, writing, math and active listening, (17) reasoning, problem-solving and ideation, (18) resilience, stress tolerance and flexibility, (19) service orientation, (20) system analysis and evaluation, (21) technology design and programming, (22) technology installation and maintenance, (23) technology selection, monitoring and control, (24) troubleshooting and user experience and (25) visual, auditory and speech abilities.

Sony *et al.* (2021) identified five motivation factors for the adoption of Q4.0: namely, reliable information, Big Data–driven QM programs, improved customer satisfaction, productivity improvement, and cost or time savings. In addition, they listed five barriers to Q4.0: high cost of implementation, lack of resources, lack of knowledge, organizational culture, and clarity of competitive advantage.

The following sections provide a summary of several I4.0 new technologies, including a brief explanation of each, examples of its usage, and a description of its benefits or opportunities.

12.4.1 Big Data

Big Data refers to large volumes of structured data (such as all the clicks users of a system make) and unstructured data (*e.g.*, social media feeds). Often associated with data analytics related to analytical techniques applied to smaller data sets (Webber and Zheng, 2020), Big Data refers to the technological ability to capture large volumes of data of great variety and to process them quickly. It includes new types of observations or measurements, in the form of big and complex data sets, obtained from transactions, emails, clicks, video streams, the worldwide web, social media, applications, public records, databases, surveys, and optically recognized electronic forms based on scanned documents, as well as data collected from devices and sensors that are internet enabled to capture data from physical units, such as radio frequency identification (RFID) and global positioning system (GPS) chips, triangulation of mobile devices using cell phone towers, and electronic payments data (Agnellutti, 2014).

A typical example of Big Data lies in predictive maintenance, which combines data from ERP systems with data from various sensors in a single processing line. The combination of data from different sources in data sets that feature the 4Vs (*i.e.*, volume, variety, velocity, and veracity) through Big Data technologies and tools is a main enabler of I4.0. Big Data technologies are developed to enhance data collection, consolidate multiple fragmented data sets, and store them reliably and cost-effectively. Big Data analysis techniques are important because of the potential business value that lies in data analysis, including machine learning techniques (Soldatos *et al.*, 2019), that can enhance the safety and quality culture through accurate execution of tasks (Rifqi *et al.*, 2021).

It is important for managers and quality practitioners to realize the potential of Big Data in terms of usage and analytics, taking into account legal, ethical, social, and privacy considerations (Agnellutti, 2014).

12.4.2 Blockchain

A blockchain comprises various connected (chained) blocks that contain uniquely identified transaction data, a communication network, and a shared ledger for data storage (Vimalajeewa *et al.*, 2010). It also consists of validity rules (logic), consensus mechanisms (protocols and algorithms), and cryptography (*e.g.*, usernames and passwords). Thus, a blockchain functions as a database located on various computers simultaneously. It continuously grows with the addition of new records or blocks, forming a chain, as each block links to a previous block (Banafa, 2020).

A ledger is software for storing transaction data or records without allowing them to be modified. A blockchain is a structure used to implement a decentralized ledger. Each block stores a list of transactions and other relevant data, including links to other blocks in the chain. Copies of updated states of blockchains are held in network nodes. Distributed ledger technology (DLT) concerns the replication, sharing, and synchronization of digital transactions across various entities in different countries (Prusty, 2018).

Blockchain technologies are still in their early stages of deployment and experimentation in industrial settings, mainly present in cryptocurrencies like Bitcoin. However, an example of a project where blockchain functions within a factory is the decentralization and synchronization of industrial processes that span multiple stations. Other examples are the use of blockchains for data security through encryption and traceability in the supply chain. Instead of using public blockchains in an industrial setting, permissioned blockchains provide higher degrees of privacy, authentication, and authorization of users and enhanced performance (Soldatos *et al.*, 2019). Prusty (2018) offered some examples of the uses of blockchain:

> trade finance, cross-border payments, digital identity, the clearing and settlement of tokenized and digital assets, provenance of ownership of a product, record keeping for critical data, signing contracts, multi-party aggregation (namely, they can be used as a shared master repository for common industry information, allowing members to query for data), payment-versus-payment or payment versus-delivery, and so on.

A blockchain facilitates transactions without a central trusted entity, secures data via cryptography, makes data truthful or transparent and indisputable, automates auditing, and reduces the risk of disputes to enable real-time settlements. Simply rerunning all transactions in a blockchain can restore a corrupted database (Prusty, 2018). It can help improve the security of transactions in banks and verification and validation of information in a supply chain and other networks. It can provide an actively distributed ledger to save time when recording transactions among various entities, eliminate intermediaries, and minimize the risk of tampering (Banafa, 2020).

12.4.3 Drones

The use of drones and unmanned aerial vehicles (UAVs) is another example of advanced technologies utilized as part of I4.0 and Q4.0. There are many applications for drones—a new and growing sector that includes parcel delivery, autonomous inventory scanning, real-time stock checks, gathering water samples and other environmental data (*e.g.,* air quality and solar energy absorption for planting trees), reaching places that are difficult for people to access, transmitting police messages of health warnings, security patrols, integration with driverless vehicles, and as a base point for dispatching multiple deliveries and recharging. The development of drones can revolutionize logistics and supply chains and reduce carbon emissions but faces different technical and regulatory challenges (Markarian and Staniforth, 2020).

12.4.4 Robotic Process Automation (RPA)

Many tasks people do nowadays are repetitive, with predictable inputs and outputs. Robotic process automation (RPA) is simply a software robot using instructions in the form of algorithms that mimic manually repetitive tasks or interactions of humans with computers, to automate them. It decreases the cost of operation, runs 24 hours a day, reduces (if not eliminates) errors, and frees up time for people to do more value-adding work. It still requires effective change management to overcome any resistance or fear of job loss, by finding smart win-win solutions. RPA is accurate and requires less effort to manage. However, it is inherently intelligent, and thus, it requires a programmer to train the robot software to record keystrokes and mouse clicks and replay them to, for example, scan a shopping website to purchase weekly groceries. Other examples include downloading different files and then using their content to consolidate regular reports to send to a group of managers, comparing hundreds of rows in an Excel file with another master document for discrepancies, basic data entry into a system, and other tasks involving reading or highly accurate typing. However, some updates in a process may affect the RPA function and require updating accordingly. Adding cognitive intelligence to RPA, using tools like language processing, text analytics, and data mining, is one emerging trend in RPA development (Mei, 2018).

RPA can help perform calculations and make decisions based on predefined rules, to accomplish tasks. Artificial intelligence (AI) enables it, using state activities that include adding triggers, conditions, and actions. Examples of technologies adopted with RPA include machine learning, language processing, and language generation. With the help of AI technologies, RPA can read images or scan documents and interpret data. RPA uses coding to capture the logical way for a human to perform a task when interacting with different applications like Oracle or SAP, validating and transforming data, as in invoice data entry. RPA covers a wide range of processes in various industries—*e.g.*, banking, telecom, travel, and logistics. Workers from within the area of work, using software platforms in the form of designed flow-charts, can easily develop RPA (Tripathi, 2018).

Its wide acceptance gives RPA various benefits, such as reduction in the cost of outsourced labor and operation; speeding up execution and response time; increasing productivity; simplifying insurance management tasks; enhancement of financial activities that include data processing and complex workflows; automation of utility-company processes (*e.g.*, meter reading or billing); improvement of health care processes, including patient scheduling or claims processing; enhancement of service quality and data accuracy; improvement of analytics through time-stamping for better pre-dictions; boosting compliance; increasing agility and scalability depend-ing on requirements; more comprehensive insight through reports; better decision-making; saving time in introducing new processes or process modification; better customer service by the robot and the freed-up work-ers; and increase in employee satisfaction from engaging in less tedious tasks (Tripathi, 2018).

As part of a value stream mapping (VSM) exercise, the improvement team can look to RPA to identify repetitive steps suitable for automation. Estimation of soft savings of workers' hours starts by listing all tasks, their frequency, and cost of manual labor per hour and then coming up with a total net impact of RPA after fairly subtracting the cost of creating the RPA algorithm.

12.4.5 Three-Dimensional (3D) Printing

Three-dimensional printing is a quick prototyping process where lay-ers of material are added together to form a 3D item. Melting material like plastic enables the creation of structural parts or subassembly elements (Nourbakhsh, 2013). It simply converts a digital model into a physical prod-uct. Another professional name for it is additive manufacturing or rapid pro-totyping (Horne and Hausman, 2017).

Three-dimensional printing can accelerate the repair process by printing the needed parts or tools instead of ordering them or keeping more inventory. It allows for flexible configuration and customization of products and production lines (Soldatos *et al.*, 2019). In addition, 3D printing is portable, with lower product waste and precise replication (Lipson and Kurman, 2013). It has now become more affordable to use than at its inception four decades ago. It is additive, with parts grown in layers in a single run instead of being subtracted from the raw material, resulting in almost no scrap. It does not require complex or expensive production tooling or handcrafting (Horne and Hausman, 2017).

Also, 3D printing is often used in prototyping to test various design iterations. Starting by digitally sk*etch*ing a 3D model and exporting it to a stereolithography (STL) file format leads to a slicing program that can read it and create coded instructions for the 3D printer to print it. Common 3D printing processes include hardening liquid resin polymers, plastic filament extrusion or fused filament fabrication (FFF), lost wax casting, and powder-based systems. 3D printing can help in making complex parts easily. However, it remains expensive for multiple prints of the same model and relatively expensive for large parts. It requires skilled designers and has a relatively limited range of materials (Ritland, 2014).

Researchers are exploring various uses for 3D printing, such as in the biomedical industry. However, viable alternatives for it still exist in the market (Horne and Hausman, 2017). Lipson and Kurman (2013) envisioned that just as people print an online document on paper and then scan and reprint it, someday they will be able to shape-shift and transform physical items from atoms to virtual bits and back again, similar to the concept of faxing and teleporting.

12.4.6 Artificial Intelligence (AI)

Artificial intelligence (AI) concerns the study of cognition and decision-making inside software systems that can carry out human-level operations, such as social interaction (Nourbakhsh, 2013). AI consists of a collection of computations a computer or a robot completes, which helps users perceive, reason, and act. It comprises illustrations of reality, cognition, information, and related methods of representation, including machine learning, representations of vision and language, robotics, and virtual reality (VR). It comprises a human-computer interface (HCI) in which bidirectional communication enables data to flow between information processors (computers) in a form convenient to a human operator using computational devices, displays, simulation, and a synthetic environment. VR is a re-creation of a real environment using digital graphics and data from multisensory devices to enable humans to interact with real and simulated objects in a synthesized environment (National Research Council, 1997).

AI concerns replicating human abilities in performing tasks. Siri is a good example of near-human results. Another example of AI exceeding human abilities is AlphaZero, which became the best chess player globally with less than four hours of self-training. AI algorithms filter, organize, and analyze data. Examples of AI technologies include statistical algorithms (used in text-based translation) and neural networks (used to train computers in image or pattern recognition) (Leehealey and Chigurula, 2019).

Fuzzy logic and expert systems are examples of how various industrial organizations have deployed AI for more than 20 years. AI can be embedded in physical systems like robots as well as in digital systems for automation. It has expanded to include deep learning associated with Big Data technologies, deep neural networks, and advanced data mining. AI can help identify complex patterns of machine degradation, product-defect causes, and failure modes more efficiently than traditional machine learning (Soldatos *et al.*, 2019).

12.4.7 Virtual Reality (VR)

Human curiosity has explored beyond reality to the recent developments in computer graphics, gaming, and social networking that have paved the way for virtual worlds to emerge. While the human senses establish real-world experience, a virtual-world experience emerges from using computer-generated illusions that create immersive environments where humans can interact, communicate, innovate, and trade (Bates-Brkljac, 2011).

VR is a technical domain that uses computer science and behavioral interfaces to enable human sensorimotor and cognitive activity in an artificial world, as a simulation of the behavior and interaction of 3D entities in real time (Fuchs *et al.*, 2011).

VR can serve in inspecting material structures and their applications, the simulation of machining processes to optimize machining parameters, development of virtual prototypes, and simulation of manufacturing processes. The next generation of enhanced simulation systems integrates VR characteristics with production process models. Also, 3D graphics and VR help provide data that is difficult to obtain using traditional methods (Bates-Brkljac,

2011). Other examples of VR and synthetic environments include remote manipulators, video games, and tele-operator systems where a human operator connects to a tele-robot that can sense, move in, and manipulate the real world. The human operator receives a transformed sensorimotor system in a virtual 3D environment to explore outer space, the ocean floor, and an internal human body (Mavor and Durlach, 1995).

In a Six Sigma Green Belt project, simulation software was used to virtually test various settings that formed a basis for a set of decisions, to see their impact on the overall recovered material from a manufacturing process. By saving the images of hundreds of boards of lumber, the Green Belt managed to run various tests with different settings or recipes to find the best one, in terms of recovered volume of greatest financial value. This method was offline and required no production interruption, and implementing the best settings in reality proved the method successful.

Another relevant technology is augmented reality (AR), useful for remote support of maintenance operators performing their service tasks. The repair instructions they receive from an expert at a distant location can guide them directly. AR can also support training operators on difficult or hazardous tasks by virtually presenting the ways experts perform them (Soldatos *et al.*, 2019).

12.4.8 *Additional Examples for Using I4.0 Technologies*

The following is a description of several examples of practical cases that illustrate the use of I4.0 technologies. Digital technologies can support automating and changing the setup of production lines faster and more flexibly than physical production systems. Digital technologies like Big Data and AI can help enhance predictive maintenance to reduce unplanned downtime, optimize overall equipment effectiveness (OEE), and prolong the productive life of equipment by scheduling maintenance and repairs at the best points in time. Obtaining and analyzing data from large digital data sets for the condition of equipment using vibration sensors, acoustic sensors, ultrasonic sensors, thermal images, power consumption, oil analysis, and quality systems achieves this. In terms of the key quality performance indicators relating to the operations and products, supply chain, and supplier material, Big Data analytics can assist improvement methodologies like Six Sigma in optimizing processes, identifying the causes of defects, employing self-learning systems, activating remedial actions, and reaching high levels of excellence. In addition, digital simulation can provide a feasible and superior approach to overcoming the inflexibility of industrial processes and trying different deployment configurations. Empowered by Big Data analytics, such tools as digital twins can provide a realistic digital model representing a physical entity and its behavioral properties, to run credible simulations, including digital data collection and analysis, prior to deploying new ideas in the physical world. The use of CPS systems and IoT technologies across the supply chain facilitates the integration of information that relates to the status of physical equipment and devices. This integration influences changes in the status of business information systems—*e.g.*, manufacturing schedules in ERP systems and material information in a warehouse management system (WMS)—which leads to an increase in supply chain efficiency. Visualization technologies, such as ergonomic dashboards, VR, and AR, help in training employees safely and tracking their work under the remote supervision of experts, within cyber representations of the physical environment (Soldatos *et al.*, 2019).

12.4.9 Essential Digital Technologies for Realizing the Vision of I4.0 and the Factories of the Future

In addition, here are some digital technologies essential for realizing the vision of I4.0 and the factories of the future (Soldatos *et al.*, 2019):

■ CPS systems are a main component of I4.0. Industrial internet of things (IIoT) systems facilitate data exchange and provide the means of connecting machines with IT systems and dealing with them as CPS systems.

■ Factories contain devices associated with I4.0 deployment—*e.g.*, sensors, gateways, encoders, actuators, and other automation devices, such as drones and autonomous guided vehicles. The need to be able to handle large amounts of data with low latency requires capabilities characteristic of 5G communication technologies.

■ The recent introduction of low power wide area networks (LPWAN) technologies supports IoT device connectivity. These technologies offer new applications, including the accurate localization of items in indoor environments.

■ To benefit from the capacity, scalability, and quality of cloud computing services, CPS systems, ERP, automation platforms, and various industrial applications are becoming cloud based. Edge computing complements cloud computing with capabilities for fast (near-real time) processing in the field, using edge nodes to support fast actuation and control of tasks.

■ I4.0 applications require cybersecurity solutions to protect data sets, ensure the trustworthiness of new devices, and protect against IT asset vulnerabilities.

12.4.10 Digital Shop Floor Properties

The following properties characterize digital shop floors that enable autonomous factories (Soldatos *et al.*, 2019):

■ End-to-end deployment of digital transformation across all the production processes.
■ Proactive optimization of operations through the prediction and anticipation of machine and product failures.
■ Real-time optimization through fast remedy of potential problems: *e.g.*, online defect repair.
■ Dynamic control of manufacturing processes supported by flexible and adaptable digital solutions, including automation and security.
■ The integration and use of standards-based solutions for interoperability utilizing IIoT.
■ Accessible solutions using open application programming interfaces (APIs) to facilitate adding more features and functionality.
■ Reduction of costs relating to manual processes, by using flexible and reconfigurable digital solutions that reduce deployment cost.
■ Addressing human factors, including aspects of product design, training, visual processes, and human safety.
■ The discipline of continuous improvement, including machines, processes, and production.

12.5 Summary of Additional Recommendations

Here is a summary of the key recommendations regarding the topics covered in this book:

■ Embed quality in the organizational culture.
■ Embed innovation in the organizational culture.
■ Use an integrated Lean and Six Sigma approach.

- Use self-assessment award models.
- Use effective tools and techniques suitable and specifically necessary for the faced challenges (Snee and Hoerl, 2018).
- Ensure management's full commitment and support.
- Ensure delivery of effective, timely, and planned training.
- Ensure to have well-defined aims and objectives for using quality tools and principles.
- Set up a cooperative environment.
- Seek backup and support as needed from facilitators or experts.

12.6 Conclusion

This book introduced various principles, concepts, pillars, and tools of quality enhancement, which, if adopted properly, can contribute and deliver great benefits to any organization, its employees, stakeholders, customers, and society at large. However, these pillars alone cannot guarantee the accomplishment of excellence without sufficiently focusing on the human element within the improvement journey. Keeping employees at the center of this effort is essential for success.

Continuous improvement (CI) is a journey that takes persistence and commitment. It is not a short-term initiative but a lifetime endeavor devoted to the pursuit of excellence. The challenge within the CI journey is not only to satisfy customers but to delight them by exceeding their expectations. Effective communication among all stakeholders is critical to success in this pursuit. Moreover, the measurement of efficiency and effectiveness; cost of quality; loss to society; quality assurance (QA); the use of a structured improvement approach; the deployment of effective programs to achieve process stability and capability; the utilization of a variety of LSS quality tools and techniques; the use of an integrated company-wide management system (ICWMS) serving as a foundation for CI, effective change management, and quality culture are all important to success on this journey. In addition, innovating with new ideas that contribute to that goal and the adoption of new trends and technological advancements of I4.0 and Q4.0, such as Big Data, blockchain, RPA, AI, and VR, are all vital to succeeding and ensuring sustained value to all society and humanity.

APPENDICES

Appendix A

Case Study A: Supply Chain (SC) Improvement Project

Implementation of Lean Six Sigma (LSS) in Supply Chain Management (SCM): An Integrated and Automated Approach

The following case study is used to illustrate some of the ideas explained in the various pillars, such as the ones in Sections 9.1 and 12.2. It is essentially a case that demonstrates the improvement of a cargo-handling process from a logistics service sector.

Introduction

Supply chain management (SCM) is vital for any organization to sustain its existence in today's modern world. There have been various changes in markets across the world, resulting from new realities related to human health, way of living, and technological advancements, which all force supply chain (SC) members to reevaluate their effectiveness individually and as a whole. A new evolution in quality management (QM) is Lean Six Sigma (LSS), which is a structured approach and a continuous improvement (CI) methodology that aims at customer satisfaction and waste reduction. SCM can utilize LSS tools and CI principles to achieve high levels of customer satisfaction regarding cost, quality, and delivery. Some researchers have considered the integration of Lean and Six Sigma with SCM. This case study extends the previous works and provides an example of how LSS, utilizing value stream mapping (VSM), can be used to improve the SC through an integrated and automated approach. The VSM approach is about enabling the team to reassess the existing system of processes from a high-level perspective, by stepping out of their limited view of the process. It enables them to identify various challenges and opportunities across the supply chain and value stream, including the basic physical operational issues (related to operators and locations, reports, and communication), information technology (IT) operating systems (related to smart data entry devices and integrated software systems), and virtual customer service and integrated stakeholders' platforms (which allows various stakeholders to interact and share data to facilitate overall communication and simplify the process). In addition, robotic process automation (RPA), which automates repetitive and manual tasks through computer programming, is considered for creating invoices, as one example of automation.

Using the VSM as Part of DMAIC LSS Structured Approach to Improve a Supply Chain

Here are some examples of improvement opportunities, which were raised as part of the VSM exercise conducted during this case study. They were grouped into the following five categories:

1. The basic and physical aspects of the operation of material handling and transportation (related to operators, layouts, and locations): Relocate all supervisors and employees who frequently interact with one another, and bring them together within the same location; shift the operator rest area to a location near to equipment parking as well as supervisors offices; eliminate unnecessary walking, and make it easier to communicate between employees; and shift the operators' current station to reduce the commuting distance, and dedicate an area for their new station near to the yard of operation.
2. Issues related to planning, scheduling, reporting, and communication: Eliminate unnecessary meetings, eliminate unnecessary repetition of communicated instructions or training, ensure all roles and responsibilities are clear for all parties involved, set up service level agreements (SLAs), and eliminate unnecessary reports.
3. IT, internal operating systems (related to electronic data interchange (EDI), smart and mobile data-entry devices as well as integrated software systems): Integrate internal operating systems with an external

platform that includes all missing fields; remove the unnecessary approval process that is built into the internal operating system; design automatic reports to replace and combine various manual ones that used to be prepared in Excel or other formats; enable the EDI features in the operating system; configure proper events to send an automated email notification to the required teams at proper moments as triggered by the process incidents; reconcile documents by mistake-proofing and enhancement of systems; design an in-house dashboard to enhance communication and integrate equipment and labor requirements; enhance the centralized resource management system, and include notification features; use barcoded inventory for all required tools in the operation; implement handheld tablets (HHT) equipped with a customized software solution (integrating the internal operating system with an automatic and real-time system for data uploading to replace several forms and eliminate the need for manual entry, reentry, and reporting); and configure the logistics-zone gate process and HHT functionality for outbound deliveries and inbound cargo.

4. Virtual customer service and integrated stakeholders platforms, which allow various external stakeholders to interact and share data to facilitate the overall communication and simplify the process: Remove the unnecessary approval process in the external platform, encourage customers to use the external platform (single window) instead of using emails to manage their orders, eliminate the waiting time by enabling customers to upload ready documents along with the initial step, stop customers from uploading redundant data by directly feeding it into the external platform, replace emails by providing options in the external platform to enable status visibility by auto-status to indicate "ready" versus "in progress" as an example, enhance the external platform to allow different stakeholders and customers to submit their documents directly, introduce an online payment method using the external platform, introduce a delivery appointment system configurable by a terminal operation team to provide delivery slot capacity using the external platform, and enable the attachment of payment receipt upon booking the delivery request.

5. Robotic process automation (RPA): Use RPA to automate repetitive manual tasks of invoicing (auto-calculate then auto-post, customer submits request and supporting documents via system, robot prepares invoices via ERP system, employee receives drafted invoice for review and approval, and invoice is issued and sent electronically to requestor).

Also, this case study provided a good example for taking an experienced operation supervisor, who is typically immersed in his day-to-day tasks, and training him to use the structured approach of LSS DMAIC utilizing VSM (current-state mapping in the measure phase and future-state mapping in the improve phase). This supervisor was successful in using VSM as a framework to help identify all gaps and voice all the pain points across the SC.

As a result of this project, various outcomes had a significant impact on several stakeholders, such as automation of manual tasks, reduction of cycle times and overall lead time, reduction of idle and wasteful operators' time, and the enhancement of communication among all stakeholders. Finally, the resulted financial savings were in the order of hundreds of thousands of dollars annually.

Appendix B

Case Study B: Revenue Assurance Project

Implementation of Lean Six Sigma (LSS) in Revenue Assurance: An Integrated and Automated Approach

Introduction

The following case study is used to illustrate the various ideas explained within the different pillars of quality discussed earlier in this book. It is essentially a case that demonstrates the digital transformation of a financial revenue assurance process from a logistics services sector.

Define Phase

Initially, the project team studied the steps of the current process under consideration for improvement. At the beginning of the process, customers visit the documentation centers to clear cargo from a port of entry. They manually submit four original documents that include the packing list, bill of lading (BoL), bill of entry (BoE), and delivery order (DO). These documents are checked and reviewed by an employee sitting at a reception counter. Once verified, an invoice is issued accordingly. The customers can initiate the payment process whenever they want to claim the cargo via any of the available payment methods (*i.e.*, cash, credit card, bank check, or wire transfer). A receipt will then be printed out and submitted to the customers to enable them to clear the cargo for delivery. Figure B.1 shows a high-level process

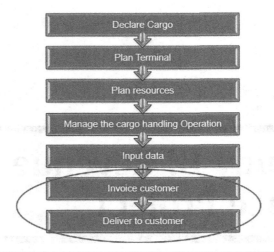

Figure B.1   A high-level process map for general cargo import and delivery, highlighting the key area of focus in the improvement project.

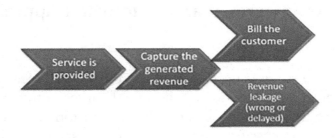

Figure B.2   Revenue leakage challenge.

map for general cargo import and delivery, highlighting the invoicing and delivery steps as the key focus area in this project. Also, Figure B.2 shows a simple illustration of the revenue leakage challenge, mainly occurring due to wrong or delayed billing. Here are some additional observations noted by the improvement team:

- A customer has to conduct multiple visits to the documentation center.
- The process is mostly paper based (including original documents, invoices, and receipts).
- An online payment option is not available.
- Reviewing the packing list takes time and effort.
- Documentation centers are not open for 24 hours a day.

- Cash and checks are collected by a paid service provider.
- Booking appointments for bringing the trucks to the terminal are arranged via email.

Measuring the Baseline and the Opportunity

The improvement team completed a detailed VSM exercise to identify all the steps in the process, including various measurements such as the cycle times, processing times, waiting and idle times, and the overall lead time from the receipt of customer order until delivery of cargo.

Here is a description of the current process. The clearing agent submits the physical copies of the cargo-related documents. Then the terminal operator verifies the DO, BoE, and packing list. The terminal operator then finalizes the total handling charges as per the packing list quantity. Then the clearing agent pays the corresponding charges at the counter and books a delivery appointment by email. The truck passage through the port gate is allowed only after payment confirmation.

Analyze

The project team conducted brainstorming sessions to identify opportunities and wasteful activities within the value stream map (VSM). Every process stage was analyzed to identify possible gaps that could be resolved and simplified using mistake-proofing and automation techniques.

Digitalization as a Key Part of the Analysis Phase

A digital transformation approach is about enabling teams to reassess the existing system of processes from an automation perspective. It enables the identification of various challenges and opportunities across the value stream, including:

- Information technology (IT)—operating systems related to the following:
  - Smart data entry.
  - Electronic submittal of service requests, such as imported and exported cargo requests.
  - Electronic upload of information and documents.
  - Online payment.

- Online booking of appointments for delivery.
- Multi-way verification of information, considering RPA for calculating revenue and creating invoices.
- Integrated software systems to allow for fetching the updated information.

■ Virtual customer service and integrated stakeholders' platforms, which allow various stakeholders to interact and share data via electronic data interchange (EDI) to facilitate the overall communication, simplify processes, and enable an easier user interface.

Improve

In this project, the following solutions were implemented. They were related to the automation of various systems as well as the enhancement of services using IT solutions:

■ An option was provided to the shipping agent to send the DO information electronically to the terminal by developing an integration between a web-based platform (*i.e.*, an online portal for trading connectivity) and the terminal operating system (TOS) for the cargo-handling operation.

■ An integration was established between customs and the TOS to ensure that the TOS receives customs clearance and BoE information that is required for releasing the cargo for delivery.

■ An option was provided to the clearing agent or importer to upload an electronic format of the packing list, BoL, DO, and BoE into the integrated system as required for the cargo-handling operation.

■ A three-way verification process was automated and enabled for the discharge list, electronic packing list, and BoE information to capture any inconsistencies in the information provided to the general cargo terminal team and, thereby, avoid revenue leakages.

■ The integration between the electronic trading platform and the TOS was enhanced to allow the platform to fetch the updated cargo inventory information as well as the charges for the general cargo operation.

■ An option was provided for the customer to pay the terminal charges online, using electronic payment (*i.e.*, eliminating the need for checks or cash).

■ An option was provided to the agent to book a delivery appointment and pay the corresponding terminal charges online, by developing an integration between the electronic platform and the TOS for general cargo operation. The appointment system helped the terminal team to effectively plan and schedule the required resources while reducing the congestion at the port of entry.

In addition, improvements included the following introduced products:

■ A new online portal for general cargo replacing the physical visits by customers and serving as a platform where customers can log in, upload supporting documents, get invoices, process the payment, and clear their cargo accordingly.
■ An electronic wallet for online payment.
■ An RPA (Robotic Process Automation) solution for repetitive and manual tasks, such as fee calculations.

The stakeholders considered and involved in this project included the following:

■ General cargo customers, such as shipping agents, clearing agents, importers, exporters, consignees, and trucking companies.
■ Documentation center employees.
■ Finance and accounting team.
■ General cargo terminal and operation team.

Here is a description of the steps of the newly improved process. The freight forwarder (FF) or the clearing agent (CA) or the customer or consignee will submit a copy of the cargo-related documents online along with a delivery plan. The terminal operator will then verify the DO, BoE, packing list, and delivery plan, and finalize the charges. Then the terminal operator will resynchronize the handling charges as per the packing list quantity and enable the delivery slots to be open in the system. The CA will book an appointment by specifying the selected time slot in the system. The appointment is approved automatically, but the operator can override that approval if required. Once the truck loading is completed, the TOS will send a cargo activity message (CAMS) confirming the execution.

Further, here is a description of the newly introduced system:

■ An online portal is developed for a customer to log in and submit all the documents online, eliminating the site visit, in addition to the portal being available all the time.

- Documents will then be immediately checked by a "bot" programmed to check all the documents, eliminating the human factor, and reducing errors. Once the documents are validated and approved by the RPA bot for further processing, the customer will receive an alert with the same information. The bot will then scan through the packing list and calculate the charges in an instant. After that, a message appears to alert an employee to proceed and post the invoice.
- Then the customer will be given payment options, which include the previously available options, in addition to internet banking and electronic wallet.
- The employee will issue the receipt accordingly, and the customer will proceed to clear the cargo and schedule the delivery appointment.

The new web-based platform included the following:

- A page to request a general cargo import transaction.
- A page to check the availability of the required equipment for the handling operation and then perform the planning and booking of that equipment.
- A page to plan and schedule the delivery of the imported cargo.
- A page to electronically request the processing of payment. Figure B.3 shows the results of the use of the new online portal to handle the processing of service payments.

By the implementation of the new system, the terminal operation team managed to add value and realize several benefits, such as the following:

- They eliminated revenue leakage: The team managed to prevent revenue leakage, because they started to block the calculated terminal

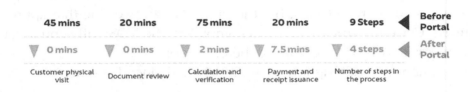

45 mins	20 mins	75 mins	20 mins	9 Steps	◀ Before Portal
0 mins	0 mins	2 mins	7.5 mins	4 steps	◀ After Portal
Customer physical visit	Document review	Calculation and verification	Payment and receipt issuance	Number of steps in the process	

Figure B.3 A comparison of some key metrics before and after improving the processing of service payment.

handling charges as well as the storage charges in advance using the electronic wallet for cash customers.

- They reduced the human-hours costs and expenses: Direct terminal visits and expenses were reduced by automating the process and submitting the documents online. Also, indirect administration costs and expenses were reduced by automating the payment process.
- They increased throughput or productivity: This was achieved by enhancing the planning process and the automation of various steps in the process.
- They enhanced customer satisfaction: The terminal team managed to provide a higher quality of service and eventually achieve a higher customer satisfaction rate by automating the process.
- They improved the utilization of resources:
  - The terminal team achieved a better usage of the available capacity of resources at the terminal.
  - They reduced congestion at the port.
  - They improved terminal operation planning and the scheduling of the resources.
  - They reduced the truck turnaround time.

Here is a description of how the implemented cargo delivery appointments' system was designed to work:

1. The terminal team would make the slots available for appointment-booking one day in advance.
2. CAs, Consignee, and FFs would all have an option to book delivery appointments by selecting the specified time slots that are available as part of a delivery plan.
3. Against each line from the delivery plan, the customer would be able to provide the detailed pickup schedule, including the number of trucks, the plate number, and the truck capacity.
4. The terminal team would be given an option to view the proposed time slot for cargo pickup. The appointments would be auto-approved by the system; however, the terminal team is able to override that approval, if required.
5. The terminal operator would have a dashboard to monitor, plan, or review the equipment and the delivery slot availability.
6. The appointment charges would be calculated by the system and would be integrated with the ERP system.

Control

In this phase, the project team met and ensured to accomplish the following steps:

- They completed the remaining tasks toward achieving the future state.
- They handed over the control plan to the process owner to ensure the gains are maintained.
- They validated the results.
- They captured the best practices and lessons learned.

Summary of the Key Results of the Project

- Automation of manual tasks, reduction of employee efforts and cycle times in the order of thousands of worker-hours (freed-up staff were relocated to fill other required vacancies), reduction of paper usage and documentation cost, enhancement of communication among all stakeholders, enhancement of revenue through new streams (like the new service fee introduced for handling the whole process on customers' behalf), and increased financial savings in the order of hundreds of thousands of dollars annually.
- Customer satisfaction, reducing customers' visits to the documentation centers and the waiting time, allowing customers to submit documents online at any time and pay the charges at their convenience, enhanced utilization of equipment, faster turnaround time for trucks, and easier information reporting.
- Introducing smart services, offering more payment options, reducing revenue collection time, and reducing errors through the automation of tasks.

Summary of the Key Conclusions Based on This Project

- LSS DMAIC can help improve the cargo-handling process as well as the revenue assurance process using VSM, to ensure the efficient flow of information among various stakeholders and to enable electronic solutions.
- Logistics processes as well as financial processes can utilize LSS principles, such as focusing on adding value to customers, reducing defects and waste, streamlining the flow of value, and improving on-time delivery of goods.

References

Agnellutti, C. (2014). *Big data: an exploration of opportunities, values, and privacy issues.* New York: Nova Science Publishers, Inc.

Ahrens, T. (2013). Assembling the Dubai government excellence program: a motivational approach to improving public service governance in a monarchical context. *International Journal of Public Sector Management, 26*(7), 576–592.

Amabile, T. M. (1998). How to kill creativity. *Harvard Business Review, 76*(5), 77–87.

American Productivity and Quality Center (APQC). (2018). Retrieved June 11, 2021, from www.apqc.org/resource-library/resource-listing/apqc-process-classification-framework-pcf-cross-industry-pdf-8.

Anderson, R., Eriksson, H. and Torstensson, H. (2006). Similarities and differences between TQM, Six Sigma and Lean. *The TQM Magazine, 18*(3), 282–296.

Antony, J. (2002). Design for Six Sigma: a breakthrough business improvement strategy for achieving competitive advantage. *Work Study, 51*(1), 6–8.

Antony, J. (2004). Some pros and cons of Six Sigma: an academic perspective. *The TQM Magazine, 16*(4), 303–306.

Antony, J. (2006). Six Sigma for service processes. *Business Process Management Journal, 12*(2), 234–248.

Antony, J. (2008). What is the role of academic institutions for the future development of Six Sigma? *International Journal of Productivity and Performance Management, 57*(1), 107–110.

Antony, J., McDermott, O., Sony, M., Fernando, M. M. and Rebeiro, R. B. C. (2021). A study on the Ishikawa's original basic tools of quality control in South American companies: results from a pilot survey and directions for further research. *The TQM Journal, 33*(8), 1770–1786.

Arnheiter, E. D. and Maleyeff, J. (2005). Research and concepts: the integration of lean management and six sigma. *The TQM Magazine, 17*(1), 5–18.

ASQ (2021). The seven basic quality tools for process improvement: excerpted from the quality toolbox. *ASQ Quality Press.* Retrieved January 23, 2021, from https://asq.org/quality-resources/seven-basic-quality-tools.

Atkinson, P. and Murray, B. (1988). Striving for excellence: the service sector. *Total Quality Management: An IFS Executive Briefing*, 171–173.

Babatunde, O. K. (2021). Mapping the implications and competencies for industry 4.0 to hard and soft total quality management. *The TQM Journal*, *33*(4), 896–914.

Banafa, A. (2020). *Blockchain technology and applications*. River Publishers. ProQuest Ebook Central. https://ebookcentral.proquest.com/lib/adportsae/detail.action?docID=6300570.

Banuelas, R. and Antony, J. (2003). Going from Six Sigma to design for Six Sigma: an exploratory study using hierarchy process. *The TQM Magazine*, *15*(5), 334–344.

Banuelas, R. and Antony, J. (2004). Six Sigma or design for Six Sigma. *The TQM Magazine*, *16*(4), 250–263.

Basu, R. (2004). Six-Sigma to operational excellence: role of tools and techniques. *International Journal of Six Sigma and Competitive Advantage*, *1*(1), 44–64.

Bates-Brkljac, N. (2011). *Virtual reality*. New York: Nova Science Publishers, Inc.

Beatty, J. R. (2006). The quality journey: historical and workforce perspectives and the assessment of commitment to quality. *International Journal of Productivity and Quality Management*, *1*(1–2), 139–167.

Bellows, W. J. (2004). Conformance to specifications, zero defects, and Six Sigma quality—a closer look. *The International Journal of Internet and Enterprise Management*, *2*(1), 82–95.

Bens, I. (2000). *Advanced team facilitation*. 1st Edition. Salem, NH: Goal/QPC.

Bendell, T. (2006). A review and comparison of Six Sigma and the Lean organizations. *The TQM Magazine*, *18*(3), 255–262.

Berling, C. (2001). The human side of continuous improvement. *International Journal of Human Resources Development and Management*, *1*(2–4), 183–191.

Bernstein, A. (2018). Net promoter score and the merchants. *Builders Merchant Journal*, *9*(1), August.

Besterfield, D. H (1994). *Quality control*. Englewood Cliffs, NJ: Prentice-Hall.

Bhasin, S. and Burcher, P. (2006). Lean viewed as a philosophy. *Journal of Manufacturing Technology Management*, *17*(1), 56–72.

Bohns, V. (2017). A face-to-face request is 34 times more successful than an email. *Harvard Business Review*, April 11. Retrieved October 20, 2021, from https://hbr.org/2017/04/a-face-to-face-request-is-34-times-more-successful-than-an-email.

Box, G. E. P., Hunter W. G. and Hunter, J. S. (1978). *Statistics for experimenters*. New York: John Wiley and Sons.

Breyfogle, F. W. (2003). *Implementing six sigma*. Hoboken: Wiley.

Bullard, F. (2022). *Power in tests of significance*. Retrieved July 5, 2022, from https://apcentral.collegeboard.org/courses/ap-statistics/classroom-resources/power-in-tests-of-significance#:~:text=The%20significance%20level%20%CE%B1%20of,of%20rejecting%20the%20null%20hypothesis.

Carvalho, A. V., Enrique, D. V., Amal Chouchenea, A. and Charrua-Santos, F. (2021). Quality 4.0: an overview. *Procedia Computer Science*, *181*, 341–346.

Castle, J. A. (1996). An integrated model in quality management, positioning TQM, BPR and ISO 9000. *The TQM Magazine*, *8*(5), 7–13.

Cavallucci, D. (2017). *TRIZ—the theory of inventive problem solving*. Cham, Switzerland: Springer International Publishing.

Chapman, R. L. and Hyland, P. W. (1997). Continuous improvement Strategies across selected Australian manufacturing sectors. *Benchmarking for Quality Management and Technology, 4*(3), 175–188.

Chen, C. C. (2007). Integration of quality function deployment and process management in the semiconductor industry. *International Journal of Production Research, 47*(6), 1469–1484.

Chen, C. C. and Chuang, M. C. (2008). Integrating the Kano model into a robust design approach to enhance customer satisfaction with product design. *International Journal of Production Economics, 114*(2), 667–681.

Chiarini, A. (2020). Industry 4.0, quality management and TQM world: a systematic literature review and a proposed agenda for further research. *The TQM Journal, 32*(4), 603–616.

Crosby, P. B. (1979). *Quality is free: the art of making quality certain*. New York, NY: McGraw-Hill.

Crump, B. (2008). How can we make improvement happen? *Clinical Governance: An International Journal, 13*(1), 43–50.

Cunningham, J. B. (1979). The management system: its functions and processes. *Management Science, 25*(7), 657–670.

CQM. (1993). A special issue on Kano's methods for understanding customer-defined quality. *The Center for Quality Management Journal, 2*(4), 3–35.

Cyger, M. (2022). *Six Sigma and costs savings*. Retrieved May 20, 2022, from www.isixsigma.com/implementation/financial-analysis/six-sigma-costs-and-savings/.

Dahlgaard, J. J. and Dahlgaard-Park, S. M. (2006). Lean production, Six Sigma, TQM and company culture. *The TQM Magazine, 18*(3), 263–281.

Dahlgaard, J. J., Kristensen, K. and Kanji, G. K. (2007). *Fundamentals of total quality management: process analysis and improvement*. London: Taylor and Francis.

Dale, B. G., Bamform, D. and Wiele, T. V. D. (2016). *Managing quality: an essential guide and resource gateway*. New York: Wiley and Sons Inc.

De Feo, J. A. and Bar-El, Z. (2002). Creating strategic change more efficiently with a new design for Six Sigma process. *Journal of Change Management, 3*(1), 60–80.

DeGroot, M. H. (1970). *Optimal statistical decisions*. New York, NY: McGraw-Hill.

Deming, W. E. (1986). *Out of crisis*. Cambridge, MA: MIT Press.

Deming, W. E. (1993). *The new economics for industry, government, education*. Cambridge, MA: MIT Press, Center for Advanced Engineering Study.

Devane, T. (2004). *Integrating Lean Six Sigma and high performance organizations*. San Francisco, CA: Pfeiffer/A Wiley Imprint.

Devor, R. E., Chang, T. and Sutherland, J. W. (1992). *Statistical quality design and control: contemporary concepts and method*. Upper Saddle River, NJ: Prentice Hall.

Dowd, C. (1988). Measuring and tracking the cost of quality. *Total Quality Management: An IFS Executive Briefing*, 37–41.

Drain, D. and Gough, A. M. (1996). Applications of the upside-down normal loss function. *IEEE Transactions of Semiconductor Manufacturing*, 9(1), 143–145.

Dubai Government Excellence Program (DGEP). (2019). Retrieved April 9, 2019, from https://dgep.gov.ae/en/program-award/award-criteria.

Dyason, M. D. and Kaye, M. M. (1995). Is there life after total quality management? (II). *Quality World*, January.

Ekings, J. D. (1988). A nine-step quality improvement program to increase customer satisfaction. *Total Quality Management: An IFS Executive Briefing*, 73–81.

Evans, J. R. and Lindsay, W. M. (2002). *The management and control of quality*. Cincinnati, OH: South-Western, a Division of Thomson Learning.

Evans, J. R. and Lindsay, W. M. (2020). *Managing for quality and performance excellence*. 11th Edition. Thomson South-Western, Mason: Cengage Learning Custom Publishing.

Farmer, E. L. and Duffy, G. L. (2017). *The ASQ CSSYB study guide*. Chicago: Quality Press. ProQuest Ebook Central.

Feigenbaum, A. V. (1991). *Total quality control*. New York, NY: McGraw-Hill.

Foster, S. T. (2007). *Managing quality: integrating the supply chain*. Upper Saddle River, NJ: Pearson Education-Prentice Hall.

Francis, D. and Bessant, J. (2005). Targeting innovation and implications for capability development. *Technovation*, 25(3), 171–183.

Friday-Stroud, S. S. and Sutterfield, J. S. (2007). A conceptual framework for integrating Six-Sigma and strategic management methodologies to quantify decision making. *The TQM Magazine*, 19(6), 561–571.

Fuchs, P., Moreau, G. and Guitton, P. (2011). *Virtual reality: concepts and technologies*. London: Taylor and Francis Group.

Gallup. (2021). *What is employee engagement and how do you improve it? Workplace*. Retrieved May 10, 2021, from www.gallup.com/workplace/285674/improve-employee-engagement-workplace.aspx.

Garber, P. R. (2008). *50 communications activities, icebreakers, and exercises*. Amherst, MA: HRD Press.

Garvin, D. A. (1988). *Managing quality*. New York, NY: The Free Press.

Gee, B., Bonney, D. S. and Journigan, W. G. (2015). *Design of experiments part 1*. Retrieved July 5, 2022, from https://businessdocbox.com/Human_Resources/91018818-Design-of-experiments-part-1.html.

Gitlow, S. H., Melnyck, R. J. and Levine, D. M. (2015). *A guide to Six Sigma and process improvement for practitioners and students*. Old Tappan, NJ: Pearson Education Inc.

Goetsch, L. D. and Davis, S. (2013). *Quality management for organizational excellence: introduction to total quality*. 7th Edition. Upper Saddle River, NJ: Pearson.

Good, P. (1994). *Permutation tests: a practical guide to resampling methods for testing hypotheses*. New York, NY: Springer.

Government Excellence System (GES). (2015). Retrieved January 30, 2017, from www.id.gov.ae/userfiles/assets/RYrCXZZnn7l.pdf.

Grossman, D. (2012). *You can't not communicate.* 2nd Edition. Chicago, IL: Little Brown Dog Publishing.

Gunasekaran, A. (2006). Editorial: productivity and quality in the 21st century. *International Journal of Productivity and Quality Management, 1*(1–2), 1–7.

Gunter, B. (1988). A perspective on the Taguchi methods. *Total Quality Management: An IFS Executive Briefing,* 99–108.

Han, C. and Lee, Y. (2002). Intelligent integrated plant operation system for Six Sigma. *Annual Reviews in control, 26,* 27–43.

Harnesk, R. and Abrahamsson, L. (2007). TQM: an act of balance between contradictions. *The TQM Magazine, 19*(6), 531–540.

Harry, M. and Schroeder, R. (2000). *Six Sigma; the breakthrough management strategy revolutionizing the world's top corporations.* New York, NY: Currency/Doubleday.

Hassan, A., Baksh, M. S. N. and Shaharoun, A. M. (2000). Issues in quality engineering research. *International Journal of Quality and Reliability Management, 17*(8), 858–875.

Hilb, M. (2006). *New corporate governance.* Berlin, Germany: Springer.

Hines, P., Holweg, M. and Rich, N. (2004). Learning to evolve: a review of contemporary Lean thinking. *International Journal of Operations and Production Management, 24*(10), 994–1011.

Hoerl, R. (2004). One perspective on the future of Six-Sigma. *International Journal of Six Sigma and Competitive Advantage, 1*(1), 112–119.

Holweg, M. (2007). The genealogy of Lean production. *Journal of Operations Management, 25*(1), 420–437.

Horne, R. and Hausman, K. K. (2017). *3D printing for dummies.* New York: John Wiley and Sons, Inc.

Imai, M. (2012). *Gemba Kaizen: a commonsense approach to a continuous improvement strategy.* New York: McGraw-Hill.

Ishikawa, K. (1983). *What is company-wide quality control?* A paper presented to Ford Executives, Englewood Cliffs, NJ, May.

Ishikawa, K. (1985). *What is quality control? The Japanese way.* Englewood Cliffs, NJ: Prentice-Hall, Inc.

Jamkhaneh, H. B., Shahin, A., Parkouhi, A. S. and Shahin, R. (2022). The new concept of quality in the digital era: a human resource empowerment perspective. *The TQM Journal, 34*(1), 125–144.

Jitpaiboon, T. and Rao, S. S. (2007). A meta-analysis of quality measures in manufacturing system. *International Journal of Quality and Reliability Management, 24*(1), 78–102.

Johnson, D. M. (2004). Adaptation of organizational change models to the implementation of quality standard requirements. *International Journal of Quality and Reliability Management, 21*(2), 154–174.

Johnson, R. A., Kast, F. E. and Rosenzweig, J. E. (1964). Systems theory and management. *Management Science, 10*(2), 367–384.

Juran, J. M. and Godfrey, A. B. (1999). *Juran's quality control handbook.* New York: McGraw-Hill.

Kaneko, N. (1988). Total quality control promotion in service industries. *Total Quality Management: An IFS Executive Briefing*, 189–194.

Kannan, V. R. and Tan, K. C. (2005). Just in time, total quality management, and supply chain management: understanding their linkages and impact on business performance. *The International Journal of Management Science, Omega, 33*, 153–162.

Kano, N., Seraku, N., Takahashi, F. and Tsuji, F. (1984). Attractive quality and must-be quality. *Hinshitsu (Quality, the Journal of Japanese Society for Quality Control), 14*(2), 39–48.

Kaplan, R. S. and Norton, D. P. (2004). *Strategy maps: converting intangible assets into tangible outcomes*. Boston, MA: Harvard Business School Press.

Kaplan, R. S. and Norton, D. P. (2006). *Alignment: using the balanced scorecard to create corporate synergies*. Boston, MA: Harvard Business School Publication Corporation.

Kaye, M. and Anderson, R. (1999). Continuous improvement: the ten essential criteria. *International Journal of Quality and Reliability Management, 16*(5), 485–506.

Keller, G. (2005). *Statistics for management and economics*. Duxbury, MA: Thomson Books/Cole, Thomson Corporation.

Keller, R. T. (1978). Dimensions of management system and performance in continuous process organizations. *Human Relations, 31*(1), 59–75.

Kepner, C. H. and Tregoe, B. B. (2006). *The new rational manager*. Princeton, NJ: Princeton Research Press.

Kiernan, D. (2014). *Natural resources biometrics*. Geneseo, NY: Open SUNY Textbooks, Milne Library (IITG PI), State University of New York.

Klefsjo, B., Wiklund, H. and Edgeman, R. L. (2001). Six-Sigma seen as a methodology for total quality management. *Measuring Business Excellence, 5*(1), 31–35.

Kolarik, W. J. (1995). *Creating quality: concepts, systems, strategies and tools*. New York, NY: McGraw-Hill.

Kotter, J. P. (2012). *Leading change*. Boston, MA: Harvard Business Review Press.

Kumar, U. D., Nowicki, D., Ramírez-Márquez, J. E. and Verma, D. (2008). On the optimal selection of process alternatives in a Six Sigma implementation. *International Journal of Production Economics, 111*(2), 456–467.

Kwak, Y. H. and Anbari, F. T. (2004). Benefits, obstacles and future of Six Sigma approach. *Technovation, 26*(5), 708–715.

Lee, D. and Hatesohl, D. (1993). *Listening: our most used communications skill, extension and agricultural information*. Retrieved October 20, 2021, from https://extension.missouri.edu/publications/cm150.

Lee, D. and Lee, D. H. (2013). A comparative study of quality awards: evolving criteria and research. *Service Business, 7*(3), 347–362.

Lee, H. L. (2004). The triple-A supply chain. *Harvard Business Review*, 102–112, October.

Leehealey, A. and Chigurula, A. (2019). *Fighting crime with Artificial Intelligence (AI)*. Proceedings of the International Conference of Artificial Intelligence (ICAI). Publication of the 2019 World Congress in Computer Science,

Engineering and Applied Computing (CSCE'19) | CSREA Press, Las Vegas, Nevada, 284–290, August 1, 2019. https://americancse.org/events/csce2019.

Lemonis, M. (2021). What people/process/product means and how it can help your business. *Marcuslemonis*. Retrieved April, 17, 2021, from www.marcuslemonis. com/budsiness/3ps-of-business.

Leonard, D. and McAdam, R. (2004). Total quality management in strategy and operations: dynamic grounded models. *Journal of Manufacturing Technology Management, 15*(3), 254–266.

Li, M.-H. C. (2003). Quality loss functions for the management of service quality. *International Journal of Advanced Manufacturing Technology, 21*, 29–37.

Lipson, H. and Kurman, M. (2013). *Fabricated: the new world of 3D printing.* New York: John Wiley and Sons, Inc.

Mangelsdorf, D. (1999). Evolution from quality management to an integrative system based on TQM and its impact on the profession of quality managers in industry. *The TQM Magazine, 11*(6), 419–424.

Markarian, G. and Staniforth, A. (2020). *Countermeasures for aerial drones.* Norwood, MA: Artech House.

Martin, J. W. (2007). *Lean Six Sigma for supply chain management, the 10-step solution process.* New York, NY: The McGraw-Hill Companies, Inc.

Martinez-Lorente, A. R., Dewhurst, F. and Dale, B. G. (1998). Total quality management: origin and evolution of the term. *The TQM Magazine, 10*(5), 378–386.

Matzler, K. and Hinterhuber, H. H. (1998). How to make product development more successful by integrating Kano's model of customer satisfaction into quality function deployment. *Technovation, 18*(1), 25–38.

Mavor, A. S. and Durlach, N. I. (1995). *Virtual reality: scientific and technological challenges.* Washington, DC: National Academy Press.

McAdam, R., Armstrong, G. and Kelly, B. (1998). Investigation of the relationship between total quality and innovation: a research study involving small organizations. *European Journal of Innovation Management, 1*(3), 139–147.

McAdam, R. and Evans, A. (2004). The organizational contextual factors affecting the implementation of Six Sigma in a high technology mass-manufacturing environment. *International Journal of Six Sigma and Competitive Advantage, 1*(1), 29–43.

McAdam, R., Leonard, D., Henderson, J. and Hazlett, S. A. (2008). A grounded theory research approach to building and testing TQM theory in operations management. *The International Journal of Management Science, 36*, 825–837.

McDonald, I., Zairi, M. and Ashari Idris, M. (2002). Sustaining and transferring excellence: a framework of best practice of TQM transformation based on winners of Baldrige and European quality awards. *Measuring Business Excellence, 6*(3), 20–30.

Mei, Y. L. (2018). *Robotic process automation with blue prism quick start guide: create software robots and automate business processes.* Birmingham: Packt Publishing, Ltd.

Mellat-Parasat, M. and Digman, L. (2007). A framework for quality management practices in strategic alliances. *Management Decision, 45*(4), 802–818.

Montgomery, D. C. (2001). *Introduction to statistical quality control.* New York: John Wiley and Sons, Inc.

Montgomery, D. C. (2010). A modern framework for achieving enterprise excellence. *International Journal of Lean Six Sigma, 1*(1), 56–65.

Morrison, C. M. and Rahim, M. A. (1993). Adopt a new philosophy: the TQM challenge. *The TQM Magazine, 4*(2), 143–149.

Motwani, J., Kumar, A. and Antony, J. (2004). A business process change framework for examining the implementation of Six Sigma: a case study of Dow chemicals. *The TQM Magazine, 16*(4), 273–283.

Nahmias, S. (2009). *Production and operations analysis.* Boston, MA: McGraw-Hill/Irwin.

Nakajima, S. (1988). *Introduction to TPM: total productive maintenance.* Portland, OR: Productivity Press.

Nanda, V. (2005). *Quality management system handbook for product development companies.* Baco Raton, FL: CRC Press.

National Research Council. (1997). *Computer science and artificial intelligence.* Washington, DC: National Academies Press.

Ng, P. T. (2004). The learning organization and the innovative organization. *Human Systems Management, 23*(2), 93–100.

Ng, P. T. (2009). Relating quality and innovation: an exploration. *International Journal Quality and Innovation, 1*(1), 3–15.

Nourbakhsh, I. R. (2013). *Robot futures.* Cambridge: MIT Press.

Oakland, J. S. (2003). *TQM: text with cases.* 3rd Edition. London: Routledge, Taylor and Francis Group.

Parthasarathy, V. A., Chempakam, B. and Zachariah, T. J. (2008). *Chemistry of spices.* Oxfordshire, UK: CAB International.

Parveen, M. and Rao, T. V. V. L. N. (2009). An integrated approach to design and analysis of Lean manufacturing system: a perspective of Lean supply chain. *International Journal of Services and Operations Management, 5*(2), 175–208.

Peters, T. and Waterman, R. H. (1982). *In search of excellence.* New York: Harper and Row.

Pfeifer, T., Reissiger, W. and Canales, C. (2004). Integrating Six Sigma with quality management systems. *The TQM Magazine, 16*(4), 241–249.

Phadke, M. S. (1989). *Quality engineering using robust design.* New York: Prentice Hall.

Pheng, L. S. and Alfelor, W. M. (2000). Cross-cultural influences on quality management systems: two case studies. *Work Study, 49*(4), 134–144.

Pries, K. H. (2009). *Six Sigma for the new millennium: a CSSBB guidebook.* 2nd Edition. Milwaukee, WI: ASQ Quality Press.

Prusty, N. (2018). *Blockchain for enterprise: build scalable blockchain applications with privacy, interoperability, and permissioned features.* Birmingham: Packt Publishing, Ltd.

Pulakanam, V. (2012). Costs and savings of Six Sigma programs: an empirical study. *Quality Management Journal, 19*(4), 39–54.

Pyzdek, T. (2003). *The quality engineering handbook.* New York: Marcel Dekker, Inc.

Pyzdek, T. (2004). Strategy deployment using balanced scorecards. *International Journal of Six Sigma and Competitive Advantage, 1*(1), 21–28.

Pyzdek, T. (2019). *What is Six Sigma.* Retrieved May 20, 2022, from www.pyzdek institute.com/blog/six-sigma/what-is-six-sigma.html.

Pyzdek, T. and Keller, P. (2019). *The Six Sigma handbook.* New York: McGraw Hill Education.

Raisinghani, M. S., Ette, H., Pierce, R., Cannon, G. and Daripaly, P. (2005). Six Sigma: concepts, tools, and applications. *Industrial Management and Data Systems, 105*(4), 491–505.

Reichhart, A. and Holweg, M. (2007). Lean distribution: concepts, contributions, conflicts. *International Journal of Production Research, 45*(16), 3699–3722.

Ricondo, I. and Viles, E. (2005). Six Sigma and its links to TQM, BPR, Lean and the learning organization. *International Journal of Six Sigma and Competitive Advantage, 1*(3), 323–354.

Ried, R. A. (2006). Productivity and quality improvement: an implementation framework. *International Journal of Productivity and Quality Management, 1*(1–2), 26–36.

Rifqi, H., Zamma, A., Souda, S. B. and Hansali, M. (2021). Positive effect of industry 4.0 on quality and operations management. *International Journal of Online and Biomedical Engineering (IJOE), 17*(9). DOI: https://doi.org/10.3991/ijoe. v17i09.24717.

Ritchie, L. and Dale, B. (2000). Self-assessment using the business excellence model: a study of practice and process. *International Journal of Production Economics, 66,* 241–254.

Ritland, M. (2014). *3D printing with sketchup.* Birmingham: Packt Publishing, Ltd.

Robertshaw, W. (1995). *Using an objective point sales measure to incorporate elements of the Kano model into QFD.* Transactions from the 7th Symposium on Quality Function Deployment, Novi, MI, 201–216.

Robison, J. (2020). *Get prepared: the security and exchange commission (SEC) mandates transparency on human capital, workplace,* December 30. Retrieved May 10, 2021, from www.gallup.com/workplace/328073/prepared-sec-mandates-transparency-human-capital.aspx.

Rosenberg, M. B. (2003). *Nonviolent communication: a language of life.* 2nd edition. Encinitas, CA: PuddleDancer Press.

Roser, C. (2021). *All about pull production: designing, implementing, and maintaining Kanban, CONWIP, and other pull systems in Lean.* Deutschland: Allaboutlean.com Publishing.

Rothwell, R. (1994). Towards the fifth-generation innovation process. *International Marketing Review, 11*(1), 7–31.

Rouillard, L. (2009). *Goals and goal setting: achieve measurable results.* Rochester, NY: Axzo Press.

Rowlands, H. and Antony J. (2003). Application of design of experiments to a spot welding process. *Assembly Automation, 23*(3), 273–279.

Salah, S. (2015). A project selection, prioritisation and classification approach for organisations managing continuous improvement (CI). *International Journal of Project Organisation and Management, 7*(1), 1–13.

Salah, S. (2017). Lean Six Sigma and innovation: comparison and relationship. *International Journal of Business Excellence, 13*(4), 479–493.

Salah, S., Carretero, J. A. and Rahim, A. (2009a). Six Sigma and total quality management (TQM): similarities, differences and relationship. *International Journal of Six Sigma and Competitive Advantage, 5*(3), 237–250.

Salah, S. and Rahim, A. (2019). *An integrated company-wide management system: combining Lean Six Sigma with process improvement.* Cham, Switzerland: Springer Nature.

Salah, S., Rahim, A. and Carretero, J. A. (2009b). Kano-based Six Sigma utilising quality function deployment. *International Journal of Quality Engineering and Technology, 1*(2), 206–230.

Salah, S., Rahim, A. and Carretero, J. A. (2010). The integration of Six Sigma and Lean management. *International Journal of Lean Six Sigma, 1*(3), 249–274.

Salah, S. and Salah, D. (2020). Comparison between the UAE government excellence system, Malcolm Baldrige national quality award and European foundation for quality management model: implications for excellence models. *International Journal of Quality and Innovation, 4*(3–4), 121–131.

Savell, R. S. and Williams, B. (1988). Internal quality: improving the service functions. *Total Quality Management: An IFS Executive Briefing,* 181–188.

Schroeder, R. G., Linderman, K., Liedtke, C. and Choo, A. S. (2008). Six Sigma: definition and underlying theory. *Journal of Operations Management, 26,* 536–554.

Scipiono, A., Arena, F., Villa, M. and Saccarola, G. (2001). Integrated management systems. *Environmental Management and Health, 12*(2), 134–145.

Sheehy, P., Navarro, D., Silvers, R., Keyes, V. and Dixon, D. (2002). *The black belt memory jogger.* Salem, NH: Goal/QPC and Six Sigma Academy.

Sheikh Khalifa Government Excellence Program (SKGEP). (2019). Retrieved April 8, 2019, from www.skgep.gov.ae/en/award/about-the-award.

Shingo, S. (1986). *Zero quality control: source inspection and the Poka-Yoke system.* Boca Raton, FL: CRC Press, Taylor and Francis Group.

Short, P. J. and Rahim, M. A. (1995). Total quality management in hospitals. *Total Quality Management, 6*(3), 255–263.

Sinclair, D. and Zairi, M. (1995). Effective process management through performance measurement: part I—applications of total quality-based performance measurement. *Business Process Re-Engineering and Management Journal, 1*(1), 75–88.

Snee, R. D. (2004). Six-Sigma: the evolution of a 100 years of business improvement methodology. *International Journal of Six Sigma and Competitive Advantage, 1*(1), 4–20.

Snee, R. D. and Hoerl, R. W. (2018). *Leading holistic improvement with Lean six sigma 2.0.* 2nd Edition. Upper Saddle River, NJ: Pearson Education, Pearson FT Press.

Sohini, G. (2020). Tips to get the most out of your RPA implementation. *PC Quest*, *11*, 22–23, November.

Soldatos, J., Lazaro, O. and Cavadini, F. (2019). *The digital shopfloor—industrial automation in the industry 4. 0 era: performance analysis and applications.* Denmark: River Publishers.

Sony, M., Antony, J. and Douglas, J. A. (2020). Essential ingredients for the implementation of quality 4.0: a narrative review of literature and future directions for research. *The TQM Journal, 32*(4), 779–793.

Sony, M., Antony, J., Douglas, J. A. and McDermott, O. (2021). Motivations, barriers and readiness factors for quality 4.0 implementation: an exploratory study. *The TQM Journal, 33*(6), 1502–1515.

Sower, V. E., Quarles, R. and Boussard, E. (2007). Cost of quality and its relationship to quality system maturity. *International Journal of Quality and Reliability Management, 24*(2), 121–140.

SPCFOREXCEL. (2017). *Dr. Ishikawa's seven quality tools*, August. Retrieved January 23, 2021, from www.spcforexcel.com/knowledge/process-improvement/ishikawa-seven-quality-tools#graphs.

Spencer, B. A. (1994). Models of organization and total quality management: a comparison and critical evaluation. *Mississippi State University Academy of Management Review, 19*(3), 446–471.

Spiring, F. A. (1993). The reflected normal loss function. *Canadian Journal of Statistics, 21*, 321–330.

Statisticbrain. (2021). *Attention span statistics*. Retrieved October 20, 2021, from www.statisticbrain.com/?s=attention+spanandid=19943andpost_type=post.

Storm, S. (2016). At Chobani, now it's not just the Yogurt that's rich. *New York Times*, April 26. Retrieved May 17, 2021, from www.nytimes.com/2016/04/27/business/a-windfall-for-chobani-employees-stakes-in-the-company.html.

Su, C. T. and Chou, C. J. (2008). A systematic methodology for the creation of Six Sigma projects: a case study of semiconductor foundry. *Experts Systems with Applications, 34*(4), 2693–2703.

Sullivan, L. P. (1986). Quality function deployment. *Quality Progress (American Society for Quality Control)*, June, 39–50.

Sullivan, L. P. (1988). The seven stages in company-wide quality control. *Total Quality Management: An IFS Executive Briefing*, 11–19.

Sun, H. (2000). Total quality management, ISO 9000 certification and performance improvement. *International Journal of Quality and Reliability Management, 17*(2), 168–179.

Suzaki, K. (1987). *The new manufacturing challenge: techniques for continuous improvement*. New York: Free Press.

Taguchi, G. (1985). Quality engineering in Japan. *Bulletin of the Japan Society of Precision Engineering, 19*(4), 237–242.

Taguchi, G. (1986). *Introduction to quality engineering*. Dearborn, MI: American Supplier Institute.

Taguchi, G., Elsayed, E. A. and Hsiang, T. C. (1989). *Quality engineering in production systems*. New York, NY: McGraw-Hill.

Taguchi, G. and Wu, Y. (1980). *Introduction to off-line quality control systems.* Tokyo, Japan: Central Japan Quality Control Association.

Tan, K. C., Lyman, S. B. and Wisner, J. D. (2002). Supply chain management: a strategic perspective. *International Journal of Operations and Production Management, 22*(6), 614–631.

Tan, K. C., Kannan, V. R. and Handfield, R. B. (1998). Supply chain management: Supplier performance and firm performance. *International Journal of Purchasing Material, Management, 34*(3), 2–9.

Tan, K. C. and Shen, X. X. (2000). Integrating Kano's model in the planning matrix of quality function deployment. *Total Quality Management, 11*(8), 1141–1151.

Tannock, J. D. T., Balogun, O. and Hawisa, H. (2007). A variation management system supporting Six Sigma. *Journal of Manufacturing Technology Management, 18*(5), 561–575.

Tapping, D., Luyster, T. and Shuker, T. (2002). *Value stream management.* New York, NY: Productivity Press.

Tapping, D. and Shuker, T. (2003). *Value stream management for the lean office.* New York, NY: Productivity Press.

Teeravaraprug, J. (2002). Incorporating of Kano's model in quality loss function. *CiteSeerX.* Retrieved April 7, 2021, from http://citeseerx.ist.psu.edu/viewdoc/summary?doi=10.1.1.19.3757.

Teeravaraprug, T. (2004). Quantification of tangible and intangible quality costs. *Proceedings of the Fifth Asia Pacific Industrial Engineering and Management Systems Conference,* 1–7.

Teeravaraprug, J. and Cho, B. R. (2002). Designing the optimal process target levels for multiple quality characteristics. *International Journal Production Research, 40*, 37–54.

Terziovski, M. (2006). Quality management practices and their relationship with customer satisfaction and productivity improvement. *Management Research News, 29*(7), 414–424.

Tidd, J. and Bessant, J. (2013). Managing innovation: integrating technological. In: *Market and organizational change.* 5th Edition. New York: Wiley.

Tripathi, A. M. (2018). *Learning robotic process automation: create software robots and automate business processes with the leading RPA tool—UiPath.* Birmingham: Packt Publishing, Ltd.

Tushman, M. L. and Anderson, P. (2004). *Managing strategic innovation and change: a collection of readings.* Oxford: Oxford University Press.

Vimalajeewa, D., Thakur, S., Breslin, J., Berry, D. P. and Balasubramaniam, S. (2010). *Block chain and internet of nano-things for optimizing chemical sensing in smart farming.* https://arxiv.org/abs/2010.01941.

Walton, M. (1990). *Deming management at work.* New York, NY: G. P. Putnam's Sons.

Watson Wyatt Worldwide. (2004). *Connecting organizational communication to financial performance.* Washington, DC: Communication ROI Study.

Webber, K. L. and Zheng, H. Y. (2020). *Big data on campus: data analytics and decision making in higher education.* Baltimore, MD: Johns Hopkins University Press.

West, M. A. and Farr, J. L. (1990). *Innovation and creativity at work: psychological and organizational strategies.* Chichester: Wiley, 3–13.

Wyckoff, D. D. (1984). New tools for achieving service quality. *The Cornell HRA Quarterly, 25*(3), 78–91.

Yang, C. C. (2004). An integrated model of TQM and GE-Six Sigma. *International Journal of Six Sigma and Competitive Advantage, 1*(1), 97–111.

Yang, C. C. (2006). The impact of human resource management practices on the implementation of total quality management—an empirical study on high-tech firms. *The TQM Magazine, 18*(2), 162–173.

Yang, H. M., Choi, B. S., Park, H. F., Suh, M. S. and Chae, B. (2007). Supply chain management Six Sigma: a management innovation methodology at the Samsung group. *Supply Chain Management: An International Journal, 12*(2), 88–95.

Zairi, M. (2002a). Beyond TQM implementation: the new paradigm of TQM sustainability. *Total Quality Management, 13*(8), 1161–1172.

Zairi, M. (2002b). Total quality management sustainability: what it means and how to make it viable. *International Journal of Quality and Reliability Management, 19*(5), 502–507.

Zairi, M. and Liburd, I. M. (2001). *TQM sustainability: a roadmap for creating competitive advantage, integrated management.* Proceedings of the 6th International Conference on ISO 9000 and TQM. Hong Kong Baptist University Press, Ayr, Scotland, 452–461, April 17–19. ISBN 962-86107-2-4.

Index

A

activity network diagrams, 14, 168, 170, 172

affinity diagram, 171

analysis of variance (ANOVA), 49, 136, 141, 142, 178, 179, 180

artificial intelligence, 257, 258, 261, 262, 267, 269

automation, 58, 106, 119, 165, 196, 197, 199, 208, 209, 212, 241, 257, 258, 259, 260, 261, 262, 262, 267, 268, 270, 272, 273, 278, 279, 280, 283, 284, 285, 287, 288

B

balance, 50, 107, 160, 206, 213, 215, 217

Big Data, xxxviii, 5, 257–264, 265, 270–272

blockchain, 257, 261, 265, 266, 274

bottleneck, 95, 196, 199, 203, 211, 213, 216

box plots, 175, 176, 177

C

capability, 5, 17, 19, 21, 24, 25, 26, 37, 54, 58, 64, 67, 116, 118, 125, 127, 142, 146, 147, 148, 149, 168, 183, 184, 186, 174

cell layout, 200, 201, 235, 236, 246, 247

central limit theorem, 127

central tendency, 125, 128, 129, 176, 179, 183

Change Management, 77, 274

changeover, 33, 116, 197, 244, 245, 246,

check sheets, 14, 134, 157

commitment, xxxviii, 8, 35, 42, 43, 47, 59, 84, 96, 99, 100, 105, 107, 199, 256, 258, 263, 274

communication, xxxvii, 3, 5, 10, 11, 15, 23, 29, 31, 42, 49, 54, 58, 61, 72, 78–81, 84, 86–87, 94, 98, 123–124, 126–128, 135, 138, 139, 141, 145, 146, 151–152, 156, 157, 166, 168–170, 177, 180, 196, 198, 200, 201, 206, 209, 210, 212, 216, 219, 220–221, 222, 226, 230, 233, 235, 238–242, 246, 248, 254, 256, 258, 259, 261, 265, 269, 272, 274, 278–280, 284, 288

concentration diagrams, 5, 173–174

confidence interval, 127, 130, 132, 137, 140–141

continuous improvement (CI), xxxvii, 3, 4, 5, 6, 7, 12, 13, 14, 17, 26, 27, 30, 31, 32, 34, 35, 36, 37, 42, 43, 49, 50, 59, 62, 75, 81, 84, 86, 92, 96, 98, 101, 160, 162, 196, 206, 218, 234, 273–274, 277

control, xxxviii, 5, 6–7, 8, 12–14, 16–17, 19, 21, 24, 25, 32, 33–34, 36–38, 47–48, 50, 58, 61, 64, 65, 67–70, 84, 96, 98, 103, 113–116, 119–120, 125, 127, 135, 137, 142–146, 149, 162, 176–177, 183–184, 189, 200, 204, 210, 211, 218–220, 222–223, 227–230, 234, 238–240, 244, 248, 255, 259, 261–262, 264, 273, 288

control limits, 137, 142, 143–144

COPQ, 20, 54, 57–58, 60, 64, 66, 116, 118, 148

correlation, 22, 150–153, 248